SOCIAL SECURITY

A CENTURY FOUNDATION BOOK

SOCIAL SECURITY: BEYOND THE BASICS

Edited by RICHARD C. LEONE
and GREG ANRIG, JR.

1999 * THE CENTURY FOUNDATION PRESS * NEW YORK

The Century Foundation, formerly the Twentieth Century Fund, sponsors and supervises timely analyses of economic policy, foreign affairs, and domestic political issues. Not-for-profit and nonpartisan, it was founded in 1919 and endowed by Edward A. Filene.

Library of Congress Cataloging-in-Publication Data

Social security : beyond the basics / Richard C. Leone and
   Greg Anrig Jr., editors.
        p.   cm.
   ISBN 0-87078-431-5
   1. Social security--United States. I. Leone, Richard
   C.   II. Anrig, Greg.
   HD7125.S599353   1999
   368.4'3'00973--dc21   99-18107
                                                        CIP

Cover Design: Claude Goodwin
Manufactured in the United States of America.

CONTENTS

1

INTRODUCTION

RICHARD C. LEONE
and GREG ANRIG, JR.

U ntil recently, Social Security operated with relatively little controversy, routinely and efficiently accomplishing the task for which it
was created—reducing poverty among the elderly. It has low administrative
costs of about 1 percent, and it even was recently declared the first government agency to have solved all potential "Y2K" computer problems.
Without the program, more than half of Americans over age sixty-five
would fall below the poverty line. However, with the retirement of
America's largest generation—the baby boomers—in sight, both Social
Security and health programs for the elderly have moved to center stage in
political and policy debates. The centerpiece of President Clinton's State
of the Union address on January 19, 1999, was his proposal for strengthening Social Security.

Perhaps because so much is at stake, the current Social Security
debate often sounds like a contest between warring ideologies or philoso-
phies of government (and antigovernment). Other times, it appears to be

an argument about which pension system will produce the highest returns. And, among specialists, it can be mistaken for an academic food fight about arcane formulas and actuarial tables. Oddly, it is rare for a discussion to focus on the two questions at the heart of the matter: How much financial risk do Americans want to take in their old age? And, how much are they willing to pay to maintain social insurance that reduces such risks? In fact, understanding the issues raised by the various proposals to change the current Social Security program is enhanced by reflecting on the basic nature of risk in the United States.

No one, of course, can be assured of a life without risk. Perhaps because so much chance is "hardwired" into the human condition, most adults, despite the rush that may accompany high-stakes activity, understand that it is foolish to take unnecessary risks, especially with regard to personal safety or economic well-being. Economists have documented the pervasiveness of risk-averse behavior—in other words, the average individual actually takes fewer risks than he or she should (should, that is, according to economists). Still, it seems true that Americans tolerate a greater degree of market risk than do members of many other wealthy societies. They do so not because they are exceptionally reckless, but rather because they place a high value on the positive results often associated with a relatively unfettered market capitalism.

Indeed, societies everywhere are converging in a belief that strong economic growth and long-term prosperity are possible only with free markets. Inevitably, they also are continuing to learn and relearn lessons about the risks that accompany free enterprise. These risks underpin the abiding importance of building strong, democratic governmental institutions that can enforce the rules of the game and deal with the abuses of the marketplace. Moreover, even in strong economies, individuals are confronted by unavoidable uncertainty about the long-term outcome of a lifetime of work, savings, and investment. Experience everywhere confirms the indispensability of a reliable social safety net, especially for our youngest and oldest. Reform of Social Security should reflect this hard-won knowledge about the workings of capitalism and democracy. We can and should assess each proposal for changing Social Security in terms of its potential effects on economic growth, inequality, fairness, and efficiency. The choices that we make about the future of social insurance will go a long way toward answering basic questions about America: What is the proper role of government in an overwhelmingly private sector economy? How can we create fairness and opportunity for all our citizens? How can we reduce inequality and poverty?

At one extreme, some argue that America will be doomed to a sharply diminished future unless radical steps are taken to change the way we support the aged. They claim that the system is near collapse and that "privatizing" it will give everybody better protection in old age. But the evidence suggests, instead, that moderate adjustments in burdens and benefits can solve foreseeable problems within the framework of the existing system.

Too often, Social Security is discussed as though it provided merely another savings or investment vehicle for workers seeking the highest possible yield on their pension savings. Social Security is more. First, it is a disability and life insurance policy that provides vital protections to virtually every member of our society. Currently, seven million survivors of deceased workers and four million disabled Americans receive income support. The Social Security Administration calculates the value of the disability insurance as the equivalent of a $203,000 policy in the private sector; for a worker aged twenty-seven, paid the average wage, and with two children, Social Security provides the equivalent of a $295,000 life insurance policy. The total value of these two policies nationally is about $12.1 trillion, more than all the private life insurance currently in force.

Second, Social Security provides a lifetime retirement annuity with benefits that rise with inflation. Many corporate pensions run out after twenty years, and most are not adjusted for inflation. The notion that these basic insurance and annuity protections would be unnecessary if we all saved more money is simply false. The truth is that neither of these protections is available in the private market at a price that the vast majority of Americans can afford.

Social Security works because virtually all of us belong to it and pay into it. Social Security, after all, does not consist of a bunch of piggy banks with our names on them. Our contributions are pooled to ensure that almost every senior citizen receives a minimum income. Although some of us need the protection more than others, all of us get some benefits. It is the nature of such pooled plans that both the most fortunate among us (the wealthy) and the least fortunate (those who die young and without a family) get the least from the program.

Some of the proposed reforms seem based on the fallacy that everyone can do better than average. Averages exist because some of us do worse and some of us better. Moreover, to the extent that higher market returns are sought—for example, by investing Social Security surpluses in higher-yielding investments—they can be achieved less expensively and with less risk within the framework of the existing system. Privatization advocates wish away the reality that individual accounts can mean high costs and risks. They also often ignore enormous transition costs—one plan would require increased taxes of $6.5 trillion during the next seventy-two years.

In the real world, there is no magic bullet that will mean more for everyone. For one thing, the system runs with great efficiency. Administrative costs are less than 1 percent of total premium flows, far, far less than the marketing and administrative costs of private insurance and pension plans. If every dollar of overhead were instead distributed to Social Security recipients—and the system somehow, magically, ran by divine guidance—the recipients hardly would notice the difference in their monthly checks.

Of course, the real route to more for all is to increase, over time, the size of the overall economic pie (and, somehow, have the current sharply unequal pattern of wealth shift). Can privatization enlarge the pie? Regardless of the return on the stock market, the only way to increase total income in the future is by higher levels of economic growth.

The reason that financial assets cannot ensure more for all is that they are claims on real production and real assets in the future. Unlike current income and current production, they don't have to add up. Financial assets are promises that can be kept only if there is enough future production. When there isn't, some asset holders are surprised: there are defaults, bankruptcies, and omitted dividends; financial bubbles burst, asset prices collapse, banks go belly-up, and people are left holding worthless paper. Real growth makes it possible to meet financial obligations.

Thus, with regard to Social Security, there is no way that any reform can make all retirees richer unless either nonretirees (workers and children) become poorer, or economic growth accelerates. The right questions about privatization or public reform are: Will a given plan increase saving and investment? By how much? Would this really boost production enough to make everyone much better off?

The major element in President Clinton's Social Security reform plan is the firm commitment of $2.7 trillion in anticipated federal surpluses. All but $700 billion of this total would be invested in Treasury obligations. In effect, this strategy would reduce the outstanding debt held by the public, arguably increasing prospects of lower interest rates and growth. And since this portion of the surplus would not be used for either new expenditures or tax cuts, overall national saving would be strengthened. The remaining $700 billion would be invested in the equity markets, for the first time diversifying the holdings in the trust funds into potentially higher-yielding assets. Those changes would keep the trust funds in the black for an additional twenty-three years—from 2032 to 2055.

Although the full impact of those proposals on the economy is impossible to predict, the lesson of the past decade is important: sustained economic growth with low unemployment can greatly ease the challenge of the aging of the population. The president was able to propose such a "painless" plan only because the economic expansion of the 1990s and the tax increases of 1993 swelled tax revenues, flipping the federal balance sheet from deep deficit to surplus. A continuation of the same levels of growth in the next century, which will be more difficult as the workforce increases more slowly, in and of itself would sustain Social Security without any changes to the system.

The proposal to allow up to 15 percent of Social Security's reserves to be invested in the stock market has aroused great consternation from critics who fear that the government will come to control corporations or force political policies on them. Those concerns seem overblown, however, when one considers that the government already has lots of ways to affect companies—regulations, taxes, legislation, and antitrust suits. Still, to avoid any risk, a diversified trust fund should be managed by a Federal Reserve-like independent board and—importantly—invest only in index funds rather than in individual companies.

Will it work? Well, state and local pension systems already own 8 percent of outstanding stock (the Social Security share eventually might reach 4 percent), and capitalism and the stock market seem to be doing pretty well.

The president also proposed the creation of new universal savings accounts (USAs). But unlike privatization schemes, USAs would not be directly connected to Social Security. Aimed at increasing household savings and economic growth, USAs would be subsidized by start-up federal grants and a matching program. Still, it's unclear whether low- and middle-income families living paycheck-to-paycheck would participate in the plans. The generous tax incentives of Individual Retirement Accounts lure only 3 percent of taxpayers earning less than $30,000 a year to contribute to those accounts. Moreover, the administrative costs of USAs would be likely to eat up a large share of the contributions of small savers.

Unlike the president's plan, which would preserve the features of Social Security that have made it so popular and effective while relying on an empirically defensible strategy for promoting economic growth, proposals to "privatize" the system by converting it into a collection of private accounts strongly resemble the ideas advocated by the supply-siders of the 1980s. Just as in the 1980s promises were made of pie-in-the-sky prosperity for all, today's Social Security supply-siders are making promises about golden years for all. The explosive real growth implicit in these promises cannot be justified by what we know about how our economy works. Just as the tax and social spending cuts of the 1980s benefited some and hurt others, every radical reform of Social Security that has been proposed will create losers as well as winners. Who will lose depends on the reform, but generally the losers are workers with low wages, people with long life expectancies, the disabled, and widows and their children. And, despite a campaign filled with factual confusion, the reality of privatization is that women, minorities, and the working poor stand to lose in almost every version.

The simple truth is that there is no magic formula that will sweep away all the issues raised by the aging of the boomers. For all but a few fortunate individuals, as well as for the nation as a whole, many problems (like life's risks in general) cannot be wished or legislated away. Over the long span of a lifetime, birthrates and medical progress are unpredictable, securities markets are sure to experience immense volatility, and even the most stable democracies are likely to undergo sweeping transformations in politics and policy. In other words, the future development of society will remain complex and uncertain. Ultimately, the inevitability of risk, when combined with the uncertainties intrinsic to the careers and health of individual workers, makes the strongest case for a safe and conservative social insurance program.

The near doubling in the next century of the percentage of the population over sixty-five does mean that all retirement programs, not just Social Security, require reexamination and fresh thinking. But, despite a superficial appeal and powerful sales programs, the most radical suggestions for change in Social Security—especially schemes to privatize it—are neither necessary nor practical. Retaining some version of the current system and the existing intergenerational compact remains the best course for ensuring that each citizen has a minimum, decent, guaranteed income during retirement. Moreover, the good news is that the necessary adjustments can be accomplished without cramping economic growth or adding to inequality and poverty.

In recent months, The Century Foundation has published a series of pamphlets titled The Basics, which provide readers with the best available facts, figures, and analysis about important but complicated public policy issues. The popularity of the Basics series convinced the Trustees of the Foundation to build on that success with new, more detailed publications under the rubric Beyond the Basics. As with the pamphlet series, these books are attempts to clarify complex policy questions, but they delve in greater depth into particular issues to dispel widespread misunderstandings and misguided conventional wisdom.

Overall, the authors of this first volume in the Beyond the Basics series reject forecasts for the next century that predict a nightmare struggle between young workers and elderly baby boomers. They believe that a healthy measure of the current confusion about Social Security is simply a result of shallow thinking by well-meaning individuals. Some of the misunderstanding, of course, may be a result of the broad assault on the public sector that lumps together *all* government activity under the heading of "fraud, waste, and abuse."

Beyond the Basics: Social Security Reform is divided into five parts. Part I is a reprint of the entire revised edition of the 1998 Basics pamphlet *Social Security Reform*. It lays out details about how the program works, its successes, the nature of the problems that may confront it, comparisons with counterparts in other countries, and overviews of ideas for reforming the system.

Part II, "Why the Sky Will Not Fall," focuses on the future impact of the retirement of the baby-boom generation. Although the aging of the American population is often described elsewhere as an impending cataclysm of biblical proportions, the essays here highlight the faulty assumptions underlying that deep foreboding.

Brookings Institution economists Henry J. Aaron and Robert D. Reischauer, in a chapter from their recent Century Foundation book, cosponsored by The Brookings Institution, *Countdown to Reform: The Great Social Security Debate*, present the economic challenges that future demographic changes pose while highlighting the political choices available to manage those challenges. Century Foundation president Richard C. Leone then shows how the nation responded when the baby-boom cohort first arrived on the scene—a period of sustained economic prosperity and extensive investment in public schools and higher education—suggesting that the retirement of the same cohort may present an opportunity for making the country stronger rather than weaker. Brandeis University economist James H. Schulz debunks claims that sustaining Social Security will undermine economic growth and victimize younger generations. And political scientists Lawrence R. Jacobs of the University of Minnesota and Robert Y. Shapiro of Columbia University evaluate myths and misunderstandings about the public's attitudes toward Social Security—myths that often have been used to support unfounded assertions that the system cannot survive.

Part III, "Rich Boomer, Poor Boomer," describes the wide economic disparities among American families and Social Security's critical role in alleviating poverty. Brookings Institution economist William Gale opens the section with an analysis of the personal finances of the baby boomers. His work indicates that roughly a third of baby-boomer families are insufficiently prepared for retirement, another third are "just hanging in there," and the remaining third are "doing well by any measure." That essay is followed by a summary of Social Security's effectiveness in addressing challenges that women are more likely to face than men: long life spans, inadequate private pension coverage, extended periods outside the paid workforce, and a history of low earnings. Finally, economist Dean Baker explains how Social Security is fundamentally an insurance program that guards against a wide array of risks. Because the system's insurance features either do not exist in the private market or would be enormously expensive to purchase, Baker argues, Social Security's value to each worker is far greater than indicated by so-called rate-of-return calculations that omit the benefits of the program's insurance coverage.

Part IV, "Is the Market the Cure?" scrutinizes the idea of transforming Social Security into a collection of individual investment accounts. In another chapter from the Aaron and Reischauer book, the authors call attention to problems of privatization ranging from high transition costs and administrative inefficiencies to erosion of Social Security's progressivity and the vulnerability of workers with little or no investment experience. John Mueller, senior vice president and chief economist with Lehrman Bell Mueller Cannon, Inc., then explains why comparisons between today's Social Security and a privatized system need to take into account differences in the risks as well as the potential rewards between the two approaches. After taking such differences into account, Mueller answers the question, "Can financial assets beat Social Security?" with the reply, "Not in the real world." Dean Baker elaborates on Mueller's analysis with a study showing inconsistencies between the claims of privatization advocates about the gains that their proposals would generate. Baker concludes that Social Security as currently structured will be a better deal than a privatized system if the economy grows more slowly in the future, as Social Security's Trustees forecast (which would reduce stock market returns), or if past growth rates continue (allowing the system to thrive without facing an eventual shortfall).

Part V, "Assessing Proposals to Save Social Security," includes an essay from former Social Security Commissioner Robert M. Ball spelling out the extent to which specific changes in the system would alleviate the shortfall now projected to occur beginning in the year 2032. This last part of the volume also contains summaries of the main features of prominent Social Security reform plans and assesses the extent to which they adhere to seven principles developed by experts on the system.

Thus, the basic message of the book is that America can sustain the fundamental promise of Social Security: when the day comes that you can no longer work because of old age, you will not have to live out your life in poverty. America is facing change, but not disaster. We can grow older gracefully.

I

The Basic Facts about Social Security and Ideas for Reforming It

2

THE BASICS:
A GUIDE TO SOCIAL SECURITY REFORM

Because the issue of Social Security concerns every American, it is critical that the debate be based on a deep understanding of the economic and social underpinnings of the system, which in January 1996 provided nearly 44 million Americans (primarily retirees and their spouses) with an average monthly benefit of approximately $745.[1] At the end of 1997, the combined reserves in the Social Security Old-Age and Survivors Insurance and Disability Insurance Trust Funds was $655 billion.[2] (Social Security took in about $458 billion and paid out more than $369 billion in 1997; the remainder went into the trust funds.)[3]

Knowing the facts is the only way to cut through the half-truths and distortions that are all too often the basis for the arguments for change offered by those with political and personal agendas. As a result, a few years ago, shortly after the issue became the subject of headlines, The Century Foundation published a pamphlet looking at this issue. What follows is the revised 1998 edition of *The Basics: Social Security Reform*. It presents the best available facts, figures, and arguments about what's right with Social Security and what's wrong with it; in addition, it looks at how the U.S. program compares to programs in other countries and the major reform proposals currently under consideration.

I. SOCIAL SECURITY IN A NUTSHELL

? WHAT IS SOCIAL SECURITY?

➤ Social Security is a contributory social insurance program providing benefits to millions of Americans. Workers contribute financially to the system during their careers and earn entitlement to family benefits upon retirement, disability, or death. Currently, nearly 44 million Americans receive benefits under the Old-Age and Survivors Insurance and Disability Insurance (OASDI) programs that make up Social Security. This group includes some 30 million elderly retirees and their dependents, 6 million disabled workers and their dependents, and more than 7 million survivors of deceased workers. (See Figure A.) Over 3 million of those receiving OASDI benefits are children.[4]

FIGURE A
Percent of Beneficiaries in Current-Payment Status, by Type, 1996

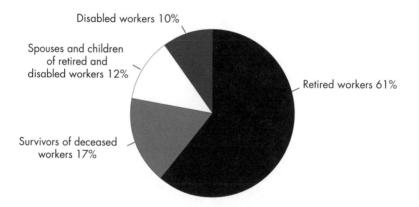

Disabled workers 10%

Spouses and children of retired and disabled workers 12%

Retired workers 61%

Survivors of deceased workers 17%

Source: Social Security Administration, "Fast Facts and Figures about Social Security," Washington, D.C.: Social Security Administration, 1997, p. 14. Hereafter cited as "Fast Facts."

? HOW IS THE PROGRAM FINANCED?

➤ About 96 percent of workers in the United States contribute to Social Security,[5] paying a flat tax of 6.2 percent of their wage income up to $68,400; their employers contribute an equal amount.[6] If, however, as many economists believe, employers shift the cost of Social Security taxes onto workers in the form of lower wages, workers in effect may actually bear a substantially larger share of the tax burden than employers.[7] Self-employed people pay both their own and their "employer's" share; their tax rate is 12.4 percent, half of which is tax deductible for income tax purposes. [8]

➤ While the payroll tax is by far the largest source of funding for Social Security, a small amount of additional revenue is raised through the taxation of the Social Security benefits of high-income beneficiaries. For single taxpayers, beneficiaries whose combined income (that is, adjusted gross income plus nontaxable interest plus one-half of their Social Security benefits) is between $25,000 and $34,000 may have to pay taxes on 50 percent of their Social Security benefits. Up to 85 percent of Social Security benefits of those whose combined income is over $34,000 may be subject to taxation (the thresholds are higher for married couples filing joint tax returns).[9] These tax revenues are channeled into both the Social Security and Medicare programs.

➤ Social Security is largely funded on a pay-as-you-go basis. Social Security is not a "piggy bank" that employees put money into and then take out of when they retire. The benefits that today's Social Security retirees receive are paid out of taxes collected from today's workers that are earmarked for the payment of these benefits. Out of this tax money, the government writes Social Security checks and mails them to beneficiaries. Any money left over after paying benefits is put into the Trust Funds, which are invested in U.S. government securities to provide funds for future use. (See Figure B, page 14.)

? WHO IS ELIGIBLE?

➤ Eligibility for benefits is earned through workers' payroll tax contributions. As noted, nearly all workers in the United States are required to contribute to the Social Security program. All citizens and those with legal alien status who work and pay contributions for the required number of years (ten) are eligible for pension benefits when they reach the minimum retirement age;[10] survivor and disability benefits also require certain minimum work credits. To qualify as disabled, individuals must have a prolonged or terminal condition and may not earn more than $500 per month.[11]

➤ Under certain circumstances, a worker's spouse, children, and parents may qualify for Social Security benefits based on the worker's contribution history. Unmarried children under age eighteen (or over eighteen if severely disabled), elderly spouses, and spouses caring for young children are generally eligible for benefits if a worker retires, becomes disabled, or dies. The elderly parents of a deceased worker may be entitled to survivorship benefits if they were financially dependent on the child for at least half their support. [12]

FIGURE B
Social Security Receipts, Expenditures, and Trust Funds at End of Period, 1940–1996

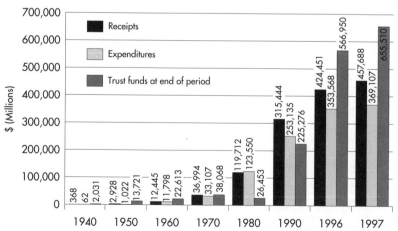

Note: Receipts include net contributions, income from taxation of benefits, reimbursements from the general fund of the Treasury, and net interest. Expenditures include benefit payments, administrative expenses, and transfers to Railroad Retirement program. These figures are for the Old-Age and Survivors Insurance (OASI) and Disability Insurance programs combined, except for 1940 and 1950, which are for OASI only.

Source: 1998 Annual Report of the Board of Trustees of the Federal Old-Age and Survivors Insurance and Disability Insurance Trust Funds (Washington, D.C.: GPO, 1998), pp. 96–97, 100–101. Hereafter cited as 1998 Annual Report of the Social Security Trustees.

? HOW ARE BENEFIT LEVELS DETERMINED?

➤ Retirement benefits are based on average earnings during a thirty-five year career. Higher lifetime earnings result in higher benefits up to an inflation-adjusted cap. The full benefit is payable at age sixty-five; workers who retire at age sixty-two get a reduced benefit based on the likelihood of their collecting benefits over a longer term. (See Figure C.) Workers who postpone retirement beyond age sixty-five, up to age seventy, get more than the full benefit. Survivorship and disability benefits are also determined by a worker's average earnings.

FIGURE C
Hypothetical Benefit Amounts for a Person Who Claimed Benefits in January 1997

Source: "Fast Facts," p. 16.

➤ Recipients of retirement and survivorship benefits who continue to work will have their benefits reduced if they earn above a certain threshold. In 1997, beneficiaries under age sixty-five lost one dollar of benefits for every two dollars of earnings above $8,640. For individuals between sixty-five and sixty-nine years of age, one dollar in benefits is withheld for every three dollars of earnings over $13,500. The benefits of individuals aged seventy and older are not subject to any earnings test.[13]

➤ All benefits are adjusted annually to keep pace with inflation, as measured by the Consumer Price Index (CPI). This means that during periods of high inflation, such as the 1970s, inflation-adjusted benefits protect Social Security recipients from having the real benefits of their Social Security check eaten away by a higher cost of living. Most private pensions do not make similar adjustments for inflation.[14]

II. WHAT'S RIGHT WITH SOCIAL SECURITY?

 SOCIAL SECURITY COVERAGE IS NEARLY UNIVERSAL

➤ About 92 percent of individuals age sixty-five and over receive Social Security benefits; an additional 3 percent, who continue to work and have not yet claimed benefits, are eligible to receive benefits upon retirement.[15] In 1997, around 147 million workers (about 96 percent of individuals in paid employment) were making payroll tax contributions to the Social Security system and building credits toward future benefits.[16]

➤ Social Security provides a substantial number of workers and their families with *insurance* against the financial risks associated with the death or disability of a breadwinner. Around 75 percent of workers aged twenty-one to sixty-four are eligible for benefits should they become disabled.[17] Nearly all children under age eighteen (98 percent) are eligible for benefits if a working parent dies.[18]

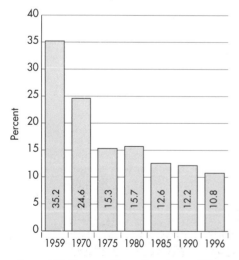

FIGURE D
Poverty Rate Among Elderly Americans

Year	Percent
1959	35.2
1970	24.6
1975	15.3
1980	15.7
1985	12.6
1990	12.2
1996	10.8

FIGURE E
Workers Likely to Lack Pension Coverage

◆ Workers in part-time jobs

◆ Workers in small firms

◆ Workers who are not members of labor unions

◆ Workers in low-paying jobs

◆ Workers who are women or members of a minority group

Source: U.S. Congress, House Committee on Ways and Means, *Overview of Entitlement Programs: 1996 Green Book* (Washington, D.C.: GPO, 1996), p.1226; figure for 1996 is from the U.S. Census Bureau's website at http://www.census.gov/hhes/poverty/poverty96/pv96e st1.html.

Source: James H. Schulz, *The Economics of Aging,* 6th ed. (Westport, Conn.: Auburn House, 1995), p. 230.

SOCIAL SECURITY BENEFITS SAVE MANY RETIREES FROM POVERTY

➤ In 1997, the benefits paid by Social Security exceeded $369 billion.[19] These benefits, in combination with Medicare health insurance, have dramatically reduced poverty for the aged in America. In 1959, the U.S. Census Bureau estimated that more than 35 percent of elderly Americans were poor.[20] During the 1960s, elderly Americans experienced twice the poverty rate of all other Americans. By 1996, in large part because of changes in the Social Security and Medicare systems, the poverty rate among senior citizens was 10.8 percent. (See Figure D.) This is slightly lower than the rate for other adults.[21]

➤ Providing workers with pensions is not compulsory for employers in the United States. In 1994, fewer than half of all workers were enrolled in private pension plans.[22] (See Figure E.)

➤ Social Security provided 66 percent of the elderly in America with benefits that represented at least half their total income.[23] Without Social Security, approximately half the elderly in America would have fallen below the poverty line in 1994.[24] (See Figure F.) A significant portion of the elderly need Social Security to survive: in 1994, 30 percent of elderly recipients relied on Social Security

FIGURE F
Elderly and Poverty Status, 1994

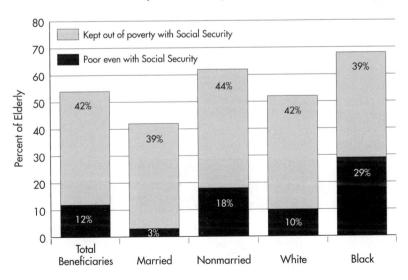

Source: "Fast Facts," p. 8.

for at least 90 percent of their total income; for 16 percent of recipients, Social Security was their only source of income.[25] (See Figure G.)

➤ Although women retirees usually receive smaller monthly checks from Social Security than do men, they typically have a greater need for Social Security.[26] Of elderly women living alone, for example, more than a third rely on their Social Security check for at least 90 percent of their income.[27] Women tend to be more reliant on their Social Security checks for numerous reasons:

◆ Women tend to earn less than men for work outside of the home. Women are more likely to have interrupted work histories, and the monetary value of women's work in raising children is not directly calculated in benefits. Thus, women often end up with lower retirement benefits than their male counterparts. The average monthly benefit for a retired woman in 1996 was $611, compared to $819 for a man.[28]

◆ Only 13 percent of elderly women receive a private pension,

FIGURE G
Percent of Beneficiaries with Social Security Benefits as a Major Source of Income, 1994

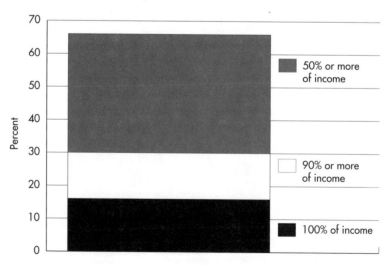

Source: "Fast Facts," p. 7.

compared with 33 percent of older men. In 1994, the median private pension or annuity income for women sixty-five or older was about $2,682 annually, compared to $5,731 for men.[29]

◆ More women than men outlive their spouses because women tend to marry older men and to have longer life expectancies. Most women are widowed and live alone after age seventy-five, while most men are married and live with their wives.[30] Indeed, more than 70 percent of those over age eighty-five are women.[31]

◆ Elderly women are nearly twice as likely to be poor as elderly men. Of the 2.3 million elderly poor living alone in 1992, 2 million were women.[32]

SOCIAL SECURITY PROVIDES BENEFITS THAT WOULD BE DIFFICULT FOR WORKERS TO MATCH THROUGH PRIVATE POLICIES

➤ More than 7 million survivors of deceased workers (including almost 1.4 million children) received Social Security benefits. About 5.5 million workers (and their spouses and children) received monthly cash benefits as a result of severe and prolonged disability. Similar retirement and disability insurance policies in the marketplace would be very expensive. For an average wage earner with a spouse and two children, the disability policy provided by Social Security is equivalent to a $203,000 policy in the private sector; Social Security's survivorship insurance is equivalent to a $295,000 life insurance policy.[33]

➤ Social Security retirement benefits are portable, following workers from job to job. In contrast, many employer-provided pension plans offer benefits only to workers who stay with the same company for an extended period of time. Social Security benefits are adjusted annually to protect against erosion caused by inflation, whereas private pension programs and insurance plans rarely guarantee such protection. Under Social Security, disability and life insurance coverage is provided without regard to the health of the individual.

SOCIAL SECURITY BENEFITS ARE WORK-RELATED AND PROGRESSIVE

➤ Because Social Security is a social insurance program, it is structured so that someone who has had a lifetime of high wages (and was therefore able save money for retirement) does not have as much of his or her income replaced upon retiring as do low-wage earners. In other words, while those who earned higher wages get a larger check than those who earned less, the check represents a smaller percentage of their average earnings. In turn, the system pays retirees who earned lower incomes benefits that replace a larger percentage of their wages. Workers with a very low wage are guaranteed a minimum benefit.[34]

This progressive feature of Social Security helps give all workers in America a chance at a decent retirement, even if the type of work they did, or personal circumstances, did not enable them to accumulate wealth or become eligible for a private pension plan.

➤ The Social Security benefits of an average-wage earner retiring in 1997 were about 44 percent of his or her average earnings, while comparable figures for low- and high-wage earners were 80 percent and 25 percent, respectively.[35] (See Figure H.)

FIGURE H
**Social Security
Wage-Replacement Rates, 1997**

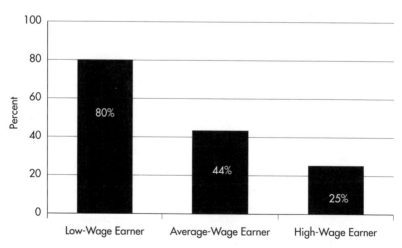

Source: David Koitz, "Social Security: Brief Facts and Statistics," Congressional Research Service Report no. 94–27 EPW, Washington, D.C., 1997, p. 10.

➤ With this structure, Social Security benefits are progressive, although benefits may be less progressive than they seem because of differing life expectancies among high- and low-income workers. People with more income tend to live longer and, as a result, collect benefits for a longer period of time.[36]

SOCIAL SECURITY IS AN EFFICIENT PROGRAM WITHOUT LOOPHOLES AND COMPLEX ADMINISTRATIVE REQUIREMENTS

➤ The program runs smoothly, regardless of political or economic events. Despite wars, economic recessions, and recent government shutdowns, Social Security checks have always reached recipients in a timely fashion.

➤ Program financing and administration are handled entirely through the federal government. Unlike other entitlements, such as Medicaid and welfare, Social Security does not require state and local governments to participate in program financing or administration.[37] Likewise, there are no interstate benefit differences for retirees with similar work histories.[38]

THERE IS LITTLE WASTE IN THE SYSTEM

➤ Administrative costs for Social Security are about 1 percent of benefits. According to the American Council of Life Insurance, administrative costs for private insurance are between 12 and 14 percent of annual benefit amounts. Public opinion polls conducted by the Roper organization, however, show that the public's "median" guess for the administrative costs of Social Security as a percentage of benefits was more than 50 percent.[39]

Social Security Has Enjoyed Broad Public Support Since Its Creation

➤ In 1935, Americans were nearly unanimous (89 percent) in their support of government assistance to needy elderly people. During the subsequent six decades, Social Security has routinely received strong support. Recent surveys affirm continued support for Social Security. In fact, many Americans advocate higher benefits and program expansions:[40]

- Significant majorities agree that Social Security provides useful benefits. In fact, nearly two-thirds of people surveyed thought that benefits were not sufficient.[41]

- Most people would be willing to pay higher taxes to maintain the Social Security system.[42] Fewer than one in ten respondents feel that the federal government spends too much on Social Security.[43]

- More than three-quarters of respondents favor universal participation in the program.[44]

What Will Your Social Security Benefit Be when You Retire?

To find out, you can call
the Social Security Administration
at 1-800-772-1213
Deaf Services 1–800–325–0778
Braille Services 1–410–965–6414

or visit the Social Security Administration's website:
http://www.ssa.gov

III. What's Wrong with Social Security?

 Without Changes, the Social Security Trust Funds May Be Depleted in 2029

➤ The Social Security Trustees' projections about the Trust Funds are based on assumptions about demographic and economic trends over the next seventy-five years. Since future conditions are uncertain, the Trustees make three sets of predictions based upon optimistic, intermediate, and pessimistic assumptions. Social Security's finances look dramatically different depending upon which assumptions are used. Under the more optimistic set, the Trustees estimate that Social Security would be adequately funded through 2035, at that point having more than $50 trillion (in 1998 dollars) in the Trust Funds; in contrast, the pessimistic assumptions yield a shortfall amounting to 5.4 percent of taxable payroll over the seventy-five-year period. Under the intermediate projection, the shortfall would amount to about 2.2 percent of taxable payroll.[45]

➤ Because of the upcoming retirement of the baby-boom generation and other demographic trends, the Social Security Board of Trustees projects (under its intermediate set of economic assumptions) that beginning in 2013 annual benefits paid to retirees will exceed payroll tax revenues.[46] (See Figure I, page 24.) Based on those intermediate assumptions, from 2013 through 2020, interest generated from the Trust Funds would be needed to meet current Social Security obligations. From 2021 through 2031, it would be necessary to use principal from the Trust Funds along with accruing tax revenues to meet expenses.[47] By 2032, under those assumptions, the Trust Funds would be fully spent. It is important to note that, contrary to many reports in the media, the system would not become bankrupt or "insolvent" when the Trust Funds run out. Under the intermediate forecast, taxes would be sufficient to pay 75 percent of the obligations to Social Security recipients at the time, declining to about two-thirds by the end of the seventy-five-year period.[48]

➤ The Trustees' intermediate seventy-five-year forecast assumes that the U.S. economy will grow at a slower rate than it has in the past. (See Figure J.) It is important to bear in mind that there is no consensus among economists today as to how the economy will perform in the twenty-first century. Few economists predicted that growth would be as high as it has been in recent years, while inflation and unemployment have remained low. The Trustees' estimate—even the intermediate forecast—errs on the side of caution.

➤ Between 1946 and 1964, people who had postponed having children during the Great Depression and World War II began to add to or start families. The oldest members of the baby-boom generation— those born between 1946 and 1964—are scheduled to become eligible for full Social Security benefits in the year 2010.

➤ At the same time, Americans are living longer. Projections of longer life expectancies and declining birth rates suggest that, after 2030, more than 20 percent of all Americans will be elderly, a larger proportion than ever before. This larger number of retirees will have to be paid their benefits from taxes collected from a smaller pool of workers, relatively speaking. In 1995, there were nearly five people between the ages

FIGURE I
Estimated OASDI Income and Outgo in Constant 1998 Dollars, 1998–2030 (in billions)

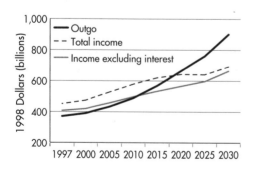

Source: *1998 Annual Report of the Social Security Trustees,* p. 177.

FIGURE J
Average of Annual Percentage Changes in Real Gross Domestic Product over Selected Periods

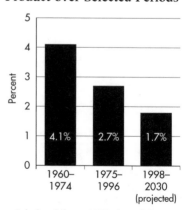

Source: Calculated from *1998 Annual Report of the Social Security Trustees,* p. 57, and data from the website of the Office of the Chief Actuary of the Social Security Administration.

of twenty and sixty-four for every person aged sixty-five and over.[49] Demographers estimate that in the year 2030, when today's young workers begin to retire, there will be slightly fewer than three persons between the ages of twenty and sixty-four for each person sixty-five and older.[50] (See Figure K.)

➤ In technical terms, the problem confronting Social Security is that over the next seventy-five years, based on the anticipated demographic changes just described and assumptions of slower economic growth, Social Security is projected to slip out of balance by an amount equal to about 2 percent of total taxable payroll (that portion of payroll subject to Social Security taxes) per year. This means that an immediate increase in the payroll tax of about 2 percent (over the current 12.4 percent combined rate) would generate adequate funds to pay full benefits through 2073. Clearly, a payroll tax increase is not the only

way to avoid the shortfall, but such an interpretation is useful for gauging the size of the problem.[51]

➤ The projected deficit has raised fear and concern and has brought numerous proposals for reform (which will be discussed in section V). In assessing any reform proposal, several factors that put the size and scope of the problem into perspective should be considered:

◆ Stronger than expected economic performance would eliminate projected shortfalls. An increase in annual economic growth of just 0.15 percentage points over the next thirty-five years would raise output by as much as the combined increase in the cost of both Social Security *and* Medicare, measured as a share of gross domestic product. Such a sustained improvement in economic performance could be accomplished through some combination of steady but not

FIGURE K
Composition of Population, by Age

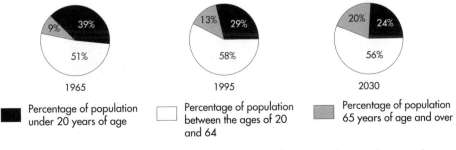

1965	1995	2030

■ Percentage of population under 20 years of age

□ Percentage of population between the ages of 20 and 64

▨ Percentage of population 65 years of age and over

Source: 1998 Annual Report of the Social Security Trustees, p. 145; the 2030 numbers are the intermediate projection.

unprecedented increases in household savings, capital investment, and labor force participation.[52]

◆ There are a number of demographic shifts that have taken place since the end of World War II that mitigate the financial burden of an increasing elderly population. For example, women entered the workforce in large numbers, and the baby-boom generation produced a baby boomlet. As a result, although there will be more retirees in 2030, the percentage of Americans in the workforce, and thus paying Social Security taxes, is projected to be greater in 2030 than it was during the 1960s at the height of the baby boom.[53]

◆ Shifts in the dependency ratio, which measures the number of workers relative to nonworkers (old and young), can move in either direction: in 1965, the year the baby boom drew to a close, for every 100 Americans of working age there were about 95 dependents, of whom about 18 were age sixty-five and over; in 1995, there were about 71, of whom about 21 were over sixty-five; in 2030, it is projected that there will be about 79, of whom about 36 will be over sixty-five. (See Figure L.)

➤ The potential problems facing Medicare are considerably more complex, especially when taking into account that the driving force behind expected cost increases is

FIGURE L
Number of Dependents (Old and Young) Supported by 100 Working-Age Individuals

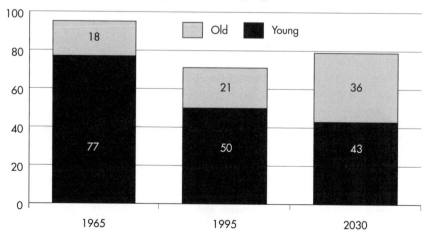

Source: 1998 Annual Report of the Social Security Trustees, p. 145.

upward pressure on health costs for people of all ages. Even after reforms under the 1997 balanced budget agreement, the Medicare Hospital Insurance Trust Fund is projected to be depleted in 2008.[54] Over the next seventy-five years, under certain assumptions, the Trustees of the Federal Hospital Insurance Trust Fund project that the Hospital Insurance Program will have an actuarial deficit amounting to 2.1 percent of covered payroll— a large funding shortfall considering that the program was financed by a 2.9 percent payroll tax in 1997.[55] While the retirement of the baby-

boom generation adds to Medicare's troubles, rapidly rising health care costs are largely responsible for the funding deficit. Of course, health care inflation is a problem through-out the medical system and not confined to coverage of the elderly. Restoring fiscal soundness to the Medicare program will be a much bigger challenge than fixing Social Security because Medicare's deficit is much larger and is not simply a by-product of population aging. (For a complete discussion of the financial problems confronting the Medicare program, see our Basics pamphlet, "Medicare Reform.")

FUTURE RETIREES WILL PROBABLY RECEIVE LESS GENEROUS BENEFITS THAN TODAY'S ELDERLY

➤ Most elderly Americans have received Social Security benefits far exceeding what they contributed in payroll taxes during their working years (plus accumulated interest), although the actual benefit-to-contribution ratio depends, of course, on one's work history and age of retirement. An average-wage employee retiring in 1997 would regain his or her Social Security tax contribution with interest after 6.2 years in retirement. A minimum-wage earner would earn back his or her portion of the tax (with interest)

in 4.4 years, while the maximum-wage earner would regain his or her tax contribution in 8.1 years, according to the Congressional Research Service.[56] (Of course, this assumes a continuation of such things as increases that match the rate of inflation.)

➤ The benefit-to-contribution ratio on Social Security contributions has been declining since the establishment of the Social Security system. Contribution rates were very low when the system was first designed: the total tax rate was 2 percent in 1937. The earliest retirees paid low taxes for a short period of time (less than their entire career) and received sizable benefits upon retirement, consequently reaping substantial "returns" on their contributions. Over time, as Social Security benefits became more generous and the number of individuals receiving benefits grew, the payroll tax was increased. The benefit-to-contribution ratio of Social Security has declined for each new cohort of retirees because later generations contributed to the Social Security system for the duration of their careers and were subject to higher payroll tax rates.[57]

➤ The benefit-to-contribution ratio for future generations of retirees is projected to decline further, assuming no changes are made to the system.[58] A single man with low earnings aged sixty-five in 2029 is expected to have an average annual real rate of return from the OASI program amounting to 2.4 percent, slightly higher than the 2 percent average real return on government bonds. A couple with one worker who earned an average income would receive a substantially higher average real rate of return, 3.75 percent, upon turning sixty-five in 2029. On the other hand, a single male with high earnings would receive a much lower rate of return (0.72 percent).[59]

 ## SOCIAL SECURITY'S PAYROLL TAX IS REGRESSIVE

➤ In 1998, Social Security's 6.2 percent payroll tax was assessed on only the first $68,400 of a worker's earnings. Because unearned income (interest and capital gains) is not subject to taxation under a payroll tax and earned income beyond $68,400 is not taxed, wealthy individuals pay a lower fraction of their total income in Social Security taxes than other people.

SOME FEAR THAT SOCIAL SECURITY DEPRESSES NATIONAL SAVING

➤ There is great concern that many Americans are not saving adequately for retirement. A low rate of saving in the United States has sparked concern because saving is generally thought to promote economic growth and higher standards of living. There are two related issues: inadequate saving by the nation as a whole—government, firms, and individuals collectively—and inadequate personal saving for retirement by individuals.

- ◆ **NATIONAL SAVING.** The U.S. national saving rate has been declining for the past thirty-five years. National saving decreased in the 1960s and 1970s because of increasing federal budget deficits (government dissavings). In the 1980s, national saving fell even faster as deficits escalated and, to a lesser extent, private saving declined.[60]

  Through its buildup of reserves in the Trust Funds, Social Security directly adds to government saving, and thus to national saving. As the Social Security Trust Funds decline, that component of national saving declines.

- ◆ **PERSONAL SAVING.** At the same time, many Americans may not be saving adequately for their own retirement. A number of economists have estimated—using a variety of economic assumptions and models— how retirees will fare in retirement. William Gale of the Brookings Institution argues that the extent to which families are prepared for their old age depends on such factors as the living standards they expect, the performance of investment and housing markets, and the growth of the economy generally. Moreover, low- and middle-income families with few assets besides their homes and little or no pension coverage are far more vulnerable than wealthier households that have amassed wealth. In his assessment of married people's retirement preparation, Gale concludes that "a third of the sample is doing well by any measure, a third is doing poorly by any measure, and the middle third is (or may be) just hanging in there."[61]

  Some suspect that Social Security may be responsible for the low rate of personal saving in the United States. By using tax revenues from workers to provide income for the elderly, some economists have argued, Social Security discourages Americans from saving for their own retirement. Workers may assume that Social Security will provide a sufficient income later and therefore neglect to save now for the future.[62]

But most studies have found little evidence that Social Security has caused a significant decline in personal saving; indeed, economists have had little success in explaining people's saving behavior at all. For example, Federal Reserve Board of Governors' economists could predict only 7 percent of the variation that exists in household saving, and no one has offered a widely accepted explanation for the substantial decline in personal saving in the 1980s.[63]

 ## SOCIAL SECURITY MAY ENCOURAGE EARLY RETIREMENT, PUTTING ADDED PRESSURE ON THE SYSTEM

➤ Over the past fifty years, older Americans have been retiring at a progressively younger age. In 1950, 83.4 percent of men aged fifty-five to sixty-four were employed; by 1990, only 67.8 percent of men in this age group were working.[64] Today, most men and women retire before age sixty-five; in fact, almost 60 percent receive Social Security benefits at age sixty-two, when reduced benefits for early retirement first become available.[65]

➤ On the one hand, earlier retirement is a trend that benefits individual workers, allowing them to enjoy a longer retirement than in the past. Most Americans say they would rather retire sooner than later. Furthermore, if individuals continue to retire earlier, this might increase the demand for younger workers. On the other hand, some economists are concerned that earlier retirement, combined with increased longevity, exacerbates the problem of economically sustaining an aging population. If the trend toward early retirement continues as the population ages, an even smaller share of workers will be supporting a larger proportion of retirees.

➤ Examining the ages at which most Americans retire suggests that the structure of the Social Security program, as well as private pensions, affects retirement decisions.

➤ **THE IMPACT OF THE SOCIAL SECURITY PROGRAM.** The two ages at which most Americans retire are sixty-two, when they first become eligible to receive any Social Security benefits, and sixty-five, when they can receive full Social Security benefits.[66] The program's primary influence on workers' decisions about when to retire are:

◆ As currently structured, Social Security benefits for those who retire after the standard retirement age of sixty-five are increased only 5 percent for each year retirement is delayed (for individuals who turned sixty-five in 1996–97), which is not enough to compensate fully for the benefits foregone; the rate will increase gradually, rising to 8 percent for those who turn sixty-six in 2009 and thereafter.[67]

◆ People under seventy who continue to work while collecting Social Security face benefit reductions if they earn more than a specified amount.

Recently, several measures have been adopted that modify the Social Security system so that it provides more incentives for older Americans to continue work:

◆ In the future, benefits will be increased for workers who retire after age sixty-five, adding to the financial incentive to work longer.[68]

◆ The amount that individuals age sixty-five to sixty-nine can earn without benefit reductions is gradually being raised over time.[69]

◆ The standard retirement age is scheduled to rise gradually from sixty-five to sixty-seven for individuals who will turn sixty-two in the year 2022, though individuals will continue to be eligible for reduced-retirement benefits at sixty-two.[70]

➤ **THE IMPACT OF PRIVATE PENSIONS.** Employer-provided pension plans appear to have a stronger impact on workers' retirement decisions than Social Security.[71] In most private pension plans, the value of a worker's pension declines substantially if he or she continues to work past age sixty-five, and often past age fifty-five.[72]

IV. HOW OUR SYSTEM COMPARES WITH THOSE OF OTHER COUNTRIES

➤ Because of increasing life expectancy and declining fertility, all of the major industrialized nations will experience substantial population aging over the next thirty years. By 2030, the elderly will make up 20 percent or more of the population in each of the seven big Organization for Economic Cooperation and Development (OECD) nations.[73] Within that group, the United States will have the smallest proportion of elderly individuals. The overall dependency ratios in those countries show similar patterns. (See Figure M.)

FIGURE M
Projected Total and Elderly Dependency Ratios Across the Seven Major Industrialized Countries, 2030

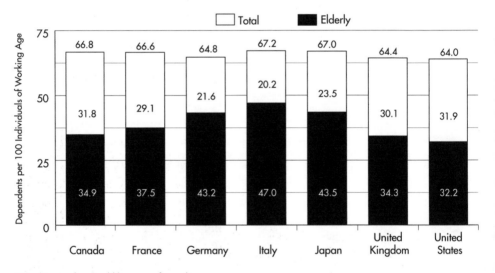

Note: Figures do not add because of rounding.

Source: Estimates and medium-variant projections from the United Nations. The total dependency ratio is the number of youths and elderly individuals per 100 individuals of working age. The elderly dependency ratio is the number of elderly individuals per 100 individuals of working age. Youth is defined as 0–14 years of age, working age is defined as 15–64, and elderly is defined as age 65 and above. Department for Economic and Social Information and Policy Analysis, *World Population Prospects: The 1994 Revision* (New York: United Nations Publications, 1995), pp. 439, 449, 451, 455.

SOCIAL SECURITY

➤ All seven major industrialized nations have social security systems that provide old-age, survivorship, and disability benefits. Each of these systems is funded on a pay-as-you-go basis; the United States and Japan accumulate some reserves for future use. Payments to current beneficiaries are financed through payroll taxes on current workers and employers. A few countries, such as Japan and Germany, use general tax revenues in addition to payroll tax collections to finance social security benefits.

➤ The level of public pension spending varies across the seven major industrialized countries. The United States spends about 6.9 percent of GDP on Social Security. Other countries, including Germany, France, and Italy, spend more than 10 percent of their GDP on public pensions. (See Figure N.) These countries also have roughly proportionate tax rates to finance their public pension programs.[74]

FIGURE N
Public Pension Spending as a Percentage of GDP, in 1990*

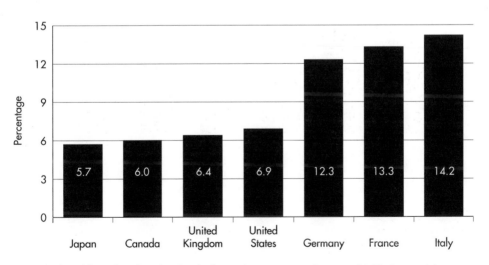

Source: Adapted from Sheetal K. Chand and Albert Jaeger, *Aging Populations and Public Pension Schemes,* (Washington, D.C.: International Monetary Fund, 1996), p. 6.

*The figures for Germany and France are for 1992.

◆ **STRUCTURE OF RETIREMENT BENEFITS.** The structure of retirement benefits varies across nations.[75] All of the seven major industrialized nations pay an earnings-related pension. The United Kingdom
and Japan also pay retirees a flat benefit based on the number of years
they made payroll tax contributions. Canada supplements its earnings-
related pension program with a noncontributory, universal pension.

◆ **SOCIAL SECURITY REPLACEMENT RATES.** U.S. Social Security
earnings replacement rates (the percentage of one's income at retirement replaced by Social Security) are low compared to the other major
industrialized nations. The maximum earnings replacement rate for a
retiree with average career earnings is 42 percent in the United States,
compared to more than 50 percent in Germany, France, and Italy.
While the maximum rate of earnings-related pensions in Canada, the
United Kingdom, and Japan are lower than in the United States,
these nations supplement their earnings-related pensions with flat
benefits that everyone receives regardless of their prior income. In
the case of the United Kingdom, however, the base amount is
extremely low.[76]

◆ **INDEXATION OF BENEFITS.** Like the United States, some industrialized nations (Italy, Canada, and the United Kingdom) index their
public pension benefits to protect beneficiaries against inflation.
Private pensions typically are not indexed in any country.[77]

FISCAL CONDITION OF SOCIAL SECURITY SYSTEMS

➤ The International Monetary Fund projects that, without changes, over the next fifty years, the social security systems in each of the seven major industrialized nations will experience a funding shortfall. The U.S. projected deficit is small compared to most of the other nations. Only the British social security system appears to face a shortfall comparable to the one projected for the United States. To restore fiscal balance, the United Kingdom and the United States would need to increase their annual revenues by less than 1 percent of GDP.[78] All of the other nations would require an increase amounting to 2 to 3 percent of GDP.[79] (See Figure O.)

FIGURE O
Projected Contributions and Shortfalls, as Percent of GDP

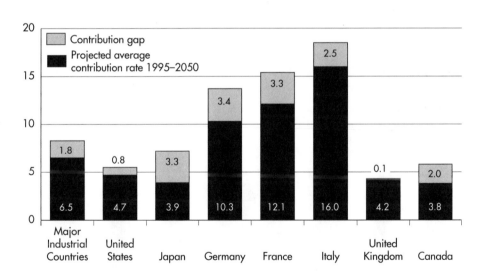

Source: Adapted from Chand and Jaeger, *Aging Populations and Public Pension Schemes,* p. 17.

COMPARING THE OTHER COMPONENTS OF RETIREMENT SUPPORT

➤ The adequacy of public pensions and the appropriate measures of reform depend, in part, on other sources of income available for seniors, including the following: earnings from work, pensions, savings, and public health care.

◆ **WORK.** Of the seven major industrialized nations, the United States, Germany, and Canada set normal retirement age at sixty-five for both men and women. In the other countries, the retirement age is lower. (In the case of the United Kingdom, men have a retirement age of sixty-five while women can retire at sixty.) The United States stands apart from other countries in that age discrimination and forced retirement are against the law.[80] Nonetheless, most workers in the United States and elsewhere are retiring at steadily younger ages, on average.[81] (See Figure P.)

◆ **PENSIONS.** In addition to public pension programs, several of the major industrialized nations have large, private pension systems. In general, countries with less generous social security systems have greater accumulations of private pension assets. The United States and United Kingdom have the largest holdings of private pension

FIGURE P
Labor Force Participation Rates of Older Males, 1977 and 1996*

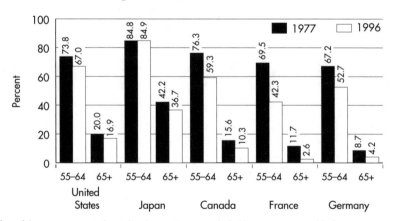

* Only five of the seven major industrialized countries are included because comparable figures are not available for Italy and the United Kingdom. In Italy, figures for participation of males 60–64 dropped from 41.6% in 1977 to 28.9% in 1995; for males 65 and older, participation rates dropped from 9.9% to 5.8%. In the United Kingdom, the earliest figures available are for 1984, when participation rates for males 55–64 was 70.0%, declining to 62.9% in 1996.

Source: Drawn from tables in Organisation for Economic Co-operation and Development, *Labor Force Statistics, 1976–1996* (Paris: OECD, 1997), pp. 532–86.

assets among the G–7 nations.[82] Total private pension assets in the United States in 1996 amounted to $7.9 trillion, slightly more than the nation's GDP of $7.6 trillion.[83]

♦ **SAVINGS.** Currently, household savings in the G–7 countries range from a low of 5 percent in the United States and Canada to more than 11 percent elsewhere. Possible explanations for the variations in saving rates range from cultural differences to tax policies and demographic distinctions.[84]

♦ **HEALTH CARE.** All of the G–7 countries have some package of health care for senior citizens. American seniors receive coverage through the Medicare program. (The United States, of course, has a much higher proportion of working-age adults and children without health insurance.) Yet, unlike citizens in other countries, American seniors incur substantial "out-of-pocket" health care expenses. About a third of medical care expenditures for elders are paid for privately.[85] It is estimated that health expenditures amount to about 21 percent of family income for seniors.[86]

Compared to many other industrial democracies, the United States spends a smaller proportion of its total health care expenditures on senior citizens.[87]

TRENDS IN REFORM MEASURES

➤ Since the 1980s, industrialized countries in general have become increasingly aware of the impending retirement of the large baby-boom cohort. Several countries, including Germany, Sweden, and Italy, have made incremental changes in their systems, restoring fiscal balance through relatively minor alterations in revenues or expenditures. These changes include increasing the retirement age, tightening eligibility requirements for early retirement or disability benefits, and lowering benefits.[88] Means-testing some or all of the public pension benefit has been implemented in Canada and Denmark, for example.

➤ More drastic reforms that alter the nature of the social insurance system have been adopted in several countries, most notable in Latin American, Asian, and African countries. The most extreme change is pension "privatization," which shifts responsibilities to the private sector and individuals. The United Kingdom has "privatized" one component of its public pension program, while Chile has moved to a substantially privatized model, albeit one that is tightly controlled by the government, including a mandatory personal pension deduction from payroll. The experiences of these countries are illuminating for the debate in the United States.

◆ **UNITED KINGDOM.** Some Americans who would like to see the Social Security system substantially reformed have looked to changes in the United Kingdom as a possible model of partial privatization for the United States.

The British pension system is now made up of two parts. The first tier, National Insurance, is a minimal, flat benefit supported by lump-sum contributions by workers and employers. In 1978, an earnings-related benefit, the so-called State Earnings Related Pension Scheme (SERPS), was put into place. SERPS is also financed by payroll tax contributions.

Unlike the current U.S. Social Security system, the British system allows SERPS contributions to be taken out of the government's retirement system and placed into approved, private defined-benefit schemes. To compensate for "contracting out," workers and their employers pay a lower rate for the National Insurance contribution.

In an effort to cut costs for the program and reduce the government's involvement with social welfare programs, the Thatcher government strengthened financial incentives for workers to "opt out" of the state-supported system for a private plan, which would lessen government obligations to future retirees.[89]

The consequences associated with this policy shift have been significant. SERPS benefits have been reduced and the pensionable age for women increased. Many Britons have found themselves with smaller pensions because of a change in the index for inflation and poor investment decisions with their private accounts. Lower pensions have led to an increase in means-tested income maintenance programs. Finally, the national government has been left with new administrative expenses, lost tax revenues, and responsibilities to bail out some failed private pension programs.

◆ **CHILE.** The degree of pension privatization in Chile has been even more dramatic than in the United Kingdom. Before 1981, Chile had a pension system that was theoretically fully funded, with most of the contributions made by employers. But the system was riddled with problems. Many individuals did not participate in the program and rapid inflation was devaluing the accumulated pensions. Moreover, benefits were calculated on the basis of an individual's earnings in only the last few years of work, creating more costly obligations than if his or her entire work history (with lower wages in the early years) were taken into account.[90]

The privatized pension scheme was put into place by a military dictator, Augusto Pinochet, and his assistant, José Pinera. In contrast to the old system, the new, privatized system is financed entirely by employee contributions, with at least 10 percent of workers' salaries going for old-age pensions and 3 to 3.5 percent for survivor and disability pensions. These personal investment accounts are managed by a small number of private companies. In addition, the Chilean government supports a minimum benefit provision (about 85 percent of the legal minimum wage), which is financed through general tax revenues. Unlike the U.S. public pension system, which has a long history, the Chilean model is still very young. Yet the system faces actual and potential problems:

- **High administrative and transition costs.** The government mandated a 17 percent across-the-board wage increase for all workers for the initial financing of the system, while assuming the obligation to support the current retirees who could not join the new system. The administrative costs, now estimated to be between 10 and 20 percent of contributions, are likely to increase when current workers begin to collect pensions from their private accounts.

- **Possible underfunding of the system.** The system's planners originally estimated that a 10 percent payroll contribution would provide workers with benefits on the order of 50 to 70 percent of their final salary. This projection was based on extremely optimistic assumptions about rates of return on the investments in the accounts. Many experts believe that more moderate rates of return in the future will seriously diminish the replacement rates of the benefits.

- **Outliving pensions.** In the U.S. Social Security program, consistent retirement benefits are guaranteed for the remainder of a worker's life. Under a so-called defined contribution plan, such as Chile's, it is possible for a worker's pension to "run out." The level of benefits received at retirement are not guaranteed to last for the retirees' lifetimes.

V. An Overview of the Major Proposed U.S. Reforms

➤ There are numerous proposed reforms of the Social Security system that would bring the system into long-run (seventy-five year) balance. Those ideas can be grouped into two general categories: changes that preserve the basic structure of the current system with minor modifications and more dramatic transformations that either would invoke means-testing of benefits or would shift part of the system from today's pay-as-you-go insurance plan to an arrangement more like 401(k) retirement plans and individual retirement accounts.

The following discussion will focus on certain reform measures that have been proposed by the 1994–96 Advisory Council on Social Security (the Gramlich Commission) as well as other ideas, such as means-testing Social Security benefits.[91]

A majority of the Advisory Council supported several incremental reforms that would reduce (but not eliminate) the projected deficit, which is estimated to be slightly more than 2 percent of projected payroll tax revenues.

1. **Increasing the working period over which a retiree's benefits are computed from thirty-five years to thirty-eight years.** Adding three years to the wage history that is taken into account when formulating a retiree's benefits would include a worker's earlier, lower-paid employment years, thereby reducing benefits. This change would close about 12 percent of the projected gap.[92]

2. **Changing the way in which Social Security benefits are taxed, so that any benefits a retiree receives beyond what he or she contributed to the system as a worker would be taxed as ordinary income.** Other retirement plans, such as some individual retirement accounts (IRAs), already are taxed in this manner. Currently, only beneficiaries with incomes above certain annual thresholds owe taxes on their benefits, and just a portion of their benefits is subject to the tax. This change would close about 14 percent of the projected gap.

3. **Extending Social Security coverage and participation to 3.7 million state and local government employees who are currently excluded from the program.** Subjecting government workers to Social Security

payroll taxes would bring more revenues into the system. This change would shrink the estimated shortfall by about 10 percent.

4. **Accelerating the scheduled increase in the retirement age so that it becomes sixty-seven by 2011; the retirement age would be indexed to longevity thereafter.** Advocates of raising the retirement age for Social Security point to the fact that Americans are living longer than before. In 1983, the Social Security Act was amended to raise gradually the age at which retirees become eligible for full benefits; under this reform, the retirement age would reach sixty-seven for individuals who will turn sixty-two in the year 2022. Speeding up this process so that the retirement age would become sixty-seven for individuals who turn sixty-two in 2011, and thereafter indexing it to longevity, would reduce how much the system pays out and improve the long-term financial picture for Social Security. This change would eliminate about 22 percent of the gap.

5. **Adjusting the Consumer Price Index (CPI).** The Bureau of Labor Statistics, which is studying possible adjustments to the CPI, announced in 1996 that it is putting in place measures that are expected to decrease the CPI by 0.21 percent per year; this change will take care of an estimated 14 percent of the gap. There is substantial controversy among economists about whether the index, even after the change, would continue to overstate inflation.

➤ These incremental changes would eliminate more than 70 percent of the projected long-term shortfall. A variety of reforms have been suggested to deal with the remainder: investing the Social Security Trust Funds in the stock market, means-testing Social Security benefits, and "privatizing" Social Security. The last of these ideas would entail switching from a system of social insurance, where everyone is guaranteed an inflation-proof benefit for his or her retirement, to a system of individual retirement accounts resembling 401(k)s, in which individuals' benefits would no longer be guaranteed by the government. The Advisory Council report agreed that means-testing should not be implemented, but members split into three groups over which reform to recommend.

INVESTING IN THE STOCK MARKET

➤ One proposed reform is to invest some of the Social Security Trust Funds in the stock market to prevent future shortfalls. Under current law, the Trustees of the Social Security Trust Funds may invest the surplus that the funds accumulate only in U.S. government securities, the debt the government issues to finance its borrowing. Because these securities are the safest investments available, they pay a relatively low rate of interest. Under one proposed plan, part of the Trust Funds would be invested in stocks through an unmanaged index fund holding a diversified portfolio of shares. (More than half of the Trust Funds would remain in Treasury securities.) An independent "investment board" nominated by the president and approved by the Senate would oversee the investments and would be allowed to invest the Trust Funds' money. Because stocks have generated higher investment returns in the past than Treasuries, diversifying might leave the Trust Funds with greater assets over time.

ADVANTAGES

◆ Preserves the current system of benefits, leaving the safety net unchanged.

◆ The system would remain progressive, with lower-income seniors receiving a higher proportion of their past earnings than upper-income retirees.

◆ If stock market returns continue to match past performance, it could leave the system healthier.

DISADVANTAGES

◆ All this plan does is change the form in which the Trust Funds' investments are held. It does not increase national saving or otherwise change the system in a way that might encourage future economic growth.

◆ The government could end up as a major stockholder in many American companies. Though reformers advocate an "independent investment board," the threat of political interference in corporate governance has raised concern.

- ◆ Stock markets are risky. Investing the Trust Funds in stocks implies taking a bet that returns will be high enough to make up the shortfall. If returns are not high enough, or the stock market falls, future generations will be left facing the bill.

MEANS-TESTING

➤ Advocates of means-testing argue that few upper-income retirees should be entitled to collect so much—or collect anything at all, in the case of the highest earners—from the government.[93] The most commonly proposed form of means-testing would be to reduce or eliminate the Social Security benefits for retirees who receive substantial investment income during their retirement.

ADVANTAGES

- ◆ By reducing benefits, means-testing could alleviate some of the future pressure on the Social Security program.

- ◆ Reducing Social Security payments to middle- and upper-income elderly would not immediately pose a threat to lower-income retirees.

- ◆ Because upper-income retirees would have their checks reduced or eliminated while the checks of lower-income beneficiaries would remain untouched, means-testing would make the system more progressive than it currently is.

- ◆ Means-testing could promote national savings by cutting benefits to higher-income workers while maintaining current tax levels, thus reducing the government deficit or increasing its surplus.

DISADVANTAGES

- ◆ Means-testing could transform the public's perception of the program from one that benefits everyone to one that serves only low-income Americans, undermining its political viability. Other government means-tested programs such as welfare, food stamps, and Medicaid are continually under political attack, in part because support is scarce for programs that primarily benefit the poor.

♦ People who earn more and save would receive lower benefits, which could be viewed as unfair as well as creating perverse incentives. Also, means-tested programs tend to motivate individuals to "hide" assets and income. The Medicaid and welfare programs have been riddled with "gaming" schemes developed by individuals who sought to receive undeserved benefits.

♦ Administrative costs would increase under a means-tested program. The administrative costs for the Social Security program are about 1 percent of total program expenditures. The administrative costs for Supplemental Security Income, the means-tested program for old people, run well in excess of 10 percent of the program.

SUBSTANTIAL PRIVATIZATION

➤ These proposals come in a variety of guises. This section focuses on one plan by some members of the Social Security Advisory Commission, using it to explore the main commonalities among the major proposals.[94] In this and the other major plans, all future retirees would receive payment from two sources: a guaranteed minimum benefit and an additional amount that reflected the returns individuals earned on their "personal security accounts" (PSAs).

➤ Both components of the benefit would be financed by the payroll tax. Because the guaranteed part of the benefit would be based only on a portion of the payroll tax, it would be significantly lower than the benefit that low-income retirees now receive. Each individual's additional benefits would depend on the performance of his or her PSA, which the worker would control.

➤ Most of the privatization plans would entail significant tax increases or newly generated borrowing to maintain current benefits for workers who will be retiring in the next ten to twenty years, as payroll taxes are shifted to the new accounts. This would be necessary because workers now in their fifties have relatively little time remaining before their retirement, and suddenly shifting to a personal account system would leave them at greater risk of ending up worse off. They would have less of an opportunity to accumulate sizable accounts, and the short-term horizon would leave them more vulnerable to a downturn in investment markets. As a result, younger workers would have to pay taxes for both current retirees' benefits and for their own future benefits.

ADVANTAGES

- People would be able to choose the risk/return combination that best suits them. The well-off could invest more aggressively while lower- and middle-income retirees could opt for more secure though lower-yield investments.

- Some individuals could obtain higher returns than they would under the current system.

- Individuals would own their own accounts, so they would face less risk if future generations defaulted on promises to pay benefits.

- National savings would likely increase if payroll taxes were raised to finance the transition to a privatized system.

- By shedding the enormous financial obligations of the government to future retirees, Social Security privatization, when fully implemented, would virtually eliminate the challenge of generating sufficient taxes to provide promised benefits.

DISADVANTAGES

♦ Social Security's success in keeping most of the elderly from poverty would be threatened. Workers who invest poorly or unwisely would not be assured of staying out of poverty.

♦ The Social Security system would become much less progressive. Research indicates that without an extensive financial education campaign, low-income workers would have lower returns on their Social Security investments, and thus smaller retirement accounts and smaller incomes than high-income workers, because they tend to make poorer investment choices.

♦ The shift to a privatized system would create huge transition costs. The current generation of workers would essentially be required to "pay twice." Today's workers would continue to pay for the benefits of current retirees. They would also be required to make contributions toward their own retirement. According to one estimate, the privatization plans backed by a minority of the recent Social Security Advisory Commission would require about $6.5 trillion in additional taxes over the next seventy-two years.

♦ Administrative costs of the Social Security program would increase, especially for individual investors, who would have to pay management fees to Wall Street investment houses on their investments.[95] Private administrative and management fees for financial portfolios are many times larger than the administrative costs for Social Security.[96]

♦ If many older Americans fell into poverty, either their families or other government programs would have to take up the slack. Many members of the baby-boom generation might find themselves supporting aging parents while trying to raise their own children.

THE STOCK MARKET: A HISTORY LESSON

While the stock market's performance over the last several years has, for the most part, been impressive, the twenty-year average for stock market performance—the approximate period of an individual's saving for retirement—has been far less predictable.

Since 1900, the 20-year average real total return on the stock market fell to about zero three times—1901 to 1921, from 1928 to 1948, and from 1962 to 1982. . . . Of course, the returns were substantially negative after paying taxes on interest and dividends. In between were periods in which the 20-year average stock market returns peaked at rates ranging from 6% to 10%. This meant that some people earned a negative real return from investing in the stock market, while others received a real pretax return as high as 10%.

—JOHN MUELLER
former economic counsel to the
U.S. House of Representatives' Republican Caucus

CONCLUSION

➤ Social Security has been one of America's most successful antipoverty programs, saving millions of elderly from living out their lives in poverty. Likewise, the program has provided important protection for families after the death or disability of the family's breadwinner.

➤ It is clear that the system will require some modifications in order to accommodate the retirement of the exceptionally large baby-boom generation. However, the debate over and implementation of policy changes must be carried out in a deliberate and responsible fashion. The financial security of America's elderly is too significant for "bumper sticker politics" or ninety-second campaign commercials.

II

WHY THE SKY
WILL NOT FALL

WILL THE BABY BOOMERS BREAK THE BANK?

HENRY J. AARON and ROBERT D. REISCHAUER

The 77 million baby boomers, born from 1946 through 1964, are marching toward retirement! Between 2008 and 2026, the fraction of the population age 62 and over and eligible for Social Security retirement benefits will increase from 15.7 percent to 22.8 percent. Unless birth rates rise sharply and unexpectedly, the elderly will form a permanently larger share of the population. How much will the baby boomers' retirement cost? Will these costs cut into the living standards of active workers if nothing is done to reduce currently promised benefits?

THE BURDEN OF SOCIAL SECURITY: PAST, PRESENT, AND FUTURE

The most widely cited indicator of the burden that Social Security places on the rest of society is the ratio of beneficiaries to workers.[1] Active workers must produce the food, clothing, shelter, health care, and other goods and services for themselves and their families, for

From Henry J. Aaron and Robert D. Reischauer, *Countdown to Reform: The Great Social Security Debate* (New York: The Century Foundation Press, 1998), Chapter 4.

Social Security beneficiaries, and for other members of the population who are not working. The higher the ratio of beneficiaries to workers, the smaller the proportion of total production economically inactive members of the population, including Social Security beneficiaries, consume.

BENEFICIARIES AND WORKERS

In 1998, there were thirty Social Security beneficiaries for every hundred workers. By 2031, when all the baby boomers will have reached the age at which unreduced Social Security benefits will be paid, projections indicate that there will be fifty beneficiaries for every hundred workers, an increase of two-thirds. This trend, although striking, is neither new nor unexpected. For the past two decades, the government's official demographic projections have painted this same picture. In other words, none of the projected long-term deficit that has emerged since 1983, when Congress last enacted major changes in the Social Security system, can be attributed to unforeseen demographic developments. The projected long-term deficit that has emerged since then is attributable to changed economic assumptions and revised methods of estimating the program's long-run costs and revenues.[2]

Looking back over six decades of Social Security history, the changing ratio of Social Security beneficiaries to workers tells a complicated story. In the early years of Social Security few people over age 65 received benefits. Most had stopped working before the system began or had been employed in one of the many jobs that were initially uncovered by Social Security. In 1945, five years after benefits were first paid, there were only two beneficiaries per hundred workers. Since then, the ratio of beneficiaries to workers has risen gradually as the proportion of 65-year-olds eligible for benefits has increased. In 1950, when only 16 percent of those 65 and older received benefits, there were six beneficiaries per hundred workers. It was not until 1958, when there were seventeen beneficiaries for every hundred workers, that over half of the elderly were receiving Social Security benefits.

Until recently, two developments helped to hold down the ratio of beneficiaries to covered workers. First, between 1946 and 1983, Congress gradually extended Social Security to domestic and agricultural workers, the self-employed, employees of nonprofit organizations, federal employees, members of the armed services, and most state and local workers—the 45 percent of the labor force initially excluded from coverage. Today, 96 percent of all civilian workers hold jobs covered by Social Security, and most of the remaining 4 percent will work in covered employment at some point in their lives and become eligible for benefits. Second, the labor force expanded rapidly as baby boomers grew up and went to work and as women increasingly took paid jobs. The influx of women more than offset a drop in male labor force participation.

A third factor—the rapid growth of worker productivity and earnings—held down benefit costs as a percent of payroll until the mid-1970s. The slowdown in growth of earnings and payroll tax revenues that started then and is projected to continue means that higher payroll tax rates will be needed to sustain any level of future benefits.

THE REST OF THE BURDEN STORY

Active members of the labor force have to support *all* economically inactive members of the population—children and nonaged adults who are not employed for pay, as well as Social Security beneficiaries. As it happens, the proportion of the population consisting of children and nonaged adults who are not working for pay has fallen over the past three decades and is projected to fall further in the future. Consequently, the number of people each worker will support is projected to rise only modestly—approximately 6 percent— between now and 2040, even though the number of elderly will soar (see Figure 1, page 54). The number of economically inactive members of the population per hundred workers was much higher in the past (156 in 1960) than it was in the mid-1990s (103 in 1995) or than it is projected to be in the future (115 in 2040).

NOT ALL DEPENDENTS ARE ALIKE

The increase in the number of mouths that active workers will have to feed is too small to attract much notice. But this way of looking at the problems created by population changes is oversimplified. First, the government pays directly for a larger share of the cost of supporting the elderly and disabled than of the cost of supporting children and economically inactive nonaged adults. While workers

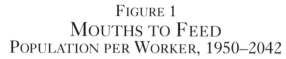

FIGURE 1
MOUTHS TO FEED
POPULATION PER WORKER, 1950–2042

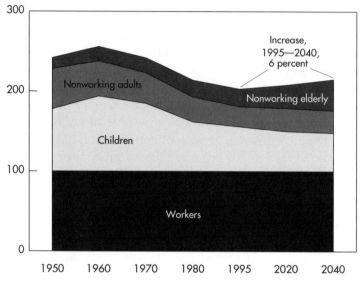

Source: National Academy of Social Insurance, "How Many People Does Each Worker Support?" *Social Insurance Update* 2, issue 4, April 1997.

eventually bear all these costs, as the government is only their agent, families *directly* bear primary responsibility for feeding, clothing, housing, and providing medical care for children and most nonretired adults. They receive help from state and local governments, which finance education, and from federal and state governments, which jointly provide income assistance, food vouchers, and health care subsidies for many low-income children and adults. As the composition of the dependent population shifts from children and able-bodied nonaged adults to retirees and the disabled, direct economic burdens on families will decline, while the costs to government of paying for the health and pension benefits of the elderly will rise.

Simply counting heads is misleading also because the average aged or disabled person costs more to support than the average child. Children and their nonworking caretakers live in families that enjoy the economies of scale available to multiperson households. A greater portion of the elderly and disabled, on the other hand, live alone or in two-person households. While children generate costs for publicly supported education, the average child consumes only about one-third as much health care as the average elderly person does.[3] On balance, projected changes in the *composition* of the dependent population will increase overall economic burdens.

THE BURDEN IN ECONOMIC TERMS

Just how large is the current burden of supporting the elderly and disabled, and how much will it grow as the baby boomers retire? In 1998, the benefit and administrative costs of Social Security amounted to 4.6 percent of GDP, about one-third more than defense expenditures and roughly the same as personal consumption spending on the purchase and operation of automobiles. By 2040, Social Security is projected to cost 6.8 percent of GDP, an increase of 2.2 percentage points in four decades. This increase is comparable to the 2 percent of GDP growth in cost of Social Security that took place between 1970 and 1982, a period less than a third as long as the 1998 to 2040 interval. It is also less than one-third of the growth of defense spending as a share of GDP—7.3 percentage points—that occurred between 1948 and 1955 when the Cold War intensified. It is slightly more than the 2.1 percentage points of GDP increase in federal spending on Medicare and Medicaid between 1980 and 1997. These increases were large but did not cause political crises or significant economic dislocation.

But Social Security is far from the whole story when it comes to the burden that retirement of baby boomers will impose on society. Between 1998 and 2040, Medicare spending is projected to increase by 3.6 percentage points of GDP. Medicaid spending, roughly two-thirds of which provides health services to low-income elderly and disabled persons, is projected to increase by about 2.4 percentage points of GDP over the next four decades. In addition, the costs of Supplementary Security Income (SSI) and food stamp benefits for the low-income aged and disabled may also rise. Finally, private expenditures on long-term care will also grow.

The projected increase in the cost of Social Security alone, or in combination with Medicare and the other programs, is significant but is not likely to overwhelm future economic growth. If real per capita income grows 1.2 percent annually—a bit slower than the rate at which per capita output has risen over the 1990s—real GDP per person will rise 65 percent by 2040.[4] Of this amount, just under one-third would be needed to deal with the projected increase in the cost of Social Security and Medicare assuming *nothing* is done to curb the growth of spending on these programs. Thus, moderate economic growth would enable future workers both to enjoy rising living standards and to pay the added taxes necessary to sustain currently projected benefit costs. The decision to levy higher taxes would, however, still be difficult and divisive.

What Can We Do About It?

Americans can act now to lighten the burden on future workers of supporting the baby boomers in two ways. Congress can scale back benefits payable in the future to retirees, the disabled, and survivors. Or Americans can adopt policies to increase economic growth.* Here we review two possible ways to boost economic growth—expanding the total number of workers and making each worker more productive.

Enlarging the Workforce

Faster population growth eventually enlarges the labor force and the economy's productive capacity. Unfortunately, few effective and politically acceptable ways exist to raise population growth. Current fertility rates will just about sustain an unchanged population. They are not projected to increase, and there is little evidence that acceptable public policy initiatives can do much to raise them. Furthermore, decades must pass before additional children that a pronatalist policy might cause to be born could be educated, reach adulthood, enter the labor force in significant numbers, and affect national production. Increased immigration could boost the labor force rapidly. But the roughly 1 million immigrants entering the United States annually are already producing economic and social strains.

Within the limits set by the adult population, the labor force can grow only if more adults choose to work for pay. The scope for such

*In Chapter 6 of *Countdown to Reform*, a package of measures aimed at restoring balance to Social Security that includes a number of reductions in future benefits is examined.

increase is limited, however, because the proportion of adults working for pay is already at a historic high. Sixty percent of women now work for pay outside the home, up from 38 percent in 1960, and Social Security's long-run projections assume that an even higher fraction of women will enter the paid labor force in the future. Large additional increases are unlikely.

The story for nonaged men is rather different. As women have moved into the paid labor force, men—especially those age 50 to 65—have moved out, largely through earlier retirement. The proportion of 65-year-old men in the paid labor force has dropped from 77 percent in 1940 to 36 percent in the mid-1990s (Figure 2). This trend reflects the fundamental economic fact that as people grow richer they want to have more leisure, which they get through shorter work weeks, longer vacations, and earlier retirement.

FIGURE 2
MALE LABOR FORCE PARTICIPATION RATES
VARIOUS YEARS, 1910–96

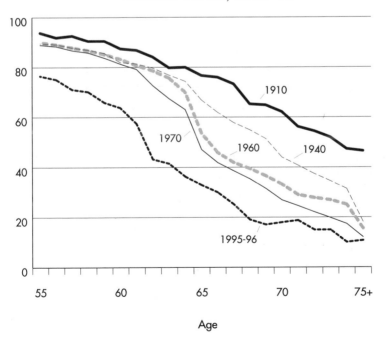

Source: Unpublished figure prepared by Gary Burtless, The Brookings Institution.

Social Security and private pensions have made earlier retirement possible for workers who have little personal savings. In fact, private pensions in the past expressly encouraged retirement of older and more highly compensated workers. To achieve this result, pensions for workers rose little or not at all after they reached a certain age. Social Security, in contrast, is roughly neutral with respect to retirement for workers up to age 65 because pensions for those who continue to work past age 61 are increased approximately enough to compensate for the foregone pensions.[5]

After dropping for decades, labor force participation rates of older males have been steady since the late 1980s. It is unclear whether the trend toward ever-earlier retirement has stopped permanently or has merely paused in response to an unusually strong economy, as happened during the boom years of the 1960s. Furthermore, policy changes have made it easier for older workers to remain in the labor force. Bans on discrimination against older workers were enacted in 1967 and 1990. Employer-imposed mandatory retirement rules were prohibited in 1986. Businesses are now required to continue pension contributions on behalf of those who work past the normal retirement age. In addition, the increment in Social Security benefits for those who work past age 65 was raised. We will not know for several years whether men have decided to work longer or are just adjusting to a new policy environment and taking advantage of the strong economy. If men could be encouraged to work even a bit longer, the effect on the labor force could be significant. For example, if men age 55 and older could be encouraged to work at the same rates as they did in 1970, the labor force would be enlarged by 2.9 million, which is one-fifth of the total projected labor force growth over the next decade.

The most obvious ways to encourage later retirement involve changing Social Security. Benefits could be cut either across the board, or just for early retirees, to encourage older workers to remain in the labor force. The age of initial entitlement could be raised. The retirement test—the reduction in benefits imposed when earnings exceed specified thresholds—could be liberalized. Or the delayed retirement credit—the increase in future benefits provided to compensate those whose benefits are cut because of the earnings test—could be increased.

Raising the "Normal" Retirement Age. The age at which unreduced retirement benefits are paid—the so-called normal retirement age—is now 65, as it has been since 1940 when benefits were first paid. In 1983, Congress approved legislation that will increase this age to 67 over the 2000 to 2022 period.[6] Many people refer to this change as an increase in the retirement age, but that designation is misleading because the change in law lowers benefits proportionally for all ages and does not increase the age of initial entitlement. Deeper benefit cuts brought about by further increases in the age at which unreduced benefits are paid might cause some older workers to defer retirement, although empirical estimates indicate that the effects would be small.

Early Retirement Benefits. The availability of Social Security benefits at age 62 facilitates early retirement, even if it does not penalize continued work. Approximately 25 percent of men still working retire at age 62, a larger proportion than at any other age. However, claiming benefits before age 65 permanently lowers benefits not only for the worker but also for the surviving spouse. A larger early-retirement penalty might cause some people to continue working but would not affect benefits for those who worked until the age at which unreduced benefits are paid. Unfortunately, it could also increase poverty among survivors of workers who retired early anyway. Already, 23 percent of women age 65 and older who live alone are poor, and just under half have incomes below 150 percent of the poverty threshold.

Age of Initial Entitlement. Neither of the two previous benefit cuts would alter the age at which benefits are first available. Although life expectancy at age 62 has increased by 3.6 years since 1961 when men first became eligible for early retirement benefits, raising the age of initial entitlement has not been politically popular. Some workers develop physical and mental limitations or are employed in strenuous jobs that make work past age 61 increasingly onerous. In addition, raising the age of initial entitlement saves little money in the long run because the increase in benefits associated with delaying retirement from age 62 to age 65 approximately offsets the shorter period over which benefits must be paid. Raising the age of initial entitlement from 62 to 63 or 64 might well encourage continued work, however. Unlike the two previous benefit cuts, it would not risk permanently lowering benefits for surviving spouses.

The Delayed Retirement Credit. In addition to raising the age at which unreduced benefits are paid, Congress in 1983 also liberalized the "delayed retirement credit"—the increase in benefits paid to those who work past the age at which unreduced benefits are paid and to those who earn enough to have their benefits reduced by the earnings test. When this change is fully phased in for those reaching age 62 in 2005, the increase will approximately compensate an average worker for the value of benefits lost because of the retirement test. In other words, the lifetime value of benefits the average worker can expect to receive will be independent of when that worker chooses to retire. Raising the delayed retirement credit still more—in effect, providing increases in lifetime benefits for later retirement—could further encourage later retirement but not without increasing program costs.

The Retirement Test. Because Social Security is intended to replace lost earnings, it has paid benefits only when the earnings of those age 62 and older are below specified thresholds. This "retirement test" has been remarkably unpopular. Many members of Congress regard the restriction as unfair and think that it has discouraged work by older men and women. Consequently, Congress has steadily raised the amounts people can earn without loss of benefits. In 1999, the retirement test for those age 65 to 69 will reduce benefits $1 for every $3 of earnings in excess of $15,500; the allowable earnings threshold will rise gradually to $30,000 by 2002. For those age 62 to 64, benefits will be reduced $1 for every $2 of earnings above $9,360, a threshold that will rise to $10,440 in 2002.[7]

Relaxing or repealing the retirement test might boost labor force participation of older workers, even though the adjustments made to the future pensions of those affected by the retirement test are analytically equivalent to repealing this test. In other words, workers with average life expectancies will receive the same total lifetime benefits whether they retire at age 62 or continue working and have their benefits reduced because their earnings exceed the retirement test thresholds. However, workers may respond less to a fair delayed retirement credit than they would to higher thresholds or a repeal of the earnings test, which would let more retirees receive pensions while continuing to work.[8] Relaxation or repeal of the retirement test would have the unintended side effect of strengthening arguments for income testing of benefits, as Social Security pensions would be paid to some people who were also taking home very high salaries, in contradiction to the traditional goal of the system to "replace lost earnings."[9] In addition, they would boost government spending in the short run.

While changes in the retirement test and delayed retirement credit are unlikely to increase work by older workers very much, delaying the availability of retirement benefits beyond age 62 would discourage retirement of people who lack the liquid assets to do so. This change in benefit structure is the one most likely to boost labor supply of older Americans.

BOOSTING THE GROWTH OF OUTPUT PER WORKER

Increasing output per worker will lighten the burden of supporting a growing aged population. How fast output per worker grows depends on changes in the skills of workers, on the quantity and quality of capital that workers use, and on managerial skill and business organization.

Skills. Improved education and on-the-job training, which increase worker productivity and earnings, are desirable for reasons that have nothing to do with Social Security, but they also can help the nation meet pension costs by raising payroll tax collections. Neither individuals nor businesses normally take this connection into account when deciding how much education or training is optimal. As important as education and training may be to economic growth, public policy in this area will continue to be driven more by the desire to expand individual opportunity than by any notion that a more skilled workforce could ease the societal burden of supporting an expanding population of retirees. Nevertheless, measures to improve the quality of education and to increase the number of young people graduating from high schools, colleges, and training programs do help ease pension costs. The benefits are very slow in coming, however, because most of the labor force for the next several decades will have completed its formal education before any improvement could occur.

Technology, Managerial Skills, and Capital. Technological advance, investment, improved management, and better business organization all boost economic growth. Public policy can promote technological advance by supporting basic and applied research and by education. Competitive and open markets, judicious and limited regulation, and a tax system that distorts investment decisions as little as possible also facilitate managerial and technological innovation, which, in turn, favors rapid economic advance.

How the nation's basic pension system is financed affects national saving, which, along with net investment by foreigners, determines the growth of the nation's capital stock. Private saving by U.S. households and businesses declined sharply and surprisingly during the 1980s and 1990s. It reached a post-World War II low of 3.8 percent of disposable personal income in 1997. As the baby boomers moved into their prime earning years in the late 1980s and 1990s and their children began to leave home, retirement saving should have risen, not fallen. Reduced tax rates and new tax-sheltered savings accounts should have amplified this trend. The fact that private saving fell is both puzzling and troubling.

The recent history of government saving is quite different and more heartening. Before the mid-1970s, combined revenues of federal, state, and local governments exceeded their spending, which meant they added to national saving. For two decades starting in the mid-1970s, mushrooming federal deficits swamped the surpluses of states and localities. The government sector as a whole became a net borrower, absorbing private saving available for investment. However, the unified federal budget has moved from a deficit of 4.7 percent of GDP in 1992 to a surplus of 0.8 percent of GDP in 1998, thereby raising national saving by over 5 percent of GDP. Official budget projections suggest that the federal surpluses should gradually rise to between 1.9 and 2.6 percent of GDP by 2008, if Congress and the president can resist the temptation to use the surpluses to cut taxes and boost spending. Surpluses should continue for almost two decades, after which rising Social Security and Medicare spending for aging baby boomers will require higher taxes, spending cuts, or both to sustain surpluses.

Budget surpluses are hard to sustain because the benefits of fiscal frugality are deferred and widely diffused, while tax cuts and program expansions produce immediate and identifiable benefits for particular groups. Nevertheless, preserving the surpluses is the most reliable way to boost economic growth and help offset the added costs of supporting the baby boomers in retirement.

CONCLUSION: POLITICS VERSUS ECONOMICS

One can hardly turn on a television or open a newspaper or magazine without encountering overwrought rhetoric bewailing the insupportable burden that the baby boomers will impose on thinned ranks of future workers. From an economic standpoint, this rhetoric is detached from reality. While there is no way to eliminate the *overall economic costs* of an aging population, sweeping structural changes are not needed to close the projected long-term deficit in Social Security if the nation enjoys normal economic growth. Measures to promote economic growth, which are desirable for many reasons, would lighten the economic burden for future workers.

The political problems of meeting the costs of population aging are more substantial, however. Whether the United States is merely as rich as it is today or even richer, it will still be necessary to shift more of what the economy produces from workers to the elderly and disabled and to survivors of deceased workers. These transfers will require increased taxes if currently promised benefits remain unchanged and the method of financing Social Security is not altered. The simplest way to reduce such tax increases is to invest Social Security's reserves in assets that generate higher yields than the current portfolio of Treasury securities. Replacing Social Security with mandatory private saving in personal accounts would in no way reduce the burden.

4

WHY BOOMERS
DON'T SPELL BUST

RICHARD C. LEONE

With the election behind us, brace yourself for the real debate about the future of Social Security and Medicare. The alarmists in this fight have a simple central argument: Many baby boomers (those born between 1946 and 1964) will live to a ripe old age, making the country a poorer place for everyone, especially those still in the workforce. In the most extreme formulation, pessimists project that, in the next century, we'll be taxing wages at an 80 percent rate to pay for entitlements. (I leave it to others to explain how, in this era of strong anti-tax sentiment, such statements get someone labeled "refreshingly realistic" whereas proposals to refinance Social Security with a 1 or 2 percentage point increase in the payroll tax are considered politically crazy.)

Reprinted with Permission. Copyright 1997 by The American Prospect, Inc. Richard C. Leone, "Why Boomers Don't Spell Bust," *The American Prospect* no. 30 (January-February 1997): 68-72 (http://epn.org/prospect/30/30leon.html).

The aging of the boomers does pose serious public policy questions, but much of the concern, especially with regard to Social Security, is overwrought. The doomsday scenario is based on the ratio of dependent aged people to the working-age population. The more meaningful comparison is the ratio of dependent people of all ages, including children, to working people. When that comparison is made, it turns out that the booming 1950s and 1960s actually had a higher dependency ratio than the ratio projected for the next century.

Longevity, of course, has been increasing since the founding of the republic. Accompanying that extension of life span has been a growth in per capita income that makes America today rich beyond the dreams of any of our forebears and fabulously rich by the standards of the world at large. Granted, we haven't gotten rich because people are living longer, but neither has longevity bankrupted the nation. Today, we're less sure than ever about when people are too old to be productive. Today's elderly are both healthier and better educated than were their predecessors. In 1974, the average educational attainment of the elderly was eighth grade; now it's twelfth grade and going up.

Our overall economic pie is a product of many things: the labor of those working; the exploitation of resources, some of them irreplaceable; and the use of capacity (capital stock) created by past generations. The real economy's goods and services are allocated in our society by, in addition to the accident of birth, a complex interaction of capitalism and democracy. If you do well in the marketplace, you can take care of yourself when you're old. If you don't, our political system has produced a limited safety net, composed largely of Social Security, Medicare, and Medicaid, that covers minimal needs.

WHEN THE BOOMERS WERE BABIES

The attack on current safety-net policy insists that we are overly generous to the elderly and that their growing numbers relative to the working population make current levels of consumption by seniors unsustainable. In the future, it's asserted, there will be too few workers to produce enough to support the social safety net. But when they were kids, the baby boomers posed a challenge that may have been even greater. There were even more of them then, and for 15 or 20 years they produced little. They made complicated demands on the real economy, and society had to respond out of the much smaller economic pie that existed at that time.

Today there are 120 million Americans at work and 140 million not working (46 percent workers). When the boomers are all retired in about 2030, there will be 160 million workers and 200 million non-workers (44 percent working). But recall that in 1964, when the boomer population peaked, there were 70 million Americans working and 120 million not working (37 percent working)—a ratio considerably "worse" than we can expect in the twenty-first century. Another way to look at the dependency "burden" is the number of young and old dependents per 100 workers. In 1993 that ratio was about 70 to 100. It will rise to 83 per 100 in 2030. But, again, in 1964 it was "worse" at 96 per 100.

Odd, isn't it, that no one, including the boomers' parents, recalls the 1960s as an era of economic deprivation?

As kids, boomers comprised over 40 percent of the population; today, they are less than 30 percent; in retirement they'll drop below 25 percent. The cost of raising the boomers was high; conservative estimates of the average cost of raising a child are about $300,000, in current dollars. (Coincidentally, this number is almost identical to the "insurance value" to a family of Social Security coverage.) But there was no free lunch: Boomers as children consumed goods and services from the real economy, just as they will as seniors. ·

In the postwar era, school systems routinely were overloaded. The market for consumer goods was transformed by the special demands of millions of children and teenagers. Boomers started changing American culture during the 1940s, and they are still at it. Rock and roll, increasing crime rates, and suburbanization are all related to the youth and numbers of the boomers. Subsequent revolutions in the labor market, family and marriage, the status of women, and the civil rights movement are also, to varying degrees, connected to the sea changes brought about by the boomer generation.

THE CHALLENGE WE MET

From the beginning, the Americans who had lived through the Great Depression and World War II expected the public sector to play a pivotal role in the adjustments caused by the arrival of 80 million boomer children. The government did produce vast programs to build schools, train teachers, and, later, to provide college loans and grants. Between 1952 and 1970, elementary and secondary school expenditures increased more than 275 percent in inflation-adjusted dollars. Between 1964 and 1980, the number of college and university students increased more than 125 percent, and the number of college instructors more than doubled. The boomers' parents, through their taxes, built these schools and colleges for their own and other people's children. Americans also provided support for the nearly 30 percent of boomers who lived some part of their childhood in poverty.

What are we to make of all this? With fewer resources, with higher marginal tax rates, the boomers were fed, clothed, educated—as Bob Dole would say, whatever. At the time, we also had a higher national savings rate—in other words, more foregone consumption by workers. Theda Skocpol emphasizes that the burden was easier to bear because the nation invested much in "upgrading" the boomers' parents, especially through the GI Bill [see "Delivering for Young Families: The Resonance of the GI Bill," *TAP*, September-October 1996]. Eight million veterans sought higher education, more than doubling the percentage of Americans who went to college. The cost was about $100 billion, in 1996 dollars. But the real purchasing power was even greater: veterans went to Princeton on the GI Bill's $500 stipend. Veterans Administration housing subsidized about a quarter of all the new residences in the nation. In fact, public investment in both people and infrastructure was very high during the entire postwar period.

Today, the success of the boomers' parents is explained largely in terms of the extraordinary economic growth for 20 years after World War II. To be sure, the psychological effect of being part of a rapidly rising tide of income was an important factor. Similarly, the sense of the nation's ability to deal with big problems through the public sphere was another unprecedented characteristic of the era. The boomers' parents, after all, had lived through the Great Depression and World War II. These back-to-back events created an overwhelming sense of America's ability, with people pulling together, to overcome obstacles. Families having more children could hardly have seemed like a catastrophe.

While growth is slower today, the economy continues to expand, and, even given modest assumptions about the future, will continue to grow. The economist Robert Eisner and others point out that, compared to 1964, we shall have triple the resources available (in constant dollars) in the next century. The boomers' parents shared a gross domestic product that, per capita, was $12,195 (inflation adjusted). We now produce $20,469 per capita, and in 2030 we'll have an estimated $35,659 per capita. These projections assume modest growth of less than 2 percent annually for the next 75 years.

In this context, the alleged fears of the future by some members of Generation X, who will inherit the largest economy in the history of the world, seem somewhat out of proportion. As far as we know, we face nothing like the Great Depression or international threats on the scale of Hitler, Imperial Japan, or the Soviet Empire. It is not given, after all, to any generation to have completely smooth sailing. A larger number of older people would seem, by twentieth-century standards, a reasonably modest challenge. A more realistic assessment of the balance between the challenges Generation X is likely to meet and the resources available to meet them should inspire optimism rather than apprehension.

Of course, there are those who insist that in the pinched, slow-growth economy of the future, it would be unjust for seniors to have so much of the pie. This argument, usually couched in terms of "generational justice," implies that we can't afford the consumption of those who contributed so much to building the economy. Remember that the boomers represent the largest workforce we've ever had—a workforce that expanded the economy more than any previous group. The boomers' children will inherit a vastly larger economy with enough resources for all. Every generation depends on others: Children must depend on parents, as well as on strangers who build bridges, plants, schools, office buildings, and industrial equipment. Even the debt a new generation must pay off is accompanied by the government bonds and other assets that it inherits. Should boomers charge rent for the portion of the nation's capital stock, including knowledge and inventions, built or dreamed up by their generation?

While boomers came into the world with nothing, on their way out they'll have a few trillion dollars in pension funds—more than any previous generation—and substantial real estate to help pay the freight. But they are not all likely to get lucky and fully fund their own retirement with no help from Uncle Sam; capitalism just doesn't work that way. Of course, if, somehow, all the elderly did turn out to be like Bill Gates, they'd be able to command all the goods and services they wanted. Then they would get more of the pie, and younger people would get less. More specifically, consider the preferences of rich seniors as consumers: It's a good bet that they buy as much or more medical care than those completely dependent on Medicare.

PAYING FOR HEALTH

Since most aging Americans are not wealthy, the question of how to finance their growing need for health care will be resolved, not only in the marketplace, but also in the public sector. A bipartisan commission to study Medicare is only a first step. The coming struggle is sure to be politically brutal, with no "winners" and lots of painful choices. The issues in health care are simply much harder to deal with than are the rather modest adjustments necessary to sustain Social Security.

By 2030 nearly 20 percent of the population will be eligible for Medicare, up from 12.8 percent today. The advance of medical technology and other trends will almost surely keep health costs rising faster than general inflation. Increasing the number of the elderly in managed care may help the short-term problems of the Medicare trust funds over the next decade, but the potential savings from managed care as we know it are not sufficient to pay for the expansion of the Medicare population and the higher costs per capita on the horizon. If America responds to the aging of the baby boomers as it did to their youth in the 1950s and 1960s, we will agree to pay the higher taxes that their medical care will cost even as the program is subjected to stronger cost controls. If, however, America responds as the alarmists urge, the program will just be cut by reducing the number of beneficiaries (for example, by means testing or raising the age of eligibility), restricting benefits, or sharply rationing care. But let us not fool ourselves: Extreme restrictions are not economic necessities; they are political choices.

To the extent that the growing Medicare expenditures reflect the preferences of consumers and voters, they are not "bad" for the nation. Health care, after all, is a high-tech domestic industry, with a growing base of domestic jobs that pay reasonably well. A population that spent even more on health care would not necessarily be worse off than we are today.

FALLACIES OF THE APOCALYPSE

Although the future will involve plenty of unpleasant surprises, a close look at the alarmists' economic projections reveals how far-fetched they are. Their pessimism—especially in terms of the likely real economic situation 30 or 40 years from now—involves numerous internal inconsistencies. The Social Security Advisory Commission, for example, already assumes reasonably slow growth for the next generation or two. The alarmists think the projections should be even grimmer. Why? Surely not because the nation will be older; there is no serious economic analysis upon which to base such a projection (take a peek at already-old Japan and Germany).

The slow-growth scenario is used selectively by those eager to dismantle the safety net. One of the remedies proposed for Social Security, for example, is buying stocks because, it is argued, equity values compound annually (apparently forever) at 7 percent a year. The continuation of such a performance for 75 years in an economy that they project to grow by less than 2 percent a year would be truly amazing!

And what about the push to recalibrate the inflation rate, thus cutting cost of living increases for the elderly? As the economist Dean Baker points out, if this guess about the inflation rate is correct, the forecast for average income in the next century should be dramatically increased. For example, the current estimate of per capita income—$35,000—for 2030 would have to be more than doubled. If we're all going to be that well off, what's the justification for arguing that we have to destroy Social Security in order to save it? In other words, when it supports their arguments, the alarmists emphasize a sluggish economy; when it doesn't, they're back to the rosy scenario.

Realism about the size of the overall economic pie and guidance derived from the lessons of the past should shape adjustments in entitlements for seniors. But our approach also should conform to basic values shared by most of the elderly. "Solutions" like privatization of Social Security that are sure to increase the already serious levels of inequality should be smoked out as ideological preferences and not fiscal imperatives.

As a society, we can continue to insist that if you work hard and play by the rules, you can count on a social safety net in old age. Let's reject plans that are likely to increase poverty among any age group. And we can stay true to tested principles by fighting harder for policies that are already part of mainstream politics: controlling the budget deficit while protecting Social Security and Medicare; increasing the minimum wage and expanding employment to bolster savings and growth; and directly addressing the corrosive effects of the growing income and wealth inequality.

The boomers' children, like the boomers' parents, will muddle through. When the boomers were kids, there were also occasional squeezes on resources: double sessions in schools all over the country and a crisis over the need for more college spaces and faculty. The boomers will get less than they want, but far more than the alarmists think is possible. Politics will continue to play the most significant role in how this shift takes place. Both the values of a democracy and the realities of capitalism support the basic soundness of the current framework for policy, albeit with changes that strike a balance among the competing demands of Americans of all ages.

America is facing change, but not disaster. We can be realistic about the future and still believe that the nation can grow older gracefully. So, we should hang on tight to the most fundamental contract we have with one another: If an American works, and then can't work because of age, that citizen will not have to live in poverty.

5

SAVING, GROWTH, AND SOCIAL SECURITY:
FIGHTING OUR CHILDREN OVER
SHARES OF THE FUTURE ECONOMIC PIE?

JAMES H. SCHULZ

Despite the repeated predictions of various social commentators, there is no intergenerational conflict in the United States today. The empirical evidence to the contrary is considerable and conclusive.[1]

But what about the future? With the American population aging and the retirement of the "baby-boom" generation not many years away, some people argue that intergenerational conflict is inevitable.[2] The truth is, however, that there is no general agreement on this question, only controversy.

The literature on socioeconomic effects of population aging is now quite large. Almost all of it starts with projecting into the next century the results of current demographic trends and pointing out the impact that this

This chapter will appear in a forthcoming collection of essays edited by Robert N. Butler, which will be published by The Century Foundation Press.

may have (or "is going to have") on the intergenerational question. This literature is dominated by dire prophecies that are now familiar to almost everyone:

- Each future worker will have to support too many retired people.

- Social Security will go bankrupt and will not be there when younger workers retire.

- The *entire* federal budget will ultimately have to go to pay for entitlements.

- Older people are being luxuriously supported at the expense of our children.

- Population aging will destroy our nation's global competitiveness, perpetuating the curse of low growth and a shrinking economic pie.

Given the apocalyptic nature of these predictions, a visitor from Mars would be likely to dismiss them and search for more balanced discussions. But the reader knows that these predictions can not be dismissed; today, they represent the accepted opinion of the bulk of the American population.

For decades now there has been waged a kind of holy war designed to "wake up" the American public to the supposed dangers resulting from the aging of America's population. Driving this war is the goal of turning Americans against one of the nation's most popular programs—Social Security. However, this war is not so much about unsustainable Social Security and Medicare or about current budget deficits. Rather, it is really about the age-old questions associated with the appropriate distribution of income in the United States—between the rich and poor, whites and nonwhites, and the strong and the weak.[3] And it is also about a medical care system with soaring costs, a lack of agreement about how these costs are to be paid, and the uneven and inequitable protection provided to individuals from the costs of major illnesses.

The current, warlike campaign against "entitlements" promotes an intergenerational conflict that does not yet exist and undermines the already tenuous sense of community and social solidarity that exists nationally. That is, it encourages long-term confrontation between age groups over the distribution of the nation's output.

"CONSUMING OUR CHILDREN" AND OTHER SUCH HORRORS

In an article entitled "Consuming Our Children?" Subrata Chakravarty and Katherine Weisman argue: "Many young people complain that they can't live as well as their parents did. They may well be right. We are witnessing nothing less than a massive transfer of income and wealth from the younger generations to the older."[4] This theme has been repeated over and over again—starting with the unsubstantiated assertion made by eminent demographer Samuel H. Preston in 1984 that the elderly were responsible for the deteriorating social and economic situation of children in the United States.[5]

The "consuming our children" theme, however, is only one aspect of the intergenerational conflict "horrors" many people write about. Another issue concerns whether the needs of a growing aged population threaten the integrity of the political system. The apocalyptic proclamations go back at least two decades. In 1978 economic journalist Robert J. Samuelson got politicians' attention by publicly attacking the elderly in the *Washington Post*. Up to that time older people were viewed by almost everyone in America as the most deserving of the poor. But Samuelson argued that the situation had changed and that there was now a "withering freedom to govern" resulting from the "soaring costs [of programs] for elderly" persons:

> The aged have handcuffed [President] Jimmy Carter. They will probably do the same for his successors well into the next century. Increasingly, invisible forces of population change will limit the freedom to govern.
>
> Put simply, the slow increase in the aged population, combined with the massive rise in assistance already promised the elderly, means that neither the president nor the Congress can afford to provide much new spending for anything else—unless they want to raise taxes or run permanently large budget deficits.
>
> . . . The seeds of conflict are obvious enough: between educators and doctors, as well as between young and old. In short, population change—slowly

and almost invisibly—is pushing Congress and the bureaucracy around with a power that has few rivals.[6]

Samuelson's article—if written today—would accurately summarize the prevailing fears. His once-deviant view is now the dominant view. What has changed since he first wrote about the topic is, first, the huge federal deficits generated in the Reagan and Bush years (frequently blamed on the elderly). Next, there is increased attention to the problems arising when the baby-boom generation retires. And, finally, we see occurring the most vicious attacks on Social Security since its creation in the 1930s.

Criticism of the elderly reached new heights when former governor of Colorado, Richard D. Lamm, in an unprecedented and almost unbelievable act, mounted a bid for the presidency in 1996 with a campaign based almost solely on attacking the elderly. He claimed that older people were making unreasonable economic demands—demands that represented a serious drain on the nation, now and especially in the years to come.

The calamitous predictions by the prophets of doom have fallen on receptive ears because these people argue that the survival of some of our most important social and economic ideals are at stake. They maintain that population aging will seriously undermine our efforts to compete in the new global marketplace—threatening future economic growth and, hence, the "American dream" that each generation will have a standard of living better than its predecessor. In fact, as noted above, they anticipate that we will end up "consuming" our own children in a sense, even as there is a progressive immiserization of future generations. And, as if that were not enough, they predict that one of America's most popular institutions, Social Security, is unsustainable and will become a "bad deal" for future generations—if it is able to survive at all.

No wonder these prophets of doom have gotten widespread attention. Who can ignore, for example, the recent statement of the well-known economist Lester Thurow: "A new class of people is being created. . . . It [the elderly class] is a revolutionary class, one that is bringing down the social welfare state, destroying government finances, altering the distribution of purchasing power and threatening the investments that all societies need to make to have a successful future."[7] Notwithstanding, this paper will make the case that these dire predictions should not be taken seriously, that they are based on simplistic and erroneous demographic analyses, and that, to the extent economics is considered, the analysis is equally simplistic and seriously deficient.

VOODOO DEMOGRAPHY

It is now commonplace to read about "dependency ratio" statistics. Almost every prediction of demographic doom starts with one basic statistic of growing dependency: in the year 2030, given current Social Security law, there will be only 2.0 workers per Social Security recipient—in contrast to the current level of 3.3 workers per recipient.[8] This is often called the aged dependency ratio, measuring the relationship between old-age Social Security recipients and those workers paying Social Security taxes. The truth is that aged dependency ratios are one-sided and very misleading. As will be explained shortly, the correct way to look at this issue is to compare the number of workers to the number of dependents of all ages (nonworkers), and then to factor in the varying costs of supporting different groups of dependents and the rising level of incomes as a result of economic growth. On this measure, there is no problem of the sort suggested by the aged dependency ratio.

In almost all industrial countries, the "total dependency ratio" (taking into account both young and old dependents) is actually quite low, much lower than in the past and much lower than in developing nations today.[9] An even better measure to use, however, is one whose ratios take into account who is actually in the labor force for all age cohorts. Projections of the "labor force dependency ratio" (measuring those who are not in the labor force against those who are) indicate that for all ages this figure is expected to decline until around the year 2010 and that it will not surpass the high levels reached around 1960. As Figure 1 (see page 78) shows, looking at people working and not working in all age-groups (children, youths, middle-aged, and the aged), increases in the numbers of aged not working are counterbalanced by declines in dependency in the other age groups. In Figure 1 (see page 78), the total labor force dependency ratio is set to decline from about 1.5 in 1960 to about 1.0 in 2010. After 2010, the total ratio is strongly influenced by the retiring baby-boom cohort and rises slightly to 1.1. After that, it levels off.

There have been all sorts of demographic statistics presented in the aging discussions to date. Most of them are worthless in assessing the economic impact of an aging society. Population analysis without economics is a kind of voodoo demographics with regard to the issues in question.[10] The parents of the "baby boomers" registered a per capita GDP of $12,195 in 1964. Assuming less than 2 percent annual growth, the retired boomers and their children will enjoy in the year 2030 a per capita income (inflation adjusted) that is almost three times as large ($35,659).[11]

Analyzing the impact of population changes on the economy is a far more difficult challenge than simply presenting demographic dependency ratios. So there may be a generally offsetting decline in the number of children as the number of older people increases (see Figure 1): What does that mean in economic terms? Is the amount of the economic resources consumed in a year the same for babies and old people? For preschoolers? For teenagers? For college students? For mothers at home with their children? Obviously not.

Very little research has been done on this question of the varying costs of supporting different groups of dependents. In one of the few economic studies to date, Allan Borowski, William Crown, and the author have statistically weighted the demographic data shown in Figure 1 to reflect the "private support costs" associated with different age groups of nonworking persons. We also looked at the potential effect of future economic growth. Based

FIGURE 1. HISTORICAL AND PROJECTED LABOR FORCE DEPENDENCY RATIOS,* UNITED STATES, 1950–2020

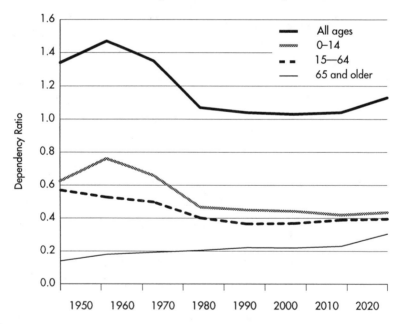

* Ratio of those (of designated ages) not in labor force to those (of any age) in labor force

Source: James H. Schulz, Allan Borowski, and William H. Crown, *Economics of Population Aging: The "Graying" of Australia, Japan, and the United States* (Westport, Conn.: Auburn House, 1991).

on this extension of the demographic statistics to incorporate economic dif-ferences, we concluded, first, "that the economic impact of demographic aging is not as bad as those doomsayers who use simplistic dependency ratios would have us believe. Second, as in other areas of social policy, relatively small increases in economic growth rates have the potential to substantially moderate the ill effects of other factors that have a negative impact."[13] In fact, our research concluded that the overall "support burden" pertaining to nonworking individuals could be less in the years 2030–50 than it was during 1950–70, assuming a relatively high rate of economic growth.[13]

Analyzing economic data over the past one hundred years for the United States and ten European countries, Richard A. Easterlin (one of the nation's top experts on population economics) also finds little sup-port for predictions that population aging will have a negative impact on economic growth and the welfare of future generations.[14] He finds a gen-erally consistent inverse relationship between trends in economic growth and population growth—economic growth rising while population growth falls. As he points out, this "is just the opposite of what one would have expected if declining population growth were exerting a serious drag on the economy." Moreover, based on the historical data, "one would be hard put to argue that dependency had much to do with the dramatic post-1973 drop in economic growth rates, and, not surprisingly, it is never men-tioned in scholarly attempts to explain this decline."

SAVING AND POPULATION AGING*

Easterlin points out that economists have paid relatively little heed in the past to demography in explaining changes in economic growth rates.[15] Instead, they have given a lot of attention to the role played by another contributor to the economic growth process—saving. If saving is reduced by population aging, then economic growth *might* be affected.

The potential impact of demographic aging on saving and growth has been a major issue in the debate over Social Security for many decades. Contemporary calls for privatization of Social Security are moti-

---

* As an economist myself, I am especially annoyed (and puzzled) by the arguments many economists use, almost by rote, to explain the supposed impact of Social Security on our national rate of savings. Therefore, this section of the chapter goes into some detail to explain and evaluate the prevailing literature, especially since the literature to date has been mysteriously deficient in articulating the limitations of past analysis.

vated in part by a desire to ensure that retirement pension programs do nothing to diminish saving and growth. Former associate Social Security commissioner Lawrence Thompson argues that the historical fact that public pensions have not been as likely as private ones to accumulate assets through saving ". . . is perhaps the most important fault line in the current world-wide debate over the costs of an aging society and the future of social security."[16]

The dialogue on this subject began in earnest with a paper published in 1974 by economist Martin Feldstein. Feldstein argued that historical data indicated that America's Social Security system depressed national saving by providing people with retirement income through collective pensions, encouraging individuals to reduce their private saving. Feldstein's empirical analysis found a sizable reduction in personal saving over the early years of the program. A big but inconclusive debate followed. Two Social Security Administration economists, Dean Leimer and Selig Lesnoy, found, for example, errors in Feldstein's calculations, reporting only small negative (and even some positive) savings effects when the errors were corrected.[17] In general, the empirical studies to date on this question have been inconclusive.[18]

Another way that demographic aging could reduce aggregate saving is if there turns out to be a general pattern of behavior among individuals, when they are old, to save less and consume more. Economists have long theorized that people would accumulate savings for old age and then spend down most or all those savings before the end of life (the "life-cycle hypothesis"). If true, the aging of a population should be associated with a reduction in aggregate saving (all other things held constant). Once again, though, the empirical evidence is very mixed. Many studies show that "savers" continue to save for most or all of their retirement years, but a few researchers find the opposite. The 1997 annual report of the U.S. Council of Economic Advisers concludes that "economists have been at a loss to explain much of the behavior of personal savings during the 1980s."[19]

But the lack of "hard evidence" and reasonable certainty with regard to the impact of population aging on saving has not stopped some advocates of privatization. They argue that Social Security is a big part of the explanation for America's currently low saving rates and part of the reason why economic growth rates have not been higher. Those voicing grave concern and dire predictions about population aging and entitlements single out one possibility (among many) as the dominant—seemingly sole—determinant of our economic future, the saving rate. For example, in a recent speech on the economic impact of an aging society, former chairman of the Federal Reserve System Paul A. Volcker focused almost exclusively on saving: "If the huge Boomer generation is encouraged to save more, the result will be a favorable and direct effect on the U.S. economy in the new century. An increase in personal savings rates beyond our historical level of four percent will favorably affect our economy."[20] Similarly, Senator Bob Kerrey and former Senator John C. Danforth, in the interim report of the Bipartisan Commission on Entitlement and Tax Reform, focused on saving: "To ensure the level of private investment necessary for long-term economic growth and prosperity, national savings must be raised substantially."[21] And the president's Council of Economic Advisers in its 1997 report states categorically that "the nation needs to raise its overall rate of saving to improve long-term economic growth."[22]

THE SIMPLISTIC NOTION THAT SAVING DETERMINES GROWTH

Why is saving so important for growth? Here is the way eminent economist James M. Buchanan explains the growth process to noneconomists:

> The act of saving allows for a release of resources into the production of capital rather than consumer goods. This increase in capital inputs into the market operates in essentially the same fashion as an increase in the supply of labor inputs. The increase in capital expands the size of the economy and this, in turn, allows for an increased exploitation of the division and specialization of resources. The economic value of output per unit of input expands, and *this result ensures that all persons in the economic nexus, whether they be workers, savers, or consumers, are made better off and on their own terms.*[23] [emphasis added]

Buchanan's certainty of favorable results from saving is not shared by economists who specialize in this subject matter. The literature on saving, investment, and growth is extensive, complicated, sophisticated, highly controversial, and generally inconclusive. But one would never know that from reading the savings *policy prescriptions* of most economists today. The complexities and ambiguities of economic theory and empiricism in this area are generally ignored.

Economists today are generally unanimous in pointing to the need to increase saving in order to promote economic growth in the United States.

The emphasis given by many economists to saving results in part from a long tradition in economics. Both traditional neoclassical growth theory and more recent growth theory focus on the role of saving. Economist Robert A. Blecker points out in a recent review article: "Since the late 1970s, mainstream macroeconomics has been dominated by a conservative policy consensus, which emphasizes raising national saving rates and avoiding government intervention in financial or labor markets."[24]

Thus, it is not surprising to find great concern about Social Security among those economists who see it as a major government program that reduces the aggregate saving needed for growth. For example, economist Edward M. Gramlich, the chair of the most recent Social Security Advisory Council, writes:

> In the end the most profound impact of Social Security on the economy, for good or ill, is its impact on national saving and investment. In the long run the most important policy-controlled determinant of a country's living standards is its national saving ratio, according to neoclassical growth models of the sort that were developed by Robert Solow. . . . The United States now saves an extraordinarily low share of its national output. The disappointing aspect of this low national saving is that as long as it persists, living standards are not likely to rise very rapidly in the future.[25]

As articulated by Gramlich, low saving translates into slow growth and lower living standards. Note that there are no ifs, ands, or buts in Gramlich's statement.

However, the point is not so much what Gramlich thinks; more important is that his opinion is highly representative of the current policy prescriptions of many other economists. For example, Martin Feldstein, in an article promoting privatization of Social Security, asserts: "There is, however, no doubt that the net effect of the transition from the PAYGO [pay as you go] system to the prefunded PRA [Personal Retirement Accounts] system would be a rise in national saving and therefore a larger capital stock and a higher level of real national income."[26] This and similar views of various economists seriously distort the discussion about population aging and economic growth. As will be shown below, such a reductionist articulation of the sources of economic growth ignores decades of research and debate since Solow's insightful but seriously deficient early modeling efforts. There are many important determinants of the rate of growth of a nation's economy.[27] To imply that saving is the only one, or that it is the most important one, is just bad economics.

Why do most economists think saving is so important? The usual answer given is that saving is necessary if there is to be investment by businesses in new factories and equipment. Saving is defined as the amount of current income that is not spent (not consumed) on finished goods and services over some specified time period. The economic resources of a nation (its land, labor, and capital) are limited and can be used to produce goods that are consumed and used up or, alternatively, to produce goods that can be used to produce greater quantities of goods in the future ("capital goods"). Saving is necessary to generate the wherewithal for investment, and investment potentially results in new productive capacity that can be the basis for economic growth in future years. So from a growth perspective, saving is a good thing. Clearly it is better than no saving or low saving.

But the definitional relationship that "saving always equals investment always equals growth" is too simplistic to base decisionmaking on. This textbook view of saving is a far cry from the real world. Recent research suggests that increasing private saving, other things being equal, does little to raise private investment. In fact, econometric analysis by David Gordon supports the view of a sizable minority of economists that investment generates saving, not vice versa.[28]

First of all, increased saving makes investment possible, but the amount and nature of the investment that actually occurs depends on a wide variety of conditions. For example, the United Kingdom, with the highest level of funded occupational pensions in Europe and more than £10 billion ($16.6 billion) in "personal saving" accounts, has not seen any appreciable increase in its recent investment rates. Nor has it achieved a higher rate of growth than European countries, such as Germany, that rely very heavily on pay-as-you-go social security pensions.[29]

Second, as Gordon points out, "saving fails to generate investment in part because increased personal saving does not appear to alter the financial constraints (credit availability) affecting investment."[30]

Third, research indicates that profitability should be regarded as a significant influence on how much actual investment occurs—along with demand, demand and profit expectations, and the relative costs of capital to labor.[31]

Fourth, there is not just one source (saving) or two (saving and investment) that are the key determinants of growth. While saving and investment are necessary, they are not sufficient to ensure that the rate of growth will be adequate to achieve any specified set of goals. There are many other factors that are as important—or perhaps more important, such as technology, know-how, and entrepreneurial drive. All economists know this, which makes one wonder why so many have chosen to ignore the other wellsprings of growth when the question of population aging comes up. As Richard Nelson remarks, "the key intellectual challenge to formal growth theory . . . lies in learning how to formally model entities that are not easily reduced to a set of numbers, such as the character of a nation's education or financial system or the prevalent philosophy of management."[32]

CREDIT CARDS AND SAVING

Before looking more closely at the other influences on growth, it is important to make clear the relatively minor role aging policies actually play in determining aggregate saving. If one were to ask people on the street what are the major considerations that influence how much they save, it is not likely that they would say much about the amount they expect to get in retirement from public and private pensions. Nor are they likely to mention the single most important source of personal saving for the majority of people—accumulation of home equity through their mortgage payments; most do not think of that as saving. Instead, people are more likely to talk about the high cost of living and the difficulties they have just "making ends meet."

In her article "The Joy of Consumption," Jane Katz points out that rising incomes do not slow our desire to spend. For most people, consumption is no longer about buying necessities. Instead, it is in large part a social phenomenon. "In a market economy, we must buy the things we need to take our place in the community."[33] As Katz notes, rising incomes do not relieve the pressures on the middle class to keep up; moreover, they probably place extra burdens on the poor to avoid the stigma of falling behind in what has been called "conspicuous consumption."

Everyone in the United States is aware of how easy it is for most individuals to borrow money to finance consumption—for stereos, televisions, vacations, automobiles, meals, and almost anything else that their fancy desires. The credit revolution in the United States is one of the most important developments of the postwar period. The expansion of revolving credit has been dramatic, with much of the growth going to credit cards. Over the past two decades, the bank credit card share of revolving credit has risen from less than half to more than two-thirds.[34]

Of course, most readers will not be surprised—since they carry around an average of three to four credit cards and receive offers of new cards every month. Credit providers have gone to extreme lengths to push people into debt. One recent letter printed by USA Today was from a parent reporting that her college student daughter had five credit cards—amassing a "tremendous amount of debt." Yet the only job the daughter ever held was working part time in a pizza shop. "I recently bought some books at my local college bookstore. The clerk put my books in the bag along with several credit card applications. Who wouldn't be tempted?"[35]

The credit card boom is, for many people, a wonderful source of credit at a cost that is high but usually lower than the costs involved in getting money from banks, "money stores," and other more traditional alternatives.[36] But using credit "to spend" is the opposite of saving; credit (when used) leads to debt.[37] Is it not reasonable to think that low saving rates in the United States are in part a result of easier credit in our consumption-oriented society—with its conspicuous consumption, television, radio, and print media advertising, and newfound ways of "buying now and paying later"? As Figure 2 (see page 86) indicates, rapid growth in consumer debt started around 1982—about the same time as personal saving rates began their sharp decline.

Is the credit boom merely a new way to finance consumption, or is it a new contributor to rising net consumption and lower personal saving? Looking to the economic literature for an informed opinion on the credit card phenomenon would only result in disappointment. A search of books and articles over a twenty-eight-year period found 4,395 citations mentioning "saving" and 213 articles mentioning "saving and Social Security." In contrast, there were 36 citations on credit cards and only one that looks at "saving and credit cards."[38]

One rarely hears prominent policymakers (or economists) worry about the impact of rising consumer debt on saving or talk about ways to stop the rise. Yet consumer debt continues to climb. The Consumer Federation estimates that, on average, households that carry a credit card balance have more than $7,000 in card debt; this results in households paying an average payment of more than $1,000 each year in card interest and fees.[39] (That is double the amount in 1990.) Figure 3 (see page 87) shows household debt payments as a percent of disposable personal income—rising from a little more than 15 percent in early 1994 to 17 percent in early 1996. "Nearly 1 in every 3 families whose household income is below $10,000 now has credit-card obligations that exceeds 40 percent of its income. . . ."[40]

Harvard economist James Medoff and financial consultant Andrew Harless argue that, "at present, the United States is locked in a situation in which Americans borrow (instead of save) to make up the difference

FIGURE 2. CONSUMER DEBT,* 1974–1994

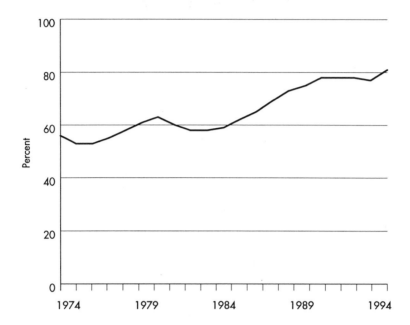

* Ratio of debt to disposable household income

Source: Based on *Economic Report of the President,* 1995 (Washington, D.C.: U.S. Government Printing Office, 1995), Chart 2–3.

between their expectations and the disappointing reality of slow growth."[41] In a frantic race to keep up, families often take on more debt than they can handle. Figure 4 (see page 88) shows the rising rate of bankruptcy filings in recent years.[42]

PERSONAL VERSUS BUSINESS SAVING

Historically, the amount of net personal saving (new saving minus new debt) by all households in the United States has been roughly equal to the amount of investment that goes into owner-occupied housing. That is, the magnitude of household saving has been just enough to allow for the replenishing and expansion of our housing stock. If that is true, where does the saving come from that allows businesses to invest in new plant and equipment?

FIGURE 3. RECENT TRENDS IN CONSUMER DEBT,*
MARCH 1994–APRIL 1996

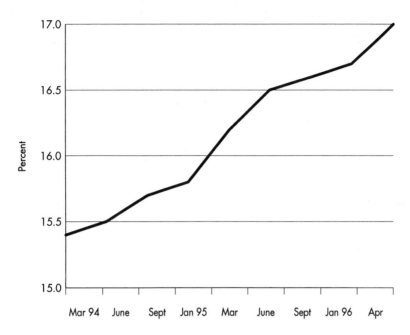

* Debt payments as a percentage of disposable personal income

Source: Federal Reserve.

Capital markets are rapidly becoming global. The savings of individuals in the United States can now be pooled with the savings of millions of others around the world. The fact that financial capital can now move easily and quickly across national borders in search of "the best returns" further changes the basic nature of the traditional interaction between saving and investment. At the same time, it creates new social problems as producers generate goods and services using globally dispersed resources, often leaving local communities to decay and local labor pools unemployed.

In the historically important growth sector of corporate production, the overwhelming majority of saving needed to facilitate new investment comes from savings generated internally by the corporations themselves in the form of retained earnings and depreciation allowances.[43] In 1994, gross business saving exceeded $800 billion, more than four times aggregate personal saving in the same year.

FIGURE 4. RECENT TRENDS IN CONSUMER BANKRUPTCY,*
MARCH 1994–APRIL 1996

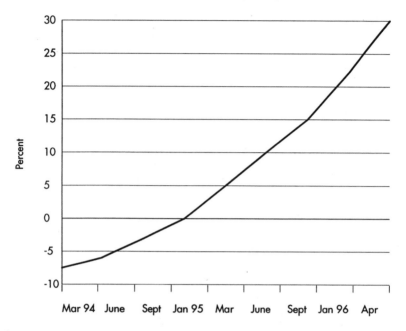

* Percentage change in bankruptcy filings from previous year

Source: Federal Reserve.

WHAT ROLE FOR SAVING?

The point is not that saving has an unimportant role to play in growth, or that policies to encourage such saving are inappropriate. Rather, the prior discussion seeks to place the issue of population aging and saving in proper perspective. As a World Bank report puts it, "Funded [pension] plans have the potential to increase household saving and productive capital formation, whereas pay-as-you-go plans do not. But this potential may not be realized . . ." unless conditions are right.[44]

Instead of qualified statements similar to the World Bank's, readers frequently are confronted with pronouncements that make it seem that the impact of population aging and Social Security on saving is the most, or one of the most, important considerations in evaluating policy options relating to growth. As just pointed out, though, saving is done by many sectors of the economy and for a variety of reasons. The significance of population aging and Social Security for the level of saving rates is certainly small in relation to that of many other determinants. As the late Arthur Okun, an eminent macroeconomist, once said, "The specter of depressed saving is not only empirically implausible but logically fake. . . . The nation can have the level of saving and investment it wants with more or less income redistribution, so long as it is willing to twist some other dials."[45]

If it is a matter of twisting some dials, why don't we just do it? A large part of the answer is that those dials are marked "Social Security," "taxation," "interest rates," "credit availability," and other highly politically sensitive issues.

ALLEVIATING THE STRAINS OF POPULATION AGING: MAKING THE PIE BIGGER

Even if Social Security reduces saving (and there is no proof that it does), people worried about future growth and the "economic pie" available to share should look elsewhere for factors determining the outcome. For example, one of the giants of economics, Alfred Marshall, once wrote: "Knowledge is the most powerful engine of production; it enables us to subdue nature and satisfy our wants."[46] His statement reminds us that the job of dealing with any economic strain arising from the baby boom and population aging does not rest solely on increasing saving.[47]

All one has to do is look around at businesses that succeed and fail to see that saving is only one of many important sources of growth. Twenty-five years ago America was the leader in tire production around the world, and Akron, Ohio, was the tire capital—with four of the five biggest tire companies in the country located there. As the *Economist* pointed out recently, "Now only one of those firms, Goodyear, remains both American and a market leader. Akron was undermined by Americans' enthusiasm for longer-lasting radial tyres after the 1973 oil shock. The problem was not that Akron's firms did not know how to make radial tyres; the technology was decades old. What they were unable to do was adjust their business model, which relied on short-lived tyres."[48]

The American tire industry did not decline because of a lack of available saving; these companies were huge and had been profitable, with lots of retained earnings. What was missing was the right combination of entrepreneurial spirit, risk taking, and successful managerial skills.

The *Economist* description of businesses currently thriving in the Silicon Valley makes for striking contrast with the American tire industry.

> To an unusual degree Silicon Valley's economy relies on what Joseph Schumpeter, an Austrian economist, called "creative destruction." Some modern writers have rechristened the phenomenon "flexible recycling," but the basic idea is the same: old companies die and new ones emerge, allowing capital, ideas, and people to be reallocated. An essential ingredient in this is the presence of entrepreneurs, and a culture that attracts them.
>
> Research has increasingly concentrated on clusters . . . where there is "something in the air" that encourages risk-taking. This suggests that culture, irritatingly vague though it may sound, is more important to Silicon Valley's success than economic or technological factors.[49]

And, as the *Economist* acknowledges, venture capital has been pouring into Silicon Valley. Low saving rates have not been a problem.

The early neoclassical growth models referred to by Gramlich are based on a primitive, unsophisticated view of business organizations, technological change, and innovation. Over the years, Richard Nelson, among others, has pointed out the complexities of growth and the key role played by parameters other than saving. Many economists' models treat businesses like machines, ignoring empirical research clearly documenting the fact that businesses are social systems that are often resistant or unresponsive to executive commands.[50] Thus, "management style," for example, can make a big difference in the success or failure of a firm.

What about knowledge—the education of the work force and the development of a scientific base for facilitating and stimulating the use of new technologies? As Marshall and many other economists have indicated, it is vitally important to spend sufficient societal resources on human capital.[51] "All over the world it is taken for granted that educational achievement and economic success are closely linked—that the struggle to raise a nation's living standards is fought first and foremost in the classroom."[52]

Investment in intangible and human capital, excluded from conventional measures of saving and investment, far exceeds in magnitude (and very likely in importance) the private saving in tangible capital.[53] Starting with the Morrill Land Grant College Act of 1862, the United States has been a world leader in government support for education and research. "As early as 1890," Theodore Schultz writes, "the ratio of university students per 1,000 primary students in America was two to three times that of any other country, and this gap was maintained and increased though the period of American industrial ascendancy."[54]

Knowledge, education, technological change, and entrepreneurship together form a powerful engine for economic growth. The Austrian School of economists (such as Joseph Schumpeter, Ludwig von Mises, and Friedrich Hayek) recognized this. This tradition continues among economists in Austria today, with a strong emphasis on the role of knowledge and discovery (what the Austrians call "entrepreneurial discovery").[55] Except for the work of a few economists (like Nelson, Schultz, and Herbert Gintis), this focus is sorely missing from American mainstream economics.

Again, it is not that economists in the United States have ignored the role of technology, risk taking, and entrepreneurship. Rather it is that the importance of these things is almost always missing from, or downplayed in, most policy discussions about issues related to economic growth and, in our case, the specific issues related to population aging and Social Security.

The discussion in this paper has only skimmed the surface of what is important to promoting economic expansion. The list of potential sources of growth is very long.[56] If increased saving were the only requirement for growth, there would be many fewer underdeveloped countries in the world today. Ask the former leaders of the USSR, or the current leaders of Russia, why Moscow's planned economy, with lots of forced saving, ended up as a disaster.

Not only is most of "the burden of the elderly" literature overly simplistic but it encourages people to look for solutions in the wrong places. Increasing economic growth rates is a very complex task and one still not well understood. Yet, good public policy requires recognizing those complexities and articulating them to the general public. Today, as ever, the most important determinants of the future economic welfare of people of all ages are those already alluded to that influence the rate of growth: technological change, entrepreneurial initiatives and risk taking, managerial skills, government provision of infrastructure, saving, investment in human and business capital, labor force participation levels, and so on. The debate over how best to make an economic system grow is not primarily an aging (or Social Security) discussion. In fact, Social Security and the aging of populations have relatively little to do with the outcome.

Economist Richard Disney, who recently undertook a comprehensive and careful review of the relevant economic literature, concludes that "there is no 'crisis of aging.' Although many countries now exhibit dramatic demographic transitions, talk of a 'crisis of aging' is overblown. . . . [T]here is no evidence of adverse effects of aging on aggregate productivity. Microeconomic and macroeconomic studies have failed to uncover any convincing evidence that differences in demographic structure between countries and over time are a major factor in determining productivity levels."[57]

Michael Cichon of the International Labor Office, using a simulation that models the demographic and economic characteristics of OECD countries, reaches similar conclusions: "There is no old-age crisis, but there certainly is an employment and public policy challenge. Those who stare at the changing pattern of the 'population tree' and conclude quickly and with a dose of Populist bravado that the present social protection has to be changed radically, are simply barking up the wrong tree." [58]

THE ENTITLEMENT MYTH:
AND CHICKEN LITTLE SAID, "THE SKY IS FALLING"

Social Security disbursements are a direct cause of our [current] federal deficit.[59]

—Peter G. Peterson

To ensure that today's debt and spending commitments do not unfairly burden America's children, the government must act now. A bipartisan coalition of Congress, led by the President, must resolve the long-term imbalance between the government's entitlement promises and the funds it will have available to pay for them.[60]

—Report of the Bipartisan Commission
on Entitlement and Tax Reform

Great myths persist with regard to deficit spending and the current state of entitlement funding.[61] These two quotes serve as a reminder of the importance of distinguishing between the short-term and long-term dimensions of the federal government's budget deficit predicament. The general view is that Social Security entitlements cause many serious problems in both the short and long run. The truth is that Social Security entitlements cause almost no problems in the short run and a few in the long run. Social Security and Medicare have *not* been responsible for the recent federal deficit. To understand this, look first at Table 1 (page 94), which summarizes the federal budget for 1993. At $461 billion, Social Security and Medicare combined are the largest entry in the table. The total budget deficit for 1993 was $255 billion. Since Social Security and Medicare represent 33 percent of total expenditures, these programs look like they might be major contributors to the deficit.

But now look at Table 2 (page 95). This table splits the federal budget into two classes, one for Social Security and Medicare and the other for all other expenditures. Budget I (the non-Social Security budget) has a deficit of $307 billion. That is, the tax revenues were insufficient to pay for these expenditures (defense, interest payments, running the government, etc.), or the expenditures were too high. In contrast, Budget II (the Social Security budget) generates a surplus of $51 billion. Thus, the overall deficit in Table 1 ($255 billion) is lower than the $307 billion deficit in Budget I solely because the Social Security surplus is factored in with the much higher deficit for the non-Social Security part of the federal budget.

Social Security was included in the federal budget for the first time in 1969. The surpluses generated during the 1960s and 1970s had the effect of helping to balance the budget. In fact, when the accounting procedure was introduced in 1969, the Social Security surplus from that year permitted President Johnson to take credit for sending a "balanced budget" to Congress instead of one with a deficit. In the 1970s and 1980s, when Social Security sometimes ran a deficit, some government officials tried to blame the very much larger *total* federal deficit (see Figure 5, page 96) on "out-of-control" nondiscretionary programs like Social Security. Currently, Social Security is generating surpluses, as it has throughout most of its history. Operating on a self-financing and partial funding basis (with current benefits mostly dependent on current taxes), Social Security taxes and expenditures must be kept in close balance. Unlike other federal programs, there is no possibility that Social Security will generate large deficits over long periods of time.

If Social Security is not the source of the deficit, what is? As a result of the major cuts in tax rates (and the indexing of ceilings to prevent inflation pushing taxpayers into higher tax brackets)[62] legislated during the Reagan years, the flow of revenues to the government has been drastically curtailed. This action coincided with a dramatic increase in defense expenditures during the 1980s (see Figure 6, page 97). While defense expenditures have declined in recent years, the defense spending legacy of the Reagan-Bush years—the interest on the huge deficits generated during the 1980s—remains to be paid for years to come. Interest payments currently represent about one-fifth of the non-Social Security budget (see Table 2).

TABLE 1. FEDERAL BUDGET, 1993

Type of Expenditure	Amount ($Billions)	Percentage of Total
Net interest	199	14
National defense	291	
Medicaid, public health, medical research	99	42
Public assistance (+ SSI, food stamps)	207	
Subtotal	**796**	
Everything else except Social Security: Internal affairs, science and space, energy, natural resources and environment, agriculture, transportation, education and training and social services, veterans, legal, general government	152	11
Subtotal	**948**	
Social Security and Medicare	461	33
Subtotal	**1,409**	**100**
Total Receipts	**1,154**	
Deficit	**-255**	

Sources: Economic Report of the President, 1995 (Washington, D.C.: U.S. Government Printing Office, 1995); Social Security Administration, *Annual Statistical Supplement* (Washington, D.C.: U.S. Government Printing Office, 1994).

In the long term, however, the Social Security surpluses will end, and the reserves of the Social Security Trust Funds will decline rapidly (see Figure 7, page 98). That is why there is unanimous agreement among policymakers that changes will have to be made in the policies governing the Old-Age, Survivors, and Disability Insurance (OASDI) programs. The controversy is over the type and magnitude of the changes to be introduced.[63]

TABLE 2. SPLIT FEDERAL BUDGET, 1993

Type of Expenditure	Amount ($Billions)	Percentage of total
Budget I		
Net interest	199	21
National defense	291	30
Medicaid, public health, medical research	99	10
Public assistance (+ SSI, food stamps)	207	22
Subtotal	**796**	
Everything else except Social Security: Internal affairs, science and space, energy, natural resources and environment, agriculture, transportation, education and training and social services, veterans, legal, general government	152	16
Total Expenditures	**948**	**100***
Total Receipts	**641**	
Deficit	**-307**	
Budget II		
Social Security Totals: OASDHI** Receipts	512	
OASDHI Expenditures	461	33
Surplus	**+51**	
Deficit	**-256**	

* Does not add to 100 percent due to rounding.

** OASDI (Old-Age, Survivors, Disability, and Health Insurance programs)

Sources: Economic Report of the President, 1995 (Washington, D.C.: U.S. Government Printing Office, 1995); Social Security Administration, *Annual Statistical Supplement, 1994* (Washington, D.C.: U.S. Government Printing Office, 1994).

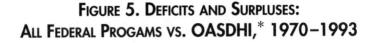

FIGURE 5. DEFICITS AND SURPLUSES:
ALL FEDERAL PROGAMS VS. OASDHI,* 1970–1993

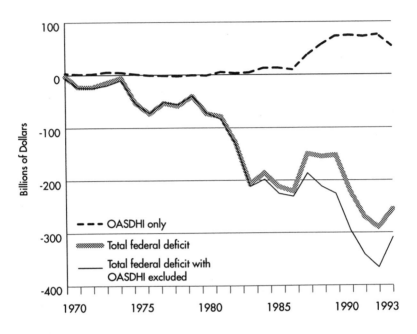

* OASDHI (Old-Age, Survivors, Disability, and Health Insurance programs)

Sources: Economic Report of the President, 1995 (Washington, D.C.: U.S. Government Printing Office, 1995); Social Security Administration, *Annual Statistical Supplement, 1994* (Washington, D.C.: U.S. Government Printing Office, 1994).

There can be no doubt that ultimately the OASDI "entitlement issue" will be resolved. Numerous proposals currently are on the table for dealing with the future shortfall. Contrary to the Chicken Little cries from some writers ("The sky is falling!"), there should be little concern that Social Security will be given a firm financial footing.

But the resolution of issues related to the health care system will not be as easy. Figure 8 (see page 99) shows, for example, that the projected big growth in future entitlement expenditures comes not from OASDI but from Medicare. When President Clinton first took office, he identified government expenditures on medical services as a "budget killer." He tried comprehensively to reform the nation's approach to health care financing but met with strong resistance. In his second term, a somewhat chastened Clinton and Congress continued to struggle with these costs, but only

FIGURE 6. DEFENSE EXPENDITURES
1970–1996

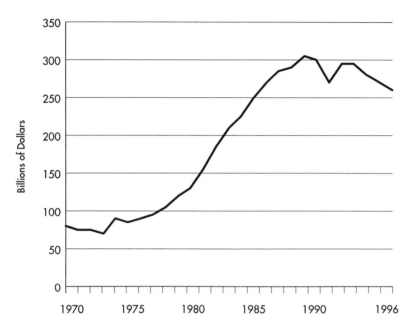

Source: Economic Report of the President, 1996 (Washington, D.C.: U.S. Government Printing Office, 1996).

incremental changes were discussed. In the absence of basic reform, there seemed to be little choice but to shift more of the costs onto private parties— especially service providers and the elderly themselves.

The medical cost issue will continue to be of much greater concern. Our health delivery system is currently undergoing dramatic structural shifts, with the final outcome and implications quite uncertain. Many experts, however, expect the costs of various services to keep rising over the long run. But that is not the focus of the current discussion. Paradoxically, much of the talk about *radical reform* has concentrated on pension reform—not on the bigger problem of national health care costs.

A variety of schemes have been proposed to privatize part or all of the mandatory public pension program in the United States. Why? For reasons discussed earlier in this chapter, proponents see public pension reform as a way to deal with the deficit, to promote more saving, and hence to promote economic growth.[64] Reform also is being pushed by those who are hostile to most government programs because of the supposed cost to

FIGURE 7. OASDI TRUST FUND BALANCES RELATIVE TO PREDICTED EXPENDITURES*

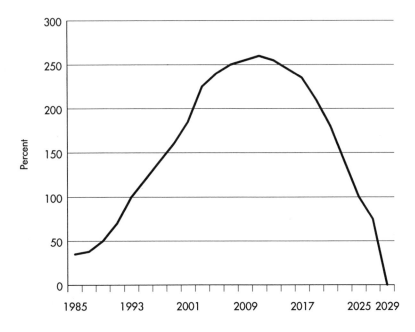

* Ratio of OASDI (Old-Age, Survivors, and Disability Insurance) trust funds assets to expenditures using intermediate economic and demographic assumptions

Source: 1997 Annual Report of the Board of Trustees of the Federal Old-Age and Survivors Insurance and Disability Insurance Trust Funds (Washington, D.C.: U.S. Government Printing Office, 1997).

individual liberty. Finally, a large number of players in the private sector investment industry are understandably anxious to increase their business by managing more of the public's retirement monies.

NOT GENERATIONAL CONFLICT BUT CONFLICT BETWEEN RICH AND POOR

Barely 10 percent of the federal budget goes to what people normally think governments do: laws, roads, natural resources, education, agriculture, transportation, general government services, and so forth. Figure 9 (see page 100) shows the trend of federal spending divided into three broad categories:

FIGURE 8. PROJECTED COSTS OF OASDHI*

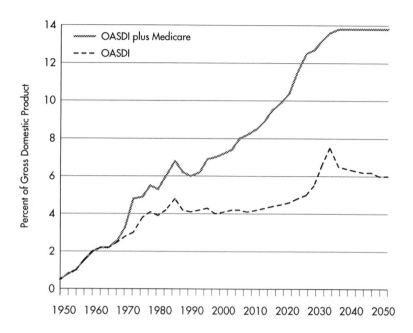

* OASDHI (Old-Age, Survivors, Disability, and Health Insurance programs)

Source: Based on data in Board of Trustees reports, Social Security Administration, using intermediate projections.

redistributive payments (transfers), expenditures on military goods and services, and expenditures on all other goods and services. The redistributive payments presented here are different from the usual numbers, including not just transfer payments to individuals but also redistribution of income through debt interest payments, grants to state and local governments, and subsidy payments. The data indicate that throughout the whole postwar period only about 10 percent of the activity of the federal government (as measured by spending) has gone to the purchase of nonmilitary goods and services. The other 90 percent has been used, first, to redistribute income and, second, to fund the defense establishment.

Thus, for the past half century or more, the issue of redistributing income has been a major activity of the federal government. Moderation

FIGURE 9. TRENDS IN FEDERAL EXPENDITURES, 1953–1994

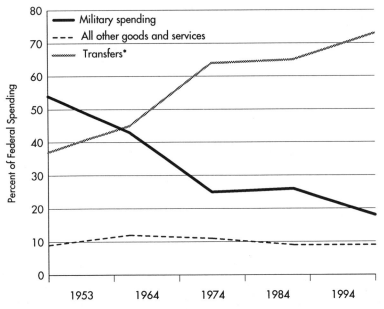

* Transfers are defined as transfers to individuals and the rest of the world plus grants-in-aid to state and local governments plus net interest plus subsidies.

Sources: Data for 1953–82 from W. C. Peterson, "The U.S. 'Welfare State' and the Conservative Counterrevolution," *Journal of Economic Issues* 19, no. 3 (September 1985). Data for 1984–94 from the *Economic Report of the President,* various years.

or elimination of poverty has been one of its primary goals, especially dealing with the poverty that arises in old age as a result of individuals' inability or unwillingness to save for retirement.

However, according to Andrew Glyn, in recent years there has been a profound shift in industrialized countries with regard to economic goals and policies—including the philosophy of income distribution.[65] According to the new, conservative orthodoxy, ". . . the equalitarian trends represented in government welfare spending had to be halted, if not reversed. This lurch in the stance of policy making throughout the capitalist world represented at bottom an attempt to claw back from workers some of the gains that the long period of high employment [during much of the 1950s and 1960s] had brought them in terms of wages, working conditions, and welfare."

In the 1980s and 1990s, with all the exaggerated concern about saving rates and budget deficits, there has been a tendency to view the redistribution of income each year through these transfer programs—especially Social Security—as a disincentive to household saving and financial prudence and as a prime culprit in the federal government's difficulties with balancing its books. At the same time, advocates of greater private saving have largely ignored the growing inequality of recent decades.

Many observers have forgotten the basic reasons for the various government programs redistributing income. Social insurance programs were first developed in the depression decade of the 1930s. But their mission is just as relevant today as it was then. Social Security is not just for helping people deal with the problems arising from big depressions (which we hope are gone forever).[66] On a more fundamental level, the need grows out of the labor-related problems (downsizing, early retirement, unemployment) arising from the successful and "efficient" operation of a market economy.[67]

Economic development holds great potential for many nations and has, in itself, decreased absolute poverty in many countries of the world. The problem with the use of market mechanisms to promote growth is the uncertainty they can bring to bear on people's livelihood and welfare—especially with regard to employment. Social Security has been a formidable resource over the years in helping market economies to thrive by "buffering" changing employment needs.[68]

With market incentives that promote efficiency, innovation, and growth also come shifting demand for products, layoffs, early retirement incentives, unemployment, inequality, bankruptcy, community decay, and social disruption. The creation of Social Security and other pensions should be seen as one of society's ways of dealing with the growing problems individuals have in finding work as they age. But, more important, these programs and initiatives should be seen in the context of ever-changing employment needs and the chronic unemployment characterizing market economies. In the words of Dan Jacobson, "more and more governments and unions have . . . come to recognize that adopting employment buffering strategies or developing worker-oriented adjustments and job-replacement strategies are a vital and, indeed, expedient element in human resource policies."[69]

Social Security offers economic protection to middle- and low-income workers that cannot be provided for efficiently and effectively through private means. The case for a program like this that deals with social inequity and insecurity has never been stronger.

Evolving Social Security benefits and early retirement policies in the United States also reflect in a significant way changing economic attitudes about labor force needs and the changing macroeconomic situation. The "early retirement" phenomenon witnessed over recent decades should be viewed as part of an uncoordinated market solution to the stagflation of 1970s, the high unemployment during the years following the OPEC oil crisis, and, more recently, the new demands of global competition and economic interdependency. Public and private pensions have been a major part of that solution.

It is important to see through the smokescreen of rhetoric about unsustainable dependency ratios (what I refer to as "voodoo demographics"), low saving causing low growth, entitlements "consuming our children," and the proliferating tales of "greedy geezers." Remember that the focus of discussions about national economic security should really be on issues such as maintaining low unemployment, cultivating the sources of growth (not just saving), and achieving a more equitable income distribution—issues that go back many years before the "Social Security debate." The debate about intergenerational redistribution and providing for people in old age can be (and should be) carried on in a totally different way from the scapegoating displayed so frequently in American society today.

6

MYTHS AND MISUNDERSTANDINGS ABOUT PUBLIC OPINION TOWARD SOCIAL SECURITY:
KNOWLEDGE, SUPPORT, AND REFORMISM

LAWRENCE R. JACOBS and ROBERT Y. SHAPIRO

Policymakers, pundits, and news audiences are bombarded every day with new public opinion polls and journalists' reports on the state of Americans' thinking about Social Security. To interpret the information, political observers rely on four assumptions about public views of Social Security. The first assumption is that the public really does not know much, if anything, about Social Security. The clear implication is that the public's preferences should be followed as a practical political matter but should be discounted as an influence on policy discussions.

No single poll on the public's attitude toward Social Security has gotten more eye-opening attention than Third Millennium's UFO poll of eighteen- to thirty-four-year-olds in September 1994. Journalists (and policymakers) followed

This chapter is an abridged version of the original paper, in which the authors reviewed hundreds of responses to survey questions from the 1970s to the fall of 1997. For a copy of the longer white paper, complete with survey data, please contact The Century Foundation.

Third Millennium's lead and pitched the poll as suggesting that young Americans considered UFOs more likely than the prospect of collecting Social Security.[1] Third Millennium's poll and its widespread use by journalists and policymakers illustrate the second assumption: Americans' confidence in the future of Social Security is dramatically changing, escaping like air from a punctured balloon. Public support for Social Security will decline dramatically now that confidence has collapsed.

The third assumption of political observers is that Americans are now turning toward radical change and would privatize Social Security as the best hope for restoring its future. Anne Willette, for example, opened her October 1, 1996, story for USA Today by heralding a poll that purported to demonstrate that almost 60 percent of Americans "want to invest some of their Social Security taxes themselves—even though they might end up with less money at retirement. Americans, particularly younger workers, are watching out for their interests and demanding their 'money's worth.'"

The final assumption is that the generations are at war over Social Security. Staving off the collapse of Social Security is the goal of self-serving seniors who are disregarding the interests of younger Americans. In a November 1994 broadcast, ABC's Jim Angle flagged younger Americans' "deep doubts about generational fairness."

We evaluated the validity of these four assumptions about public opinion by reviewing hundreds of responses to survey questions from the 1970s through fall 1997. We were especially interested in survey items that were worded in an identical or similar manner over a long period of time. As is well known, poll results are extremely sensitive to the wording of questions; survey responses can be an artifact of how poll questions are phrased. Examining similarly worded questions allows us to identify genuine patterns and trends in public opinion.

The conclusion of our analysis is that the evidence on public opinion is at odds with important aspects of the conventional presumptions regarding Americans' thinking about Social Security. The public is, in fact, better informed about Social Security than is commonly presumed. Areas in which the public is wrong often represent plausible conclusions based on the available information. The public may simply be echoing the choices it is presented. Although large proportions of citizens understand Social Security's operations, this knowledge is generally much more prevalent among the more affluent and educated.

In addition, Third Millennium's notorious UFO report is both fabricated and provides no new information about public opinion—Americans have had low confidence in Social Security since the 1970s. Despite this low confidence, the public's support has remained strong, according to available trend data.

The third assumption, that Americans welcome the opportunity to restructure Social Security, similarly lacks a clear grounding in the available evidence. Responses to balanced survey questions show no support for individualized privatization. Politicians who emphasize this kind of structural reform place themselves in the vulnerable position of pressing an option that a comparatively well informed public opposes.

The fourth assumption, that of intergenerational warfare, is overstated. Although seniors are more sensitive to threats to Social Security, younger Americans are consistently just as supportive (if not more so) of the overall program. Forgotten in the rush to condemn seniors as "greedy geezers" are the differences that divide the elderly. Opinion surveys suggest that education, economic circumstances, and other factors both divide seniors and draw them together with other segments of the population, including younger cohorts. A broad cross section of Americans support Social Security not because it satisfies a simple calculation of its "money's worth" to any individual but because it provides insurance against the risk of low income in retirement and protection from bearing the burden of financially drained parents.

WHAT THE PUBLIC KNOWS

Although Americans' overall political knowledge is "modest at best," Social Security constitutes an exception.[2] The public appears to know more about Social Security than about national defense or basic government institutions. Thus, while the public cannot be characterized as a fully informed citizenry, its knowledge of Social Security is much higher than is widely assumed. Surveys since 1973 show that at least half of the Americans questioned have consistently reported that they are "very" or "fairly" well informed.[3] The degree to which Americans perceive themselves as informed varies significantly by age and somewhat by education and income. Seniors consistently rank themselves the best informed, and those below thirty rank themselves the least informed. But Social Security is apparently sufficiently well understood through interpersonal contacts and media coverage to counteract the typical advantage of the affluent.[4]

Americans' confidence in their knowledge apparently springs from the information they receive through the media. Surveys by Princeton Survey Research Associates in January and February 1997 found that about half or more of Americans claim to be following news reports on Social Security "very" or "fairly" closely.[5] Of course, whether Americans' confidence in their understanding of Social Security is justified remains a separate issue; the public may be overestimating its competence or the information conveyed to the public by policymakers and journalists may be inaccurate.

The evidence suggests that the public's confidence is not unwarranted. Many of the basic rules and procedures of the Social Security system are known to half or more of the public. Eight surveys since 1978 indicate that generally two-thirds or more of Americans accurately understand that Social Security is a "pay-as-you-go" system.

A collection of individual survey items since the 1970s reveals that a majority or a solid plurality of the public accurately understands important facts about Social Security. The public recognizes that its funds are invested in government bonds rather than in stocks, or rather than being placed in a bank account; that exhaustion of the trust funds in 2029 will result in fewer assets and reduced benefits rather than the system becoming completely broke and unable to pay any benefits; and that its future financial problems stem from fewer workers and increased life expectancy. These are comparatively detailed and technical issues.

There are, however, some significant gaps in the public's understanding. Only one American in ten, or at best three Americans in ten, understands that Social Security is one of the federal budget's most expensive items; that fraud and abuse have not caused the program's financial trouble; and that Social Security is not facing financial difficulty because it is a "Ponzi scheme" to finance other programs.

Although Americans are wrong on a number of facts, their responses are either plausible or reflect the information that policymakers and journalists have fed them. For instance, the public's false impression that Social Security is poorly administered likely stems from a general distrust of government and from the media's widespread coverage of administrative slipups; Social Security is guilty simply by association with government. In fact, less than 1 percent of Social Security outlays are consumed by administrative costs, and independent auditors have never charged that its rolls of retirees are bloated by bureaucratic bumbling and government incompetence. Yet only 7 percent realize that Social Security's financial problems do not stem from fraud and abuse.[6]

The public also errs in believing that foreign aid and food stamps are more costly than Social Security in the federal budget, an impression created by politicians and the news media. The 1996 presidential election, for instance, cautiously steered clear of Social Security but gave ample play to the burden on taxpayers of funding welfare and—in the Republican primaries—foreign "giveaways." With this background, concluding that food stamps and foreign aid are significant budgetary burdens is not so far-fetched.

Other Social Security issues on which the public appears off base are actually points of contention on which reasonable people disagree. For instance, only 8 percent of Americans do not attribute Social Security's financial difficulties to unwise investments. At the same time, in the context of the future (in contrast to the past, where Social Security's pay-as-you-go system with a small contingency reserve invested in government bonds has worked well), observers are deeply divided over funding and investment issues, with some arguing that accumulating a larger reserve and investing in stocks now represents a wiser strategy.

In short, Americans' knowledge about Social Security is far from complete and certainly does not conform to the ideal of a democratic citizen, but it is more extensive than is commonly assumed, and wrong answers to poll questions are often reasonable conclusions based on available information.

STRONG SUPPORT FOR SOCIAL SECURITY

No survey question has repeatedly asked Americans over time if they support Social Security. The only modest exception occurred in two surveys by the Cato Institute in spring 1996, which found that about two-thirds of Americans were "very" or "mostly" favorable toward Social Security.

Nevertheless, indirect survey questions confirm sustained and very strong support for Social Security. Respondents have been asked a series of questions over a number of years about whether "we [are] spending too much, too little, or about the right amount on . . . Social Security." The answers to these questions make two very important points. First, an extraordinary nine out of ten Americans support the view that spending on Social Security is "about right" or "too little." Second, the high support has been remarkably stable even though 7 percent of respondents have shifted from the "too little" to the "about right" category since 1986.

When Americans have been asked to set spending priorities in the federal budget, they have expressed overwhelming support for maintaining or expanding the Social Security program. Support remains enormous and opposition to cutting back massive. Since the mid-1980s, fewer than one out of ten Americans have favored decreasing Social Security's funding in wrestling with the competing demands on the federal budget, though about 10 percent of respondents have shifted from favoring increased funding to keeping funding the same.

A series of surveys that used quite different wording to ask Americans whether the federal budget deficit should be reduced by cutting spending on Social Security showed that, over the last fifteen years, two-thirds of Americans or more have opposed cutting the program to achieve budget reductions. Six polls in the mid-1990s asked respondents, after they indicated support for a balanced budget, if they would favor cuts in Social Security to achieve it; between 58 percent and 71 percent opposed balancing the budget if it meant cuts in Social Security.

A nearly identical pattern of steadfast support for Social Security appears in surveys on benefit reductions as a means to trim the federal budget. Since 1982, majorities of 61 percent to 78 percent have opposed reductions in cost-of-living adjustments (COLAs) to reduce the federal budget deficit, though the proportions favoring the reform have increased over time. Other surveys find similar opposition to cuts in Social Security to reduce taxes.

The public has been more open to taxing the Social Security benefits of the wealthy as a means for reducing the federal budget deficit. No matter how the questions in various surveys are worded, Americans have sent a strong and sustained message to budget cutters: while taxing the wealthy is acceptable, the basic structure of Social Security is off-limits in the competition for federal funding.

The public supports Social Security benefits for seniors because it represents an insurance against the risk of low income in retirement, a right earned by paying in during working years, and a protection from the burden of financially drained parents. Americans do not view the program in terms of individual profit and loss like a private investment, but as a protection like fire insurance against known risks. For example, a 1997 survey by the Public Agenda Foundation found that 84 percent of the public agreed that Social Security "forces people who would otherwise neglect to save for their retirement to at least save something for it, and that 77 percent of the public polled supported the program because it guarantees a minimal income even if you face financial disaster in retirement."[7] A 1996 survey by DYG, Inc. reported similarly lopsided majorities in all age groups who supported Social Security as insurance "just in case" it is needed.[8]

Social Security is also considered a benefit that is earned rather than doled out on the basis of need. Although a 1997 *Washington Post* survey found that 64 percent of those surveyed favored "reducing benefits paid to upper-income retirees in the future" in order to strengthen Social Security's finances, evidence indicates that the public favors the principle that all Social Security contributors earn a right to its benefits. Princeton Survey Research Associates discovered in a January 1996 survey that 63 percent of Americans surveyed approved of having their "tax dollars used to help pay" for the Social Security benefits of better-off retirees. Tellingly, the young were more supportive than were seniors.[9] Americans consider canceling benefits to any retirees to be tantamount—as participants in the National Issues Forum (NIF) explained—to "breaking the promise." These surveys, combined with the evidence on popular support for taxing the benefits of the wealthy, suggest that the public is reaching a subtle distinction: they acknowledge the principle that the wealthy—like all others who have paid in—have earned Social Security benefits.

Another source of Social Security's support is that working Americans count on it to support their retired parents. DYG surveys in 1985, 1995, and 1996 confirmed that three-quarters of Americans surveyed supported Social Security because it relieved them of the financial burden of caring for their parents.[10]

Americans from quite varied personal circumstances express substantial support for Social Security, and even the differences among groups defy straightforward classification. Generally, supermajorities of 70 percent to 90 percent of Americans from different educational, income, and age backgrounds opposed reductions in Social Security spending to reduce the federal budget deficit. Within this overall consensus, however, some standard differences emerge. Individuals who were better educated, more affluent, and younger were less opposed to spending cuts. On the other hand, a 1997 survey finds the most advantaged reverse positions and become possibly the greatest defenders of Social Security, perhaps because of a growing sense that the federal budget is under greater control.[11] Variations in the wording of questions complicate comparisons over time.

These views defy any presumption of self-interest. Surveys taken throughout the 1990s show that, repeatedly, seniors, the affluent, and the better educated depart from their expected positions to offer strenuous support for Social Security: the better educated were more protective of Social Security spending in 1991 and 1997 than the least well educated; the most affluent were equally opposed to cuts in 1994 as were the poorest; and, despite breathless media accounts of intergenerational warfare, the younger cohorts were as protective of Social Security spending (if not more so) as the oldest in 1993, 1995, and 1996.

Further evidence that Americans persistently act against their narrow self-interest is available in a series of individual surveys in 1997. A March 1997 *Washington Post* survey reported that the young were the most concerned that Social Security benefits to average retirees were so small that they needed to struggle to get by; older groups were least likely to hold this view. A February 1997 *Los Angeles Times* survey found that the young were the most supportive of the existing arrangements for financing Social Security, with no clear differences among educational and income groups.[12]

THE PUBLIC REMAINS SUPPORTIVE DESPITE ITS LOW CONFIDENCE

A common assumption is that low confidence in Social Security's future erodes support for the program. The conventional wisdom says that, as confidence drops, support is also expected to dip. In fact, neither low confidence nor downward shifts in confidence consistently coincide with declining support.

Confidence crashed from the 60 percent to 50 percent range in the mid-1970s to 39 percent in 1979 and then 32 percent in 1982, yet support for the program did not change appreciably. The 1990s produced a similar pattern of plummeting confidence but relatively steady support.

The conventional wisdom that the public's backing for Social Security is crumbling under the strain of low confidence is simply not supported by available evidence. The explanation for this apparent paradox lies in three factors that extend far beyond the particular challenges facing Social Security: economic anxieties, mistrust of government, and disproportionately negative news coverage. Supermajorities support Social Security but fear that politicians or an economic downturn will ruin it.[13]

Indeed, overwhelming proportions of Americans fear that economic bad news will hurt their financial situation in retirement. A 1997 survey by the Public Agenda Foundation found that 79 percent worried about inflation, 74 percent were concerned about high health care costs, and 66 percent expected a souring economy to undermine retirement plans.[14]

The confidence of Americans in Social Security is unavoidably colored by their distrust of government in general. Confidence in government in general recently has been at or near its all-time low, with the most disaffected concentrated among the young (who are the least confident in Social Security). The National Issue Forums, which convened focus groups around the country, found in 1997 that general "cynicism about government competence and trustworthiness" has fueled specific concerns about Social Security's ability to handle the retirement of baby boomers. NIF participants simply assumed that politicians would "play politics" with Social Security.[15] A forty-year-old New Mexico man captured the pervasive skepticism toward government when he complained in a Public Agenda Foundation study, "I don't think the politicians up there should have any control over it—I don't trust them."[16] Concern about Social Security is a symptom of a larger problem.

Finally, the media's systematic framing of Social Security in terms of its problems and unending need for change can only increase Americans' anxiety about whether it will be there for them. Our analysis for the National Academy of Social Insurance of thousands of stories in the Associated Press and leading broadcast and print outlets found a persistent pattern: Social Security received large but relatively brief bursts of extensive media coverage that disproportionately zeroed in on its problems and on the need to reform the program.[17] The message in the mass media is that Social Security is difficult to sustain without constant doctoring. The public's confidence in Social Security, then, is most likely a function of dread of government, media coverage, and economic fears.

III

RICH BOOMER,
POOR BOOMER

7

ARE AMERICANS SAVING ENOUGH FOR RETIREMENT?

WILLIAM G. GALE

The baby-boom generation—the roughly 76 million people born between 1946 and 1964—has had a major influence on American society for five decades. From jamming the nation's schools in the 1950s and 1960s to crowding labor and housing markets in the 1970s and 1980s, boomers have reshaped economic patterns and institutions at each stage of their lives. Now that the leading edge of the generation has turned fifty, the impending collision between the boomers and the nation's retirement system is naturally catching the eye of policymakers and the boomers themselves.

Retirement income security in the United States traditionally has been based on the so-called three-legged stool: Social Security, private pensions, and additional household saving. The system has served the elderly well: the poverty rate among elderly households fell from 35 percent in 1959 to 11 percent in 1995.

But problems loom in the future. Partly because of the demographic bulge created by the baby boomers, Social Security faces a long-term imbalance.

This chapter also will appear in a forthcoming collection of essays edited by Robert N. Butler, which will be published by The Century Foundation Press.

The solution, even if it involves privatization, must in some way cut benefits or raise taxes.[1] Thus, the future economic status of the elderly hinges critically on the adequacy of private saving and private pensions.

The private pension system has changed dramatically in nature, shifting away from traditional defined benefit plans to defined contribution plans, which provide workers with much more discretion over participation, contribution, and investment decisions. Naturally, this invites questions about the future ability of pensions to help finance retirement.

The personal saving rate has remained low for more than a decade, and net personal saving other than pensions has virtually disappeared over the past ten years.[2] A significant proportion of people currently reaching retirement age has low levels of financial assets.[3] A large proportion of younger households may also be saving too little to finance their retirement.[4]

People who do not provide for themselves now may be more likely to put pressure on public assistance programs in the future. In addition, a number of trends—including increased life expectancy, earlier retirement age, escalating health care costs, likely reductions in Social Security, and the longer-term deterioration of family networks—will make retirement preparation more difficult in coming years.

These developments would be enough to raise concern about retirement preparation under the best of circumstances. But the prospect of a huge generation edging unprepared toward retirement raises particular concerns about the living standards of the baby boomers in old age, the concomitant pressure on government policies, and the stability of the nation's retirement system.

SOME CONCEPTUAL ISSUES

Whether Americans are saving adequately for retirement depends in part on a number of definitional and conceptual issues. First and foremost, what is meant by "adequate?" One definition of adequate retirement wealth is to have enough resources to maintain preretirement living standards. A common rule of thumb, often used by financial planners, is that retirees should be able to accomplish this goal by replacing 60–80 percent of preretirement income.[5] Retiree households can maintain the same standard of living with less income than when working because they typically have more leisure time, smaller family size, and lower expenses. Their taxes are lower, both because they escape payroll taxes and because the income tax is progressive. And most have already paid off their mortgages and debts relating to other durable goods. On the other hand, older households may face higher and more uncertain medical expenses, even though they are covered by Medicare.

Maintaining living standards, though, raises some important conceptual problems. For example, retired people have much more leisure time and so literally can substitute time (leisure) for money (consumption expenditure) in maintaining living standards. Understanding the rate at which households make this trade-off is a difficult task. Also, what does it mean to maintain standards of living when health is declining as people age? If the definition is that retirees are restored to the health status they enjoyed as twenty-two-year-olds, clearly enormous expenses would be required, and virtually no one could be said to have "enough" to maintain living standards by that definition. Implicitly, people probably have in mind some age-appropriate health status as a benchmark, but what that benchmark is may vary dramatically across the spectrum of retirees.

In part, the right definition of "enough" depends on why the question is being asked. For example, from a policy perspective, it may be sufficient if boomers maintain, say, 90 percent of their living standards. If that level were achieved, people might decide that there were more pressing uses of limited public resources.

Depending on why the question is asked, other plausible definitions of saving "enough" include having enough resources to stay out of poverty, keeping income above 150 percent of the poverty line, and so forth. There is no hard and fast definition that will satisfy all purposes. Moreover, any measure of what it means to save enough may vary across households in relation to their risk aversion, health status, expectations, preferences for saving, income uncertainty, family size, and other factors.

A second issue is which assets or income sources to include in any measure of how well baby boomers are preparing for retirement. There is near universal agreement that financial assets targeted to retirement, Social Security, and pensions should be included. There are disagreements about whether housing wealth, other assets, labor income earned in "retirement," inheritances, or government benefits should count. As before, to some extent the decision whether to include a certain form of income hinges on what question is being asked.

Some studies focus only on how much retirees are putting aside in personal saving for retirement. There, the outlook appears bleak. James Poterba, Steven Venti, and David Wise found that, in 1991, the median household headed by a sixty-five- to sixty-nine-year-old had financial assets of only $14,000.[6] But expanding the measure to include other assets paints quite a different picture: adding in Social Security, pensions, housing, and other wealth, median wealth was about $270,000.

A third issue—crucial but as yet little explored—is that concerning which baby boomers are not providing adequately for retirement and how big the gap is between what they have and what they should have. Some boomers are doing extremely well, others quite poorly. Summary averages for an entire generation may not be useful as descriptions of the problem or as suggestions for policy.

PREVIOUS RESEARCH

The Congressional Budget Office (1993) recently compared households aged twenty-five to forty-four in 1989 (roughly the boomer cohort) with households the same age in 1962. Boomer households, it turned out, had more real income and a higher ratio of wealth to income than the previous generation. Though this finding initially seems optimistic, in fact the CBO study implies that baby boomers are going to do well in retirement only if the current generation of elderly is thought to be doing well, if the retirement needs of the two generations are the same, if the experience from middle age to retirement is the same for both generations, and if boomers will be satisfied to do as well in retirement as today's retirees.

None of these conditions is guaranteed. First, although the current generation of elderly are generally thought to be doing well in retirement, some 18 percent were living below 125 percent of the poverty line in 1995. Second, retirement needs may be higher for boomers because they will live longer than the previous generation and will likely face higher health costs.

Third, whether the boomers will have a similar experience from middle age to retirement is an open question. The previous generation prospered from the growth of real Social Security benefits in the 1970s. They also benefited from the inflation that caused a dramatic increase in house values in the 1970s and reduced the real value of mortgage debt. However, if housing is not to be included in the wealth measures of adequacy, as many would argue it should not be, then it is unclear why an increase in housing values should be thought of as having helped the previous generation.

Other "onetime" events favor the boomers. First, the stock market fell in real terms in the 1970s, but the S&P 500 has risen by more than 500 percent since 1982. Second, more female boomers are working, and those that do earn more, than women in the previous generation. This will raise their pension coverage and benefits. It also implies that boomers will have a bigger drop in work-related expenses in retirement. Third, pension coverage and pension tenure, including 401(k)s, may be higher for male boomers as well because of the maturing of the pension system. Fourth, boomers are having fewer children than their parents did, reducing their living expenses during working years. Fifth, lifetime earnings may peak later for boomers than for the previous generation because boomers are more likely to be in white-collar jobs than in jobs that emphasize physical effort. This means that at any given age, relative to the previous generation, boomers have a greater proportion of their lifetime income (from which to save) ahead of them and will be more likely to be able to work longer if they wish.

Finally, doing as well as the previous generation may not be considered a satisfactory accomplishment either on personal grounds or as a policy goal. For example, living standards tend to rise over time as productivity growth makes workers more efficient. Thus, telling a thirty-five-year-old worker that he or she has the same living standard now as a thirty-five-year-old worker did thirty years ago is not likely to elicit much cheer. A more plausible measure of what constitutes adequate saving is to compare the living standard of boomers in retirement to the one boomers enjoyed during their working years. For all of these reasons, how to interpret the CBO's result is unclear, even if the result itself is unambiguous.

The most comprehensive study of these issues was undertaken by Stanford professor Douglas Bernheim in conjunction with Merrill Lynch. Bernheim developed an elaborate computer model that simulates households' optimal saving and consumption choices over time as a function of family size, earning patterns, age, Social Security, pensions, and other characteristics.[7] He then compared households' actual saving with what the simulations suggested they should be saving. His primary finding, summarized in a "baby boomer retirement index," is that boomers as a whole are saving only about one-third of what they should be to maintain preretirement living standards.

While this finding has generated substantial attention, it is not well understood. The index does not measure the adequacy of saving by the ratio of total retirement resources (Social Security, pensions, and other assets) to total retirement needs (the wealth necessary on the eve of retirement to maintain preretirement living standards). Instead, it examines the ratio of one type of "other assets" to the portion of total needs not covered by Social Security and pensions.

Table 1 (see page 118) helps explain how Bernheim's index is constructed. In case A, a hypothetical household (or group of households) needs to accumulate 100 units of wealth. It is on course to generate 61 in Social Security, 30 in pensions, and 3 in other assets.[8] Total retirement resources are therefore projected to be 94 percent of what is needed to maintain living standards.

TABLE 1. ALTERNATIVE MEASURES OF THE ADEQUACY OF RETIREMENT SAVING

CASE	SOCIAL SECURITY (1)	PENSION (2)	OTHER ASSETS (3)	TOTAL RETIREMENT RESOURCES (1) + (2) + (3)	NEEDS (4)	BOOMER INDEX (%) (3)/[(4) - (1) - (2)]	TOTAL RESOURCES INDEX (%) [(1) + (2) + (3)]/4
A	61	30	3	94	100	33	94
B	0	0	33	33	100	33	33
C	20	20	20	60	100	33	60
D	61	0	33	94	100	85	94
E	61	0	17	78	100	44	78
F	61	30	3	94	95	75	99
G	61	30	3	94	93	150	101

Definitions: *Total Retirement Resources* = Social Security + pensions + other assests.
Needs = accumulated wealth on the eve of retirement that keeps living standard in retirement equal to living standard in working years.
Boomer Index = (other assets) / (needs – Social Security – pensions).
Total Resources Index = (total retirement resources) / (needs).

Source: Author's calculations.

But, according to the boomer index, the household is saving only 33 percent (that is, 3/[100–61–30]) of what it needs.

Thus, one problem is that the level of the boomer index provides little information about the overall adequacy of retirement preparations. In particular, having the boomer index stand at one-third does not imply that, in the absence of changes in saving behavior, boomers will have living standards in retirement equal to one-third of their current living standard. It could mean that (as in case B), or it could mean retirement living standards will be 60 percent of current ones (case C), or 94 percent (case A), or even more than 99 percent (if Social Security and pension benefits were 99 and other saving were 0.33).

A second problem is that changes in the boomer index over time, or differences across groups, do not correspond to changes or differences in the adequacy of overall retirement saving. If, as in case D, the household in A rolls over its pension into an IRA, the boomer index rises dramatically though total retirement resources are unchanged. If, as in case E, household A rolls over half of its pension into other assets and spends the rest on a vacation, the household clearly is less prepared for retirement—its stock of total retirement resources falls—yet it obtains a higher boomer index than in case A.

A third problem is that the boomer index can be extremely sensitive to estimates of retirement needs. In case F, retirement needs are 5 percent lower than in A, but the boomer index rises from 33 percent to 75 percent. In case G, retirement needs are 7 percent lower than in A, and the boomer index rises to 150 percent.

Bernheim points out that biases in his model cause it to understate the retirement saving problem. The wealth measure, he notes, includes assets the household has earmarked for retirement as well as half of other nonhousing wealth. The model also assumes that there will be no cuts in future Social Security benefits or increases in Social Security taxes, and that life expectancy will not be extended.

But other factors cause the model to overstate the problem. Pension wealth is probably understated. Pension coverage is almost surely understated because any male not covered at the time of the survey, when the respondents are thirty-five to forty-five years old, is assumed never to be covered. Data from Current Population Surveys, however, suggest that pension coverage rates rise by 20 percent from age thirty-five to age fifty-five.[9] Pension benefits may also be understated: Bernheim uses an 18 percent replacement rate of earnings between ages sixty-one and sixty-three, based on data from the 1970s. Because the pension system grew rapidly from the 1940s to the 1970s, workers retiring in the 1970s likely had fewer years in the pension system and hence lower benefits than the boomers will upon retiring. Somewhat more recent data using the 1983 Survey of Consumer Finances suggests replacement rates of 25 to 30 percent and possibly higher.[10]

The basic model excludes all housing wealth; Bernheim's calculations show that including housing would raise the index to 70 percent. The model also excludes all inheritances. A substantial minority of boomers are expected to receive inheritances, typically estimated to be in the range of $10,000 to $30,000.[11] The model assumes that people will retire at age sixty-five, though the Social Security normal retirement age will be sixty-six for most boomers and sixty-seven for the youngest. It excludes all earnings after "retirement," though about 17 percent of the income of the elderly in 1988 came from working.[12] Some portion of this income is earned by people who "need" to work, but casual evidence suggests that a good number of people would like to continue working even if they do not need to. With partial retirement on the increase, boomers may work even more in their senior years, regardless of the adequacy of saving.

There is no allowance in the model for reductions in work-related expenses for those who do retire. This may be an especially important consideration for the growing number of two-earner families. Nor are there allowances for the fact that people eventually pay off their mortgage and hence can continue to consume the same amount of housing services but at greatly reduced cash cost. Data from the 1992 Survey of Consumer Finances indicate that 90 percent of baby boomers that owned homes had outstanding mortgages, compared to about 7 percent of homeowners aged seventy or higher. Similar qualifications apply to other durable goods—furniture, carpets, appliances, cars, clothes. The model used by Bernheim assumes that people rent these items and therefore have to pay for their use every year. In reality, people usually have purchased such items and so do not need to continue making payments after retirement.

Finally, the model also does not allow for any decline in living standards, though a small decline hardly seems like an important policy concern. This is important because, as noted, the boomer index can be extremely sensitive to small changes in assets or needs.

Whether these biases are larger or smaller than the countervailing ones observed by Bernheim is not obvious. Owing to the current uncertainty over the effects of these various influences on our perception of retirement security, measuring and identifying biases accurately is an important area for future study.

SOME NEW RESULTS

Despite the extant research, fundamental questions remain not only unanswered but also in some cases unasked: What proportion of households is saving adequately for retirement? How has the proportion changed over time? What are the characteristics of such households? Among those not saving adequately, how big is the problem?

I have developed preliminary estimates in response to these questions using data from the 1983, 1986, 1989, and 1992 Surveys of Consumer Finances. These are nationally representative household surveys undertaken by the Federal Reserve Board. The sample consists of married households where the husband is aged twenty-five to sixty-four and works at least twenty hours per week.

To determine whether a household is saving adequately requires comparing its actual wealth to a measure of its target wealth. The measures of actual wealth are taken from the surveys. Target wealth indicates how much a household needs to have accumulated, given certain characteristics, to be "on track" for saving enough for retirement. The characteristics that affect this calculation include age, earnings, education, and pension status. People that are older or have higher earnings need to have accumulated more wealth; those with pensions need to have accumulated less (nonpension) wealth than those without. Controlling for the other variables, those with higher levels of education need to have accumulated less than those with lower levels of education. The reason is that workers with higher levels of education tend to have earnings paths that rise more steeply with age and peak later in life. Thus, at a given age and level of earnings, a worker with more education would be expected on average to have more future income than a worker with less education.

To determine target wealth for each household, I use results from Douglas Bernheim and John Karl Scholz,[13] who calculated target wealth-to-earnings ratios as a function of household age, education, and pension status. This ratio can be multiplied by household earnings to determine each household's target wealth level. Because the figures from Bernheim and Scholz use Bernheim's model, the estimates presented here suffer from the same biases as discussed above.

Table 2 (see page 122) shows that in 1992, not counting housing equity, about 47 percent of all households—and 48 percent of baby boomers—were saving adequately. When half (or all) of housing equity is counted, the adequacy rate climbs to 61 percent (or 70 percent) for all households and about the same for baby boomers. All three measures have fallen since 1986. This may be a little misleading, since the 1986 sample was a reinterview of selected respondents of the 1983 survey rather than a random cross section.

TABLE 2. ADEQUACY RATES
Percentage of Households Deemed to Be
Saving Adequately for Retirement

All Households in the Sample

	WEALTH DEFINITION		
Year	Narrow	Intermediate	Broad
1983	44.0%	65.7%	75.9%
1986	52.7	71.3	77.7
1989	43.3	63.0	71.5
1992	46.8	61.1	69.7

Baby Boomer Households

Year	Narrow	Intermediate	Broad
1989	47.7	66.7	72.8
1992	48.1	63.0	71.0

Sample: Married couple where the husband is aged 25–64 and works at least 20 hours per week.

Definitions: *Baby Boomer Households* = households where the husband was born between 1946 and 1964.

Narrow Wealth = Financial assets (checking and money market accounts, CDs and savings accounts, IRAs and Keoghs, mutual funds, stocks and bonds, trusts,cash value of life insurance, and employer-related thrift account balance) plus nonfinancial assets (business, other real estate, and other assets) minus total debt (lines of credit, credit card debt, other real estate debt, other debt).

Intermediate Wealth = Narrow Wealth plus 50 percent of housing equity.

Broad Wealth = Narrow Wealth plus 100 percent of housing equity.

Source: Author's calculations from the 1983, 1986, 1989, and 1992 Surveys of Consumer Finances.

However, in 1992 the intermediate and broad wealth measures were below their 1983 levels, which is more troubling.

In any given year, adequacy rates are prone to rise with education and income. Within the baby-boom generation, adequacy rates generally decline somewhat with age. This is consistent with a point made by Bernheim that the older boomers should be saving at a higher rate but do not appear to be doing so. Adequacy rates tend to be higher for boomers with pensions than for those without, either because pensions raise households' overall wealth or because people more oriented toward saving and thinking about retirement are also more likely to have jobs with pensions.

Interestingly, high adequacy rates do not necessarily require high levels of observed saving. For example, suppose annual retirement needs are 75 percent of final earnings. According to the Social Security Administration, Social Security benefits replace about 47 percent of final earnings for the average worker with thirty-five years of experience who earns $40,000 at retirement and has a nonworking spouse. With pensions typically replacing 25–30 percent of final earnings, a household with Social Security and a pension would not need much more saving to maintain adequate living standards, especially if at least one member of the household can work for a time in "retirement," expects to receive bequests, or expects to use housing equity to support retirement consumption.

Table 3 (see page 124) examines the difference between current target wealth and current actual wealth among households that are not saving adequately (ignoring all housing equity). For many such households the wealth shortfall is relatively small. The median inadequate saver has a shortfall of $22,000, or about six months of earnings—a problem that could be solved either by postponing retirement for six months or by accepting a relatively small reduction in retirement living standards. Even among sixty- to sixty-four-year-olds, the median inadequate saver could obtain a sound retirement by working for an additional two years.

Thus, the glass can be viewed as half full or half empty. When housing equity is ignored, the typical household seems to be either just barely saving enough or just missing the target. When housing is included, more than two-thirds of households appear to be above the minimum wealth they need, given age and other considerations. Roughly speaking, a third of the sample is doing well by any measure, a third is doing poorly by any measure, and the status of the middle third is ambiguous. Both of the following statements are true: up to two-thirds of the households in the sample are now saving at least as much as they should be; and two-thirds are "at risk" in that any deterioration in their situation could make it impossible for them to maintain their current living standards in retirement.

In short, two issues matter tremendously to any characterization of the problem: the heterogeneity of saving behavior across households and uncertainty concerning the right measures of wealth to use and the future course of the boomers. The results examined here refer only to a sample of married couples where the husband works full time. Other married couples and singles are likely to be faring worse.

TABLE 3. ADEQUACY GAPS, BY AGE, 1992
Inadequate Savers, Using Narrow Wealth Measure

Age	GAP IN DOLLARS			GAP/ANNUAL EARNINGS		
	25%	50%	75%	25%	50%	75%
25–29	1,710	2,960	4,850	0.068	0.117	0.239
30–34	1,900	3,400	5,920	0.071	0.100	0.176
35–39	8,020	13,180	23,390	0.227	0.367	0.491
40–44	14,260	26,940	51,220	0.425	0.734	1.100
45–49	19,300	33,500	56,420	0.404	0.824	1.396
50–54	24,770	65,100	82,450	0.888	1.252	1.816
55–59	32,510	51,800	98,670	1.049	1.496	1.900
60–64	29,140	75,470	153,420	1.022	2.166	2.914
All Households	5,920	22,480	51,880	0.199	0.519	1.252
Baby Boomer Households	4,450	13,480	29,099	0.150	0.378	0.732

Sample: Married couples where husband is aged 25–64 and works at least 20 hours per week for households saving inadequately.

Definitions: *Narrow Wealth* = Financial assets (checking and money market accounts, CDs and savings accounts, IRAs and Keoghs, mutual funds, stocks and bonds, trusts, cash value of life insurance and defined contribution pension account balance) plus nonfinancial assets (business, other real estate, and other assets) minus total debt (lines of credit, credit card debt, other real estate debt, and other debt).
Broad Wealth = Narrow Wealth plus 100 percent of housing equity.
No College = Head's highest educational attainment less than or equal to 15 years of schooling.
College = Head's highest educational attainment greater than 15 years of schooling.
Pension = Head covered by a defined benefit or defined contribution pension (not including 401[k]s).
Gap = Target wealth level–actual wealth level.

Source: Author's calculations based on the 1992 Survey of Consumer Finances.

THE UNCERTAIN FUTURE

The uncertainty of forecasts about the adequacy of saving should be a predominant concern. There are several reasons why it is difficult to make projections with confidence. First, as a society, we have as yet little understanding of the dynamics of retirement. Only one or two generations have had lengthy retirements, and crucial aspects of retirement living standards—pensions, health care, asset markets, Social Security, life span, family living arrangements, retirement age—have changed rapidly over time. Two well-known recent phenomena—the anemic saving rate and the soaring stock market—send diametrically opposing messages about the status of retirement preparation in the United States.

Relatively long-term predictions are inherently fraught with error. Consider the difficulty of predicting, in 1982, the fate of people who were to retire fifteen years later. In 1982, the country had just finished a decade marked by high personal saving, two major oil shocks, several recessions, skyrocketing house prices fueled by inflation, high tax rates and interest rates, and a disastrous performance by stocks. Since then all of those economic parameters have reversed themselves: personal saving has plummeted, energy prices have similarly fallen sharply, house prices have stagnated as inflation, tax rates, and interest rates have fallen, and the stock market has increased many times over. The economy has suffered only one recession in the past fifteen years. In addition, health care costs rose dramatically, there was a major Social Security reform, and numerous tax changes influenced the treatment of retirement funds.

Of course, every generation has faced uncertainty with regard to its future. It is not obvious that the boomers' prospects are riskier than those faced by previous generations at similar stages in the life cycle or those to be faced by "generation X." It is, however, worth focusing on some of the major sources of uncertainty.

Retirement patterns. The "adequacy of saving" can be flipped around to become nothing more than an "age of retirement" issue. In the extreme, if people never retire, they do not need any retirement saving. More generally, working longer reduces the length of retirement and therefore, even if the extra earnings are not saved, raises the adequacy of retirement wealth preparations.

Average age at retirement, which fell throughout the twentieth century for men, may start rising regardless of the adequacy of saving. Many of today's jobs do not depend on "brawn" and can thus be done by older people. The normal Social Security retirement age will rise to sixty-six by 2008 and sixty-seven by 2025 even in the absence of further changes to the program.

There is also increasing evidence that people would prefer to reduce their hours worked gradually rather than abruptly. There are some obvious institutional problems here, but Christopher Ruhm finds evidence that only 36 percent of household heads retire immediately at the end of their career jobs and nearly half remain in the labor force for at least five additional years.[14] About 47 percent of workers eligible for a pension continue to work after leaving their career job. If people choose to continue to work even after "retirement," this will bolster the resources available to support living standards in retirement.

Life expectancy. A related uncertainty involves life expectancy. Expectations about remaining years of life for sixty-five-year-olds have risen significantly in the past two decades and are projected to grow further. From a retirement saving perspective, living longer means having to stretch resources over a longer period.

Home equity. Uncertainty regarding home equity is twofold. First, how will housing prices evolve? Both easing demographic pressures and the long-term reduction in tax rates in the 1980s may diminish the value of housing.[15] The second issue is the extent to which housing should be conceived as part of the wealth used to support living standards.[16] Excluding housing wealth is sometimes defended on the grounds that people do not like to move when they are old, but this is somewhat misleading. Households can extract equity without moving, via reverse mortgages.

Other reasons to include or exclude housing equity in wealth depend on the underlying purpose. For example, as a public policy concern, a retired couple that lives in a $300,000 house and has little cash or financial assets but refuses to dip into housing equity may not be considered to have very pressing needs.

In the 1970s, housing was a highly profitable investment, so people would naturally have put more money into housing rather than less. In the 1980s and 1990s, as housing has become a less attractive asset to hold for demographic and tax reasons, people may be more willing to extract equity from their houses. The elderly in the 1970s had lived through World War I, the Great Depression, and World War II and so may have had different attitudes toward the importance of maintaining a precautionary stock of wealth. Baby boomers, in contrast, have always been willing to countenance financing through housing equity. In fact, boomers have been among the major loan recipients in the booms in home equity lending in the 1980s and 1990s.

The issue becomes whether the boomers, when they are elderly, will behave more like they did when they were young or more like today's elderly. Recent policy changes have eliminated the taxation of the first $500,000 of capital gains on a house. This may induce more retired people to sell their homes in the future and allow them to consume their housing wealth. The fact that the current generation of the elderly have not already done so may just indicate that they are doing quite well; that is, they have adequate saving from other sources.

The evolution of asset markets. Equity values cannot continue to grow at the rapid rates experienced in 1996 and 1997. And even if the boomers accumulate what seem to be sufficient retirement funds under standard rate-of-return assumptions, they will—loosely speaking—all want to cash in those funds at roughly the same time. That might mean massive sell-offs of securities that could depress asset values and reduce stock market returns. Conceivably, asset prices could fall sharply, but since equity markets are forward-looking, it may be more likely that they would remain stagnant for a long period, as in the 1970s.[17]

Inheritances. The current generation of elderly has amassed tremendous wealth. Although a substantial portion is in the form of annuities—Social Security and pensions—that cannot be bequeathed, a large amount of resources will be passed on to the baby-boom generation. This will be a boon for selected families. It will not in and of itself "solve" the saving problem for the boomer generation, but it certainly will not hurt. In terms of dollar value, most inheritances involve extremely wealthy decedents giving to very wealthy recipients. Relative to retirement income needs, the typical boomer household will likely gain little if anything from inheritances, perhaps on the order of $10,000–$30,000.

THE ROLE OF PRIVATE PENSIONS

The retirement status of future generations of Americans will depend to a large extent on the evolution of the private pension system. Pension wealth is a sizable component of total household resources. In 1993, 47 percent of civilian nonagricultural workers participated in pension plans.[18] The present value of future income flows from private pensions accounted for 20 percent of the wealth of households aged sixty-five to sixty-nine.[19]

The private pension system grew rapidly in the twenty-five years after World War II. In 1940, 15 percent of private sector workers were covered by pensions. By 1970, the figure had risen to 45 percent.[20] Since then, however, pension coverage has either remained constant, fallen a bit, or increased slightly depending on the definition of coverage, the data source, the sample, and the end years chosen.[21]

Stagnating pension coverage, however, masks a major shift in the composition of private pensions toward defined contribution plans and away from defined benefit plans. In defined benefit plans, annuity benefits are stipulated as a percentage of years worked, average or maximum salaries, and other considerations. In defined contribution plans, contributions are stipulated. The account balances build up over time, and whatever is in the account at the time of retirement is available for retirement consumption. From 1975 to 1992, the share of defined contribution plans rose from 29 percent to 60 percent of all active pension participants, and from 35 percent to 72 percent of all contributions.

Since the early 1980s, almost all of the rise in defined contribution plans has taken the form of 401(k) plans. For example, total contributions to defined contribution plans rose by $49 billion from 1984 to 1992, of which $48 billion represented increased contributions to 401(k)s. A recent, related trend is the evident growth in hybrid retirement plans, which combine features of defined benefit and defined contribution plans. While less is known about these plans, they may be seen as an attempt generally to balance the costs and benefits of defined contribution and defined benefit plans.

Two main hypotheses have been examined concerning the secular rise of defined contribution plans: increased regulation of defined benefit plans following the passage of the Employee Retirement Income Security Act (ERISA) in 1974; and the changing composition of the workforce. These hypotheses, of course, need not be mutually exclusive.[22] The appeal of plans with 401(k) characteristics undoubtedly springs in part from the fact that employees may make tax-deductible contributions. Further, Richard Ippolito also shows that the matching features of 401(k) plans are likely to be relatively more attractive to more productive workers, so that 401(k)s can help firms attract and retain the right type of people.[23]

The implications for retirement saving of the shift to defined contribution plans can be divided into two parts: first, the effects of pensions on saving behavior generally; second, differences in the effects of defined benefit and defined contribution plans on saving. The interaction between pensions and other saving can be complex. In the simplest life cycle models, workers save only for retirement. Changing the form of workers' compensation from current wages to future pension benefits has no effect on consumption, and no effect on overall (pension plus nonpension) wealth or saving. Increases in pension wealth are offset completely by reductions in other wealth. A number of issues in the real world, however, complicate this analysis. First, unlike conventional, taxable assets, pensions are typically illiquid, tax-deferred annuities. Second, people save for reasons other than retirement. Third, alternative models of saving have been proposed, in which households make saving decisions based on psychological or behavioral models[24] or people lack the basics of economic literacy.[25] Given all of the theoretical variants, the range of possible outcomes is wide: pensions can have any effect from reducing nonpension wealth by more than pension wealth adds to raising nonpension wealth.

Taken at face value, the literature to date suggests with only a few exceptions that pensions raise household wealth overall and cause almost no reduction in households' nonpension wealth. However, my previous research notes that several features of earlier empirical work impose a series of systematic statistical biases, implying that such previous studies overstate the effect of pensions on other wealth.[26] Correcting for none of the biases, the author estimated that a dollar increase in pension wealth reduces other wealth by 10 percent or less. Correcting for five (of the eight) biases yielded the finding that a dollar increase in pension wealth reduces other wealth by forty to eighty cents, depending on the specification of the regression equation. Some analyses also suggest considerable heterogeneity in how households respond to pension wealth.[27] Thus, there remains substantial uncertainty concerning the impact of traditional pensions on households' wealth accumulation.

Like the literature on traditional pensions, studies examining the impact of 401(k)s have produced disparate results.[28] Estimates from this literature also suffer from a series of econometric biases, most of which tend to overstate the impact of 401(k) plans on saving but at least one of which may lead to an understatement of the effects.

There are several significant differences in the operation of defined benefit and defined contribution plans that could influence the adequacy of retirement saving.[29] In defined contribution plans, employees typically have much more control over not only whether to participate but also how much to contribute, where to invest, and how and when to withdraw funds. All of these options raise concerns about the adequacy of retirement saving. Participation rates among workers eligible for 401(k) plans hover around 70 percent. This is much higher than, say, IRA participation rates but of course lower than the almost 100 percent participation rates that prevail for defined benefit plans. There is also concern that workers in defined contribution plans are not contributing enough and are investing too conservatively (and hence earning too low a return).

In addition, defined contribution plans are more liquid than defined benefit plans. Workers can make use of the money in 401(k)s under circumstances of personal hardship and other considerations and can access all of the funds, subject to a penalty, should they leave the firm. Evidence suggests that most people with the option of taking an early, lump-sum distribution choose to take the funds in cash. But these are mainly younger workers who have built up only small amounts in their accounts. Most of the funds that are eligible for lump-sum distribution are in fact rolled over into other retirement accounts.[30] Although defined benefit plans can be cashed in upon exiting the firm in certain circumstances (mainly when the present value of future benefits is low), the benefits offered are in general much less liquid than benefits in defined contribution plans.

The increased liquidity of defined contribution plans may make them more attractive relative to defined benefit plans. This would attract contributions to defined contribution plans, but the contributions would be more likely to be removed before retirement. The net effect on saving seems to be uncertain.

Defined benefit and defined contribution plans create different kinds of risks. In the former, benefits are linked to the highest few years of earnings, whereas in the latter, benefits are essentially a weighted average of earnings over many years. Rules regarding (nominal) benefits in a defined benefit plan are set by the employer, typically many years in advance. Benefits in a defined contribution plan depend on the rate of return earned on pension assets, based on choices made by the participant. Both types of benefits are subject to inflation risk. Andrew Samwick and Jonathan Skinner conclude that defined contribution plans present less overall risk than defined benefit plans do.[31] If so, then defined contribution plans may well engender less precautionary saving and so have a larger negative impact on other saving.

Accruing balances and account statements are probably simpler to understand in defined contribution plans than in defined benefit plans. Whether increased visibility of earnings raises or reduces households' other saving depends in part on whether the household accrues more or less than its members would otherwise have expected in its plan. An added effect is that by providing periodic updates on balances, defined contribution plans may do a better job of constantly reminding households of the need to save for retirement. Of course, there is no reason why such updates could not also be provided in a defined benefit plan.

Although it is in general quite difficult to pin down the implications of these differences for how pensions affect wealth, several points are worth emphasizing. First, the mechanisms through which pensions affect wealth can be exceedingly complex. Second, there is no reason to expect defined benefit and defined contribution plans to have identical impacts on the level or struc-ture of household wealth, even if the benefit levels are held constant. The shift toward defined contribution plans creates opportunities as well as risks. Secular shifts in preferences in the pension system may be altering the way pensions affect retirement wealth accumulation.

A final consideration concerns substitution between 401(k) plans and other pension plans at the firm level. Many 401(k)s appear to have been converted directly from previously existing pension or thrift plans. Because 401(k)s were not popular until the IRS issued clarifying regulations in 1981, most plans created before 1982 are thought to have been conver-sions. In 1985, these plans accounted for 39 percent of the 401(k) plans, 85 percent of balances, 65 percent of participants with nonzero balances, and two-thirds of contributions.[32] Even as recently as 1991, the majority of assets, 42 percent of participants, and 47 percent of contributions were in plans created before 1982. This suggests the possibility that much of 401(k) wealth in 1991 would have existed in other pensions even in the absence of 401(k) plans.

For 401(k)s created after 1985, other mechanisms may be at work. Leslie Papke uses panel data from 1985 to 1992 and estimates that for every ten plan sponsors that started out in 1985 with no 401(k) or other defined contribution plan and then added a 401(k) over time, the number of defined benefit plans offered by those sponsors fell by at least three more than it otherwise would have over this period.[33] Plan-level estimates imply that if a 401(k) plan is added by a sponsor, the probability that a defined benefit plan is terminated approximately doubles or increases from about 18 percent to about 36 per-cent. These results imply that a sizable minority of 401(k) plans are replacing defined benefit plans.[34]

Another channel of substitution can occur on the margin—firms may cut back on existing plans in other ways such as restricting or reducing benefit increases. Casual observation suggests that this form of substitution could be quite important, but there is as yet no hard evidence.[35] It is also possible (but difficult to verify) that some 401(k) plans are being established at firms that would have created another plan had 401(k)s not existed. Taken together, these trends and possibilities suggest that a substantial portion of 401(k)s may be replacing other pensions.

To the extent that 401(k)s displace other plans completely or at the mar-gin, an additional issue comes into play. All workers covered by traditional plans participate, but workers may well opt out of a 401(k). Thus, the saving impact of the 401(k) may be less than that of the traditional plan it displaces.[36] If so, a 401(k) plan that substituted for a terminated defined benefit plan could actually reduce private saving on average.

CONCLUSION

Retirement prospects for the baby boomers are marked by heterogeneity and uncertainty. The heterogeneity stems from the fact that some households save much more than others. While some part of this difference is likely the result of government policies, much of it must ultimately be attributed to households' observable characteristics—number of children, age, income, and others—and, just as important, households' unobserved characteristics—their patience, risk aversion, valuation of the future. There are several sources of uncertainty, including what policymakers and boomers themselves will accept as a reasonable goal for retirement living standards and the functioning of the economy as a whole. This diagnosis of the problem indicates that the adequacy and distribution of retirement saving will continue to be an important topic in policy debates in the future.

8

THE IMPACT OF SOCIAL SECURITY REFORM ON WOMEN

W ith reform of Social Security under serious consideration in Washington, one important criterion for scrutinizing proposals for change is the particular effect they would have on women. On average, women earn less and live longer than men. Because of those two characteristics, elderly women are more likely than elderly men to become impoverished and face financial strains during their retirement. But Social Security helps to offset those vulnerabilities in ways that neither private pension plans nor personal savings accounts offer:

◆ Benefits continue to be paid throughout the lifetime of retirees and are indexed to increase as prices rise. In contrast, pensions and personal savings accounts are rarely indexed to inflation, and retirees may outlive those assets.

◆ Social Security's benefits are progressive—they replace a larger share of the past earnings of low-income retirees than of those who earned more.

Reprinted from a Century Foundation issue brief.

In contrast, low-income workers are much less likely to have any pension or nest egg to draw on.

♦ Social Security provides a widow's benefit equal to 100 percent of the payment a deceased spouse was receiving.

♦ For women who spend their lives or curtail their careers by taking care of their children, Social Security provides a retirement benefit equal to 50 percent of their spouse's benefit (which is based on his earnings history). And homemakers who become divorced after at least ten years of marriage are entitled to a benefit tied to the earnings of the former spouse.

These unique features of Social Security are largely responsible for the program's success in limiting poverty among elderly women. *Without Social Security, more than half of older American women would be living in poverty.* Only 13.6 percent of women aged sixty-five and over were impoverished in 1995—still, that's more than double the 6.2 percent poverty rate among elderly men (see Figure 1).

FIGURE 1
POVERTY STATUS OF PERSONS 65 YEARS AND OLDER BY SEX, 1995

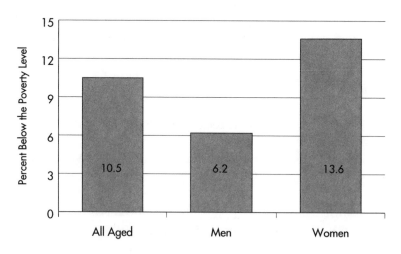

Source: U.S. House of Representatives, Committee on Ways and Means, *1998 Green Book,* May 19, 1998, Table A-6.

Some proposals for reforming Social Security would weaken some of the features of the current system that particularly help women. For example:

♦ Converting the program to one based primarily on private investment accounts could erode protections for women by 1) reducing or eliminating today's guaranteed lifetime, inflation-adjusted benefit; 2) making payouts more dependent on time spent in the workforce and earnings levels, which would determine how much each worker contributes to his or her account; and 3) leaving those with low incomes dependent on the performance of the investments in their accounts for a secure retirement.

♦ Reducing the cost-of-living adjustment would, over time, erode the value of benefits relative to prices. Again, women would be most vulnerable.

♦ Extending the number of working years used to calculate retirement benefits from thirty-five now to thirty-eight in the future would, in essence, add more nonearning years that would be factored into the computation for women who left the workforce for extended periods. The consequence is that working women would experience deeper benefit reductions than men.

In order to understand how Social Security reform could pose more risks for women, it is important to identify the differences between the financial circumstances of men and women and Social Security's role in reducing poverty among elderly women.

WOMEN VERSUS MEN

♦ Women tend to spend fewer years in the workforce than men, since they are much more likely to interrupt their careers to care for young children or elderly parents. For the same reasons, they are more likely to work at part-time rather than full-time jobs. And even when they work full time, women are likely to be paid less than men. As a result, median earnings for women are far below those for men (see Figure 2, page 136).

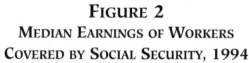

FIGURE 2
MEDIAN EARNINGS OF WORKERS
COVERED BY SOCIAL SECURITY, 1994

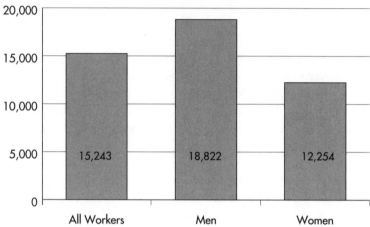

*Source:*From the Social Security Administration website, online version of Social Security Bulletin, *Annual Statistical Supplement,* 1997, Table 4.B6, see: http://www.ssa.gov/statistics/supp97/pdf/t4b6.pdf (as of September 8, 1998.)

♦ More than 70 percent of Americans aged eighty-five and over are women. Among those aged seventy-five and over, most women are widowed and live alone while most men are married and live with their wives. This is because, in addition to differences in life expectancies (see Table 1, page 137), women are more likely to marry older men than vice versa.

♦ Only 13 percent of elderly women receive a private pension, compared with 33 percent of older men. Among current workers, only 22 percent of all women are covered by a pension, compared to 49 percent of men. In 1994, the median annual private pension or annuity income for women 65 or older was about $2,682, compared to $5,731 for men.

♦ Women save, on average, about half as much as men.

WOMEN, SOCIAL SECURITY, AND POVERTY

♦ In 1995, the average annual Social Security benefit for retired women age sixty-five and over was $6,971—well below the poverty line of about $7,500. For men, the annual benefit was $9,376.

TABLE 1
LIFE EXPECTANCY AT AGE 65, FOR INDIVIDUALS REACHING 65 IN SELECTED YEARS, 1997–2025

	LIFE EXPECTANCY (IN YEARS)	
YEAR	MALE	FEMALE
1997	15.6	19.2
2005	16.0	19.5
2015	16.4	19.8
2025	16.8	20.2

Source: U.S. House of Representatives, Committee on Ways and Means, 1998 Green Book, May 19, 1998, Table 1–53.

♦ One-fourth of women age sixty-five and over rely on Social Security for at least 90 percent their income (twice the rate as for men). Social Security comprises 100 percent of the income for more than 20 percent of elderly women living alone.

♦ The female poverty rate increases with age. By age eighty-five, 19 percent of all women live in poverty.

♦ In 1993, women age sixty-five and over had a median net worth of $9,560, compared to $12,927 for men and $44,410 for married couples.

♦ The majority of women rely on Social Security's spousal or widows benefits. In 1996, 63 percent of women beneficiaries sixty-two and older were receiving wives or widows benefits. Almost 40 percent couldn't qualify for worker benefits and were only eligible as wife/widow recipients. Social Security actuaries predict that even among those retiring in 2015, only about 20 percent of widows will have earned benefits greater than those of their husbands.

♦ On average, separated and divorced older women are substantially poorer than widows, and all are poorer than wives. Among those aged sixty-five and over, 19 percent of widowed women and 24 percent of other unmarried women lived below the poverty line in 1995. (Only 9 percent of widowers aged sixty-five and over lived in poverty.) Eighty percent of widows in poverty become poor only after their husbands die.

Because Social Security is projected to face a shortfall between promised benefits and revenues in the year 2032, almost all proposals for reforming it involve some combination of benefit reductions, tax increases, or additional federal borrowing. The question with each plan is whether those burdens are fairly shared, and whether the most vulnerable Americans would continue to be able to count on the system to help them stay out of poverty. Clearly, a great deal is at stake, particularly for American women.

9

THE FULL RETURNS FROM SOCIAL SECURITY

DEAN BAKER

EXECUTIVE SUMMARY

A major concern in the current debate on restructuring the Social Security system has been the rate of return that the program will provide to the current generation of young workers and the generations that will follow. Most analysis of the rate of return has focused on the core Social Security program, often ignoring the benefits provided by the survivors and disability insurance portions of the program. In addition, prior calculations of rates of return have assessed the value of benefits at their actuarial value. This ignores the fact that Social Security benefits are provided as insurance, which could be purchased in the market only at a substantial premium above their actuarial value. For example, the benefit for retired workers and their spouses is provided as a real valued annuity (an annual payment that is adjusted upward as prices rise).

This report, which was a joint project of The Century Foundation and the Economic Policy Institute, originally appeared as a white paper published by The Century Foundation Press.

Recent research indicates that individuals would have to pay a premium of 15 to 20 percent above the actuarial value to purchase a standard annuity from an insurance company. A real valued annuity, which provides protection against inflation, would presumably require a still higher premium, although real valued annuities are still not widely available in private markets, so the actual cost cannot yet be determined. By ignoring the insurance aspect of Social Security, other calculations have underestimated the returns provided by the program.

The calculations in this study evaluate rates of return for different types of workers in the age cohort born in 1975 by adding together all aspects of the program and assessing benefits at their insurance value.

This age cohort was selected because the last round of Social Security tax increases was fully phased in before it entered the labor market, and it will therefore bear the full brunt of all the currently mandated changes in the Social Security program. In addition, the higher normal retirement age will also be fully phased in before these workers are old enough to retire.

The calculations show that:

♦   Claims for high rates of return from privatizing Social Security—namely, that they would match the stock market performance over the past seventy-five years, or 7.0 percent after inflation—are vastly overstated. First, forecasts by the Social Security Trustees of slower economic growth imply that future stock market returns will be around 3.5 percent over the next seventy-five years. Second, administering private accounts would eat up between 1.0 and 2.0 percent of the return. Third, most people would probably invest in a mixture of stocks and low-yielding bonds. Fourth, converting to privatized accounts would require large transition taxes amounting to about 1.6 percent. When all these factors are taken into account, the rates of return on a privatized system would fall below 2.0 percent, and perhaps even below 1.0 percent.

♦   Weighing the value of the four insurance features of the Social Security program makes the current system a much better financial deal than any private substitute could hope to offer. These features—the inflation-adjusted retirement annuity, survivors insurance, disability insurance, and protection against retiring in poverty as a result of a lifetime of low earnings—are either unavailable in a private market or very expensive. In most cases, taking these benefits into account raises Social Security's rate of return enough so that it is more than a full percentage point higher than what a privatized plan could offer. In most circumstances, the real rate of return under the current system is 3.0 percent or higher.

◆ Under the current system, medium- and low-income Americans will receive the highest rates of return. A two-earner couple with medium/low earnings histories (probably the most common situation) will receive a real rate of return (in excess of inflation) of 3.2 percent. A two-earner couple where both workers have low earnings histories will receive a return of 3.5 percent. A one-earner couple with a low earnings history will receive a real return of 5.0 percent on their Social Security taxes.

◆ Even if taxes are raised immediately to bring the system into long-term balance, most workers would still receive a real rate of return close to 3.0 percent, and relatively few would be pushed below the 2.0 percent threshold.

In sum, the calculations in this paper suggest that Social Security provides returns that are quite competitive with private sector investment instruments when the full value of the program—including the value of all the benefits associated with the program as well as the fact that these benefits are provided as insurance—is taken into account. Recognizing that the benefits are provided as insurance requires assigning a premium to Social Security benefits that is comparable to what would be charged to get the same insurance in private markets.

INTRODUCTION

Much of the current debate over the future of the Social Security system has been driven by the concern that Social Security would provide a poor rate of return to the present generation of young workers and future generations of workers. Although the benefits received by the first beneficiaries of Social Security were very large relative to the taxes they paid into the system, the return has dwindled substantially through time, as tax rates have increased. By some calculations, single high-income young workers can actually expect to receive less back in benefits than the taxes that they paid into the system. Many of the proposals for the privatization of Social Security are motivated by the desire to raise the return to such workers.

However, comparing the returns to Social Security, as they are usually calculated,[1] to returns in the private financial markets presents an incomplete picture. The Social Security system provides more than just income to retired workers. It also provides survivors insurance to the spouses and children of deceased workers. It provides disability insurance to workers who become unable to work. And it provides retirement income in the form of a real valued annuity, a product that is just now becoming available in the private market. To compare fairly the returns on Social Security taxes with the returns on money invested in private financial markets, it is necessary to incorporate all the benefits provided by the Social Security program. Furthermore, to calculate accurately the return on Social Security taxes, these benefits should be calculated based on their value as *insurance*, not just on the expected value of the benefits themselves. The financial sector charges substantial fees on the insurance policies it offers. A full assessment of the value of the Social Security program would include the fees that workers would otherwise have to pay to acquire comparable insurance in the private sector.

This study calculates the returns workers can expect to receive on their Social Security taxes when all the benefits are assessed at their market value. The inclusion of survivors and disability benefits significantly increases the rates of return, compared with calculations that include only the benefits for retired workers and their spouses. Assessing all benefits at their insurance values raises the rate of return further. These adjustments raise the rates of return for most types of workers to levels comparable to those available in private financial markets. This makes the program appear far more equitable to today's young workers and those yet to enter the labor force.

THE CONCEPT OF SOCIAL INSURANCE

Much of the current debate over Social Security has focused on the rate of return that the program provides on the taxes workers pay. Most calculations indicate that the return on Social Security taxes received by young workers, and those yet to enter the labor force, will be quite low, and in some instances even negative. It is often noted that private sector investment instruments, such as mutual funds, have been paying considerably higher rates of return. This basic point underlies much of the push to privatize all or part of the existing program. However, this sort of simple comparison of the returns on Social Security taxes and private sector investment instruments misrepresents the benefits provided by the Social Security program. The Social Security program provides a comprehensive system of insurance throughout the life of working adults. A fair comparison of Social Security with private sector alternatives must incorporate all aspects of this insurance and value each component at its market price.

The fact that the Social Security program provides several different forms of insurance, and not just retirement income, is very important. When insurance is purchased in the market, there is always a cost passed on to the consumer. The expected value of the insurance (the value of the claims multiplied by the probability of collecting on the policy) will always be less than the cost of the insurance policy. The reason is that the insurance company must cover its administrative expenses and earn a profit. Therefore, it must charge fees that are higher than what it anticipates its customers will collect in benefits.

If an economist were to analyze the payback on insurance policies just by comparing the money that an insurance company pays out on its policies with the money the customer paid in (discounting both payments for the time at which they are made), she would always find that the customer was getting back less than he or she paid in. However, it would be wrong to conclude that a person buying insurance was simply giving away money to the insurance company and getting nothing in return. In purchasing insurance, an individual is buying a form of protection for herself and her family. This protection has real value. Individuals can, and do, quite rationally determine that it is worth paying a premium to ensure that unfortunate events (car accidents, home fires, severe illness, etc.) do not have devastating financial consequences. A comparison of the payback from the Social Security program with private sector alternatives must treat the insurance value of the program in the same manner it would treat insurance provided by the private sector.

There are four distinct types of insurance that are provided by the Social Security program. The first is the retirement benefit, which is most frequently associated with the program. This benefit is provided as a real valued annuity to workers and their spouses based on their earnings history. A real valued annuity is an annual payment (e.g., $10,000 per year) that is adjusted upward as prices rise. The annuity provided by Social Security is adjusted each year for the rate of inflation as measured by the consumer price index. The fact that the benefit is a real valued annuity is very important. This means that retired workers and/or their spouses can expect to receive a benefit, which is adjusted for inflation, for as long as they live. Since the benefit is provided as an annuity, the retiree is assured that she will not outlive her savings. In the private sector, people pay a substantial premium to have their accumulated wealth turned into annuities. A recent study estimated that workers on average had to pay 15 to 20 percent of their savings to purchase an annuity in the private market.[2] This means that an accurate comparison of the Social Security retirement benefit with private sector investment instruments must factor in this savings to workers.[3]

It is important to note that the Social Security benefit is provided as a real valued annuity, not a simple annuity. The latter, which is the product most typically sold in private markets, provides a fixed sum of money every year, regardless of the inflation rate. For example, a simple annuity may provide a retiree with $10,000 every year for as long as she lives. If inflation is very low, this payout schedule may be roughly what the worker expects. However, if inflation were consistently high, or were to jump up at some point in the worker's retirement, she would eventually find herself in a situation where the purchasing power of the $10,000 annuity had eroded substantially. One of the most important features of the insurance provided by Social Security is that it protects against this possibility. Social Security benefits are indexed to the inflation rate. This means that the amount of money that an individual receives each year will move in step with inflation. This protects retirees against the possibility that the actual value of their benefits will be eroded by inflation. It is not easy to determine exactly how to price this insurance against inflation. Real valued annuities are still not generally available in the private market, although it is likely that financial institutions will begin to offer them in the near future.[4] However, at present, their relative scarcity makes it difficult to find a basis on which to determine the market price of a real valued annuity. Clearly, the protection against inflation that Social Security provides is of considerable value. For this reason, this study uses 20 percent, the high end of the estimated range of the cost of purchasing simple annuities, as the value of receiving Social Security retirement benefits in the form of real valued annuities.

It is often argued that the cost of annuities will fall dramatically if there is a partial privatization of Social Security, since the demand for annuities will increase enormously. This will reduce the problem of adverse selection, which is one of the factors that currently drives up the price of annuities.[5] While this is a possible outcome, and even a likely one, if the market for annuities is effectively regulated, there is no guarantee that privatization will lead to this result. There are many cases in which financial institutions succeed in charging very high fees even in relatively well developed markets; for example, the administrative costs for operating mutual funds. The estimates in this paper can be seen as pricing the annuity provided by Social Security based on the current annuity market. How this will change if Social Security is partially privatized is a matter for speculation at present.

In addition to providing the retirement benefits that are most often associated with it, the Social Security program provides a survivors benefit to the children or disabled spouses of workers who die prior to retirement. This is in effect a life insurance policy that covers the family of every worker who pays Social Security taxes. This policy would provide more than $15,000 a year in benefits to the family of an average-income worker with two children who dies at an early age. (This sum will also be adjusted for inflation each year to protect its purchasing power.) Most workers are probably not even aware that the program provides this benefit, since it doesn't receive much attention in public discussion of the program.

To assess the value of this benefit, the expected survivors benefit paid out by Social Security was multiplied by 1.18 to approximate the cost of purchasing this insurance in the private market. The 18 percent premium was obtained by calculating the amount that the life insurance industry spends on administrative costs and takes as profits as a share of the revenue it receives each year. This should give a reasonable approximation of the difference between actual insurance payments and the premiums paid by consumers.[6] This figure may understate the true value of the insurance provided. Many workers, if they had to buy insurance as individuals, would have to pay higher fees or be unable to buy it altogether because of their health status. As a universal program, Social Security is providing insurance to all workers covered under the program, regardless of their current health.

The third type of insurance provided by Social Security is disability insurance. This insurance provides benefits to workers and their families if they become unable to work because of injury or illness. The benefit schedule is comparable to that provided under the survivors insurance. An average-wage worker with two dependent children could expect to receive approximately $15,000 a year if she became disabled for some reason. Unlike many private life insurance policies, this payment is not capped. The worker will receive the benefit as long as she is disabled, if necessary until the point at which she reaches retirement age.

In addition, for this study, the expected value of disability benefits was multiplied by 1.18 in calculating the full value of the insurance provided by Social Security. This calculation also probably understates the true value of this insurance considerably. Disability insurance is not often purchased in the private market, primarily because there are large problems of adverse selection and fraud, which drive up the cost of these policies. The issue of adverse selection arises because those individuals who have particularly dangerous jobs (e.g., miners or construction workers) or bad family health histories might be especially likely to buy disability policies. Since these people would drive up the costs for insurers, insurers would have to charge premiums that assume they are getting an accident-prone population. The issue of fraud arises because it often is not easy to verify that someone is disabled to the point of being unable to work. (Death does not pose the same ambiguity.) Insurance companies would have to incur large expenses to prevent people from defrauding them and collecting on phony claims of disability. For these reasons, disability policies tend to be expensive and are not often purchased in private markets.

The last form of insurance provided by Social Security is the protection against retiring in poverty as a result of a lifetime of low earnings. The Social

Security payback structure is extremely progressive. A worker who had an average income of $12,000 a year during his working life would receive an annual retirement benefit equal to 60 percent of this amount, or $7,160 a year. This represents a high return on the taxes this worker has paid into the system. By contrast, the annual benefits going to a high-wage worker would be a much lower percentage of his average wage, giving him a far lower return on his taxes. For example, a worker with average earnings of $68,000 a year would receive $18,900 a year in benefits, less than 28 percent of his average wage.

The fact that low-wage workers get a very good deal under Social Security, while high-wage workers don't fare as well, provides protection against the possibility that a worker will have low earnings throughout his working life. Whether or not a person is able to earn a high wage throughout his life clearly depends on many factors, including persistence and talent. However, luck also plays a very large role in this equation. Technological change, chance economic events, or chronic illness can impose hardships on even the most talented and dedicated workers. The higher returns that Social Security provides to low-wage earners is a form of protection against having the bad luck to spend one's life as a low-wage worker. This type of insurance is not available at all in the private market, and it is not clear how it would be priced if it were.[7] This analysis does not assign any price to this form of insurance in assessing the benefits of the Social Security program. Nonetheless, it is important to note that the strongly progressive payback structure of the existing system provides a valuable type of insurance to the covered workforce. As a result of this insurance, workers can know that a downturn in their employment prospects will have considerably less serious consequences for their retirement income or at least for the portion provided by Social Security.

THE INSURANCE ASPECTS OF SOCIAL SECURITY UNDER PARTIAL PRIVATIZATION

The insurance aspects of Social Security have not figured prominently in the recent debate on restructuring the system. While some of the proposals for restructuring the core retirement program also propose changes to the survivors or disability program, most recommend leaving these programs largely intact. For this reason, the treatment of benefits other than the core retirement benefit has not received much attention. However, it is still appropriate to examine the prospects for the survivors or disability benefits under partial privatization, even if it may be the intention of the proponents of Social Security restructuring plans to leave these programs unchanged.

There are two reasons for believing that these programs may face pressure for change in future years, if the core Social Security program is largely replaced by a privatized system. The first reason is political. The current Social Security program enjoys enormous political support because it is a universal program that provides benefits to nearly every voter at some point. Because of this widespread support, it is difficult politically to propose cuts to any portion of the program, even if most beneficiaries may not be directly affected by the cuts. This situation would change if most people came to depend less, or not at all, on the retirement portion of the Social Security system. Even though survivors and disability insurance may provide protection to all workers, most likely, only those who actually receive benefits under the program will appreciate its true value. This may create a situation in which the survivors and disability portions of Social Security come to be viewed as welfare programs for the poor, rather than universal programs that benefit all workers. Programs for the poor have historically been easy targets for budget cutters. If the survivors and disability programs are separated from the core Social Security retirement program, their long-term political prospects would certainly become more questionable.

The second reason why partial privatization would make these programs more vulnerable is a simple economic one. They would be much less administratively efficient if separated from the core Social Security program. As the system works now, a common administrative apparatus can be used to administer all three programs. The result is that the administrative costs of the whole system are less than 0.9 percent of the benefits paid out each year. In 1997, the combined Social Security and Disability programs paid out $358.3 billion in benefits and had expenses of $3.21 billion.[8] Under the current system, a disproportionate amount of the expenses is associated with the disability program. The disability program paid $1.21 billion in administrative expenses, or 37.7 percent of the cost of the combined program, even though disability accounts for only 12.7 percent of the total benefits paid.

If a substantial portion of the core retirement program were stripped away, the amount of record keeping and processing for the remaining portions of the program would be virtually unchanged from what it is at present. This means that the remaining program would have to bear the exact same administrative expenses as the current Social Security program. The ratio of administrative expenses to benefits in a stripped-down system may exceed 2.0 or even 3.0 percent, depending on how much of the Social Security program is privatized. While this expense-to-benefit ratio is still low compared with that of private insurers, it would be substantially higher than what it is currently. This increase in the expense ratio could lead to pressure to cut back on those areas of the remaining program that are particularly costly to administer, such as the disability program.

In short, the current system of insurance that constitutes the Social Security program has a certain degree of political protection as a result of the popular support for the system as a whole. Each individual component is also cheaper to operate as a result of the fact that a single administrative apparatus can be used for all three parts of the program. If the retirement portion of the program is partially or completely removed, the political support for the remaining programs is likely to dwindle. In addition, the administrative costs would soar relative to the benefits paid out. Even if the current group of advocates of Social Security restructuring actually want to maintain the other portions of the program in their current form, the process set in place by restructuring may still lead to their dismantlement at some point in the future.

THE RATE OF RETURN ON SOCIAL SECURITY

Before considering the returns provided by the Social Security program, it is important to establish some framework for comparison. Proponents of privatization have often juxtaposed the returns to Social Security with the returns in the stock market, which have averaged 7.0 percent over the last seventy-five years. This figure is grossly inflated for four reasons. First, the returns in the market will be much lower over the next seventy-five years (approximately 3.5 percent), if the economic growth projections of the Social Security Trustees prove accurate.[9] Second, there are substantial administrative costs associated with private accounts, usually estimated at between 1.0 to 2.0 percent annually. Third, most people will not hold all their money in stock through their whole life, but rather in a mixture of stock and lower yielding bonds (the usual assumption is a fifty-fifty mix). Finally, the switch to a privatized system will require substantial transition taxes. The size of these taxes will depend on the time period for the transition and the extent of the privatization, but they could be as high as 1.6 percentage points. There is a zero rate of return on these transition taxes. When all these factors are properly accounted for, the rates of return on privatized plans are likely to fall below 2.0 percent, and possibly below 1.0 percent. This should be the backdrop in assessing the projected returns on Social Security discussed below.

The methodology used for calculating rates of return in this section is modeled on the methodology of two earlier studies.[10] These studies examined the rates of return of the Old-Age and Survivors Insurance portion and the Disability Insurance portion of the Social Security program, respectively. The main difference between the calculations here and the ones that appear in these studies is the assignment of an insurance value to benefits, as explained above. The earnings levels that have been selected for analysis correspond to the "low earnings," "average earnings," and "high earnings" scenarios modeled by the Social Security Administration.[11] The methodology is described in more detail in the appendix.

It is worth noting that the earnings histories assumed for the stylized individuals examined in this study are highly unrealistic. For example, they assume that a medium-wage earner will earn roughly the average wage in the economy every year throughout his or her working lifetime. Wages rise only in step with the average wage in the economy, not with a worker's growing experience. This stylized earnings pattern is in keeping with the analysis in studies by C. E. Steuerle and J. M. Bakija.[12] The same stylized earnings pattern was also assumed in the analysis of the various options considered by the President's Advisory Council in its 1997 report.[13] This pattern is clearly quite unrealistic, since most workers will start their careers with a relatively low wage. Typically, as workers go through their twenties and thirties and gain experience in the workforce, their wages will rise. Eventually, wages level off and may decline slightly as workers near retirement. The stylized earnings path assumed in this analysis is also unrealistic in assuming that people work a full year each year from age twenty-one until their retirement at age sixty-seven. Most people will spend at least some period of time out of the paid labor force. A worker with a history of rising earnings, or one who spends a limited period of time out of the labor force, would receive a higher rate of return from the Social Security program than is indicated in these calculations.

The calculations discussed below give rates of return for the 1975 birth cohort, the members of which would be twenty-three in 1998. The calculation for this birth cohort will incorporate the full impact of all previously legislated changes to the Social Security program. These workers will have paid the current tax rate throughout their working lifetimes. This birth cohort will also feel the full impact of all currently scheduled increases in the normal retirement age, since they will not be able to receive full benefits until age sixty-seven.

RETURNS FOR MARRIED COUPLES

Most workers will not be single throughout their working lives and most will also have children. For these workers, the benefits provided to spouses and children in the event of early death or disability will be important aspects of the program. Unfortunately, much of the discussion of rates of return has ignored these aspects of the program and focused excessively on the less typical case of single workers. Table 1 shows the benefits calculated for a one-earner couple.

Following the studies by Steuerle and Bakija, the calculations shown in this table assume that the spouse with earnings is the man. The benefits to spouses and children are broken up into three types. Type I benefits are retirement benefits received by a spouse in the event that the worker lives to normal retirement age. Type II benefits are the old-age benefits received by a spouse over age sixty-five where the worker died before age sixty-five. Type III benefits are the survivors benefits received by the spouse and children in the situation where a worker died before age sixty-five. (See the appendix for a more detailed description of these calculations.)

TABLE 1. ONE-EARNER COUPLES

	Low Earners	Medium Earners	High Earners
OASI taxes	116,894	243,530	389,644
DI taxes	12,525	26,093	41,748
Worker's benefit actuarial value	144,282	236,087	305,406
Worker's benefit insurance value	173,138	283,304	366,487
Family benefits Type I	93,182	152,473	205,366
Family benefits Type II	32,331	53,671	71,263
Family benefits Type III	7,772	12,568	16,540
Total family benefits actuarial value	133,285	218,712	293,169
Total family benefits insurance value	159,787	262,203	351,472
DI benefit actuarial value	30,591	50,409	73,006
DI benefit insurance value	36,097	59,483	86,147
Total taxes	129,419	269,623	431,392
Total benefits actuarial value	308,158	505,208	671,581
Total benefits insurance value	369,022	604,990	804,106
Rate of return—OASI actuarial value	4.1	3.3	2.8
Rate of return—OASI insurance value	4.7	4.2	3.4
Rate of return—OASDI actuarial value	4.4	3.6	3.0
Rate of return—OASDI insurance value	5.0	4.2	3.5

All numbers are in 1995 dollars. Taxes and benefits were calculated assuming a 2.0 percent real discount rate. See the appendix for a full explanation of the methodology.

The inclusion of the additional benefits available to married workers with children makes a very large difference in the rate of return. The rate of return on the benefit package for a one-earner couple with low earnings is 4.4 percent when using actuarial values and 5.0 percent when the benefits are assessed at their insurance value. Since Social Security is structured to benefit low-wage earners and one-earner couples disproportionately, a one-earner couple with low earnings can expect to see the highest payback on their taxes.

One-earner couples with medium and high incomes also fare relatively well under the existing payback structure. The rate of return for a medium-income one-earner couple is 3.6 percent using actuarial values for Social Security benefits. It is 4.2 percent when using insurance values. The return for a high-income couple is 3.0 percent using actuarial values and 3.5 percent using insurance values.

In the current debate on restructuring Social Security, there seems to be general agreement on reducing the bias toward one-earner couples in the current payback structure. For example, all the members of the President's Advisory Council supported the recommendation to reduce the spousal benefit from 50 percent of the worker's benefit to 30 percent. Insofar as the generous spousal benefit is simply a residue of traditional conceptions of the family, in which only the man worked outside the home, this change would seem quite appropriate. There is certainly no reason for the government to show a preference for this type of family over a two-earner family.

However, the enormous rise in women's labor force participation over the last three decades has already made the traditional one-earner family virtually extinct. There will be very few women in future years who will not have spent a significant period of time in the paid labor force. The exceptions might be less likely to be women who are filling a traditional role of mother and homemaker, but rather women who take the responsibility for being the primary caregiver to a chronically ill child, parent, or relative. In such situations, a generous spousal benefit can be seen as an additional form of insurance for families that must deal with such illnesses. Although it may still be appropriate to reduce this benefit in the manner advocated by the Advisory Council, it is worth noting that the spousal benefit may have a real rationale rather than just being an archaic relic of a different era.

Table 2 (see page 152) shows the returns calculated for two-earner couples. The combinations are the same as those analyzed in a study by C. E. Steuerle and J. M. Bakija.[14] In all three cases, the returns are considerably lower than for one-earner couples. The rate of return for a couple consisting of two low earners is 3.2 percent when using actuarial values and 3.5 percent when assessing the benefits using insurance values. For a couple where the man is a medium-income earner and the woman is a low-income earner, the rate of return is 2.5 percent when using actuarial values and 3.2 percent using insurance values. In the case where the man is a high-income earner and the woman is a medium-income earner, the return is 1.9 percent using actuarial values and 2.4 percent using insurance values.[15] It is worth noting that in all these cases, the calculated rates of return using insurance values are well above the 2.0 percent threshold. This means that in the vast majority of real world situations, the Social Security program as currently structured will provide workers with a positive rate of return when applying the standard of a 2.0 percent real discount rate.

TABLE 2. TWO-EARNER COUPLES

	Low/Low Earners	Medium/Low Earners	High/Medium Earners
OASI taxes	229,381	351,242	618,483
DI taxes	24,577	37,633	66,266
Worker's benefit actuarial value	260,582	334,584	482,264
Worker's benefit insurance value	312,698	401,501	578,717
Family benefits Type I	0	44,301	33,451
Family benefits Type II	0	17,601	17,272
Family benefits Type III	7,052	11,074	15,173
Total family benefits actuarial value	7,052	72,976	65,896
Total family benefits insurance value	8,321	87,350	78,772
DI benefit actuarial value	57,219	76,937	116,720
DI benefit insurance value	67,518	90,786	137,730
Total taxes	253,958	388,875	684,749
Total benefits actuarial value	324,853	484,497	664,880
Total benefits insurance value	388,538	579,636	795,218
Rate of return—OASI actuarial value	2.5	2.0	1.6
Rate of return—OASI insurance value	3.1	2.9	2.2
Rate of return—OASDI actuarial value	3.2	2.5	1.9
Rate of return—OASDI insurance value	3.5	3.2	2.4

All numbers are in 1995 dollars. Taxes and benefits were calculated assuming a 2.0 percent real discount rate. See the appendix for a full explanation of the methodology.

RETURNS FOR SINGLE MEN

Table 3 shows the returns from the Social Security program for single men of the 1975 birth cohort. The low-earner male is assumed to have an annual wage of $12,000 in 1995 (in 1995 dollars) and to have his wages rise in step with the projected growth in average wages throughout his working career. He is assumed to work every year from age twenty-one to age sixty-six and to retire upon turning age sixty-seven in 2042. His probabilities of paying taxes and collecting retirement and disability benefits are based on the Social Security Trustees' projections of death and disability probabilities. The medium-earner male and high-earner male are assumed to have wages of $25,000 and $40,000, respectively, in 1995 (in 1995 dollars). In both these cases, wages are assumed also to rise in step with the projected growth of the average wage. As with the low-wage earner, the probabilities of paying taxes and collecting benefits are based on the Social Security Trustees' projections of death and disability probabilities. The wage cutoffs picked for this analysis are the standard

TABLE 3. SINGLE MALE WORKERS

	Low Earners	Medium Earners	High Earners
	12,000	25,000	40,000
OASI taxes	112,487	234,348	374,953
DI taxes	12,052	25,108	40,173
Retirement benefit actuarial value	116,300	190,302	246,177
Retirement benefit insurance value	139,560	228,362	295,412
DI benefit actuarial value	24,387	40,187	58,199
DI benefit insurance value	28,777	47,421	68,675
Total taxes	124,539	259,456	415,126
Total benefits actuarial value	140,687	230,489	304,376
Total benefits insurance value	168,337	275,783	364,087
Rate of return—OASI actuarial value	2.1	1.4	0.8
Rate of return—OASI insurance value	2.6	1.9	1.3
Rate of return—OASDI actuarial value	2.5	1.8	1.0
Rate of return—OASDI insurance value	3.0	2.2	1.6

All numbers are in 1995 dollars. Taxes and benefits were calculated assuming a 2.0 percent real discount rate. See the appendix for a full explanation of the methodology.

cutoffs for analysis of Social Security. Benefit payments at these break points are given in each issue of the Social Security Trustees Report.[16] While designating $40,000 as the average wage for high-earning workers may appear low, relatively few workers actually have average wages over their lifetime that exceed this level. Approximately, 6.0 percent of men and just over 1.0 percent of women currently fall into this catergory.[17] (The cutoff is indexed to average wage growth, so the percentages should not be expected to increase over time.) It is also important to note that the vast majority of workers will be married at some point in their lives. This means that they will be entitled to survivor and disability benefits for their spouses and children, if they have any. Very few workers will actually be single their whole life, so the returns for single workers will actually be applicable to very few people.

Table 3 also gives the value of all cumulative tax and benefit payments using a 2.0 percent real discount rate. It is standard to use discount rates to evaluate payments made at different points in time, and 2.0 percent is the rate most often used in evaluating Social Security benefits and payouts.[18] A 2.0 percent discount rate means that an implicit real interest rate of 2.0 percent is assigned to all tax payments and benefits received. For example, a tax payment made ten years ago is treated as though it has been collecting 2.0 percent interest each year, so that it would be worth 1.22 times as much as a tax payment made today ($1.02^{10} = 1.22$).

The calculations that appear in the table indicate the extent to which the inclusion of disability benefits and pricing Social Security benefits at their insurance value affects the rate of return on Social Security taxes. For example, in the case of a low-income male, the actuarial value of the retirement benefit taken by itself would provide a return of just 2.1 percent on the taxes paid into the system. Including disability taxes and the disability benefit raises the rate of return to 2.5 percent. This result should not be surprising since the disability program is projected to run a very large deficit over this time horizon, which implies that its benefits will be considerably larger than the taxes collected for the program. Even though the disability tax is less than 10.0 percent of the combined OASDI tax (1.2 percentage points out of a 12.4 percentage point tax), over the next fifty years, the shortfall in the disability program is projected to be 21.9 percent of the total shortfall in the combined program (0.30 percentage points of covered payroll out of a total shortfall of 1.37 percentage points).[19] Since the disability program is usually lumped together with the rest of the Social Security program in discussions of the long-term revenue shortfall facing the system, to be consistent, the benefits from the disability program should be included in any assessment of the rates of return provided by the Social Security program.

Valuing the benefits of the Social Security program at their insurance value raises the rate of return in the case of low-earning males by an additional 0.5 percentage points to 3.0 percent. This places the rate of return for the system roughly even with the projected rate on long-term government bonds.

The returns in all categories are lower for medium- and high-earnings males in keeping with the progressive payback structure of Social Security. However, both adjustments—the inclusion of disability taxes and benefits, and pricing benefits at their insurance values—significantly improve the rate of return. For the medium-earner male, these adjustments push the rate of return slightly above the 2.0 percent threshold, which is often viewed as the breakeven point in assessments of Social Security paybacks.

The payback for high-income earners falls below this threshold even after making these adjustments. Their rate of return from the program using the actuarial value of benefits is just 1.0 even after incorporating the value of disability benefits. Using insurance values raises the rate of return to 1.6 percent, still considerably below the 2.0 percent threshold. While this rate of return may appear unattractive, it is in keeping with the logic of Social Security as a system of social insurance. High-income earners were fortunate enough to have enjoyed relative prosperity during their working lifetime. They are more likely to have a pension or to have accumulated some amount of savings during their working lifetimes than more moderate income workers, and therefore would be less dependent on their Social Security benefits. Even with a lower rate of return, they still are receiving higher absolute benefit levels guaranteeing them a significant base retirement income. A small amount shaved off the return received by high-wage workers can make a large difference in the returns of low- and moderate-wage workers.

Returns for Single Women

Table 4 (see page 156) shows the rates of return for low-, medium-, and high-earner women from the 1975 birth cohort. In each case, the return calculated is somewhat higher than for men with the same wage history. The reason that women are projected to receive higher returns is their longer life expectancy. Currently, at age sixty-five, women have a life expectancy that is 3.5 years longer than men. While this gap is projected to narrow somewhat in the next seventy-five years, this difference in life expectancy means that women would receive benefits over a longer period of time on average than men.

TABLE 4. SINGLE FEMALE WORKERS

	Low Earners	Medium Earners	High Earners
	12,000	25,000	40,000
OASI taxes	116,894	243,530	389,644
DI taxes	12,525	26,093	41,748
Retirement benefit actuarial value	144,282	236,087	305,406
Retirement benefit insurance value	173,138	283,304	366,487
DI benefit actuarial value	21,230	34,983	50,566
DI benefit insurance value	25,051	41,280	59,668
Total taxes	129,419	269,622	431,392
Total benefits actuarial value	165,512	271,070	355,972
Total benefits insurance value	198,190	324,584	426,155
Rate of return—OASI actuarial value	2.6	1.9	1.3
Rate of return—OASI insurance value	3.1	2.4	1.8
Rate of return—OASDI actuarial value	2.7	2.0	1.4
Rate of return—OASDI insurance value	3.3	2.6	2.0

All numbers are in 1995 dollars. Taxes and benefits were calculated assuming a 2.0 percent real discount rate. See the appendix for a full explanation of the methodology.

The table shows the same pattern as Table 3. Including the value of disability benefits raises the rate of return by approximately 0.2 percentage points for each category of wage earner. The inclusion of disability benefits adds less to the returns for women than men, because women face considerably lower probabilities of being disabled. Therefore, the returns on this aspect of the program are lower for women. Assessing benefits at their insurance value raises the return for women by an additional 0.6 percentage points. The rates of return shown for different categories of wage earners are again quite progressive. The projected rate of return for low-earning single women is 3.3 percent when assessing all the benefits of the program at their insurance value. This compares to a rate of return of 2.0 percent for high-earning single women. While the rate of return that high-earning women can expect from Social Security is considerably less than that for low-earning women, it is worth noting that it hits the 2.0 percent threshold viewed as a break-even point.

RETURNS IN A BALANCED PROGRAM

The returns calculated above all assume that the current tax and benefit schedule remains in effect through the working lives and retirement of the cohort born in 1975. Of course the projections from the Trustees indicate the program will not be balanced through this period. According to the 1998 Trustees Report, it would take an immediate tax increase of 2.19 percentage points to bring the program into balance over its seventy-five-year planning horizon. Given the current direction of the political debate on Social Security, it is virtually inconceivable that the Fund would be balanced by an immediate tax increase of anything close to this magnitude. Still, it is worth examining how the rates of return for the program would be affected if the funding gap were closed by a tax increase. Table 5 shows the returns for a two-earner couple assuming that the payroll tax was immediately increased by a sufficient amount

TABLE 5. TWO-EARNER COUPLE WITH TAX INCREASE

	Medium Earners
OASI taxes	402,229
DI taxes	43,096
Worker's benefit actuarial value	334,584
Worker's benefit insurance value	401,501
Family benefits Type I	44,301
Family benefits Type II	17,601
Family benefits Type III	11,074
Total family benefits actuarial value	72,976
Total family benefits insurance value	87,350
DI benefit actuarial value	76,937
DI benefit insurance value	90,786
Total taxes	445,325
Total benefits actuarial value	484,497
Total benefits insurance value	579,636
Rate of return—OASDI actuarial value	2.3
Rate of return—OASDI insurance value	2.8

All numbers are in 1995 dollars. Taxes and benefits were calculated assuming a 2.0 percent real discount rate. See the appendix for a full explanation of the methodology.

to balance the program.[20] The calculations assume that the man is a medium-income worker and the woman is a low-income worker.

The table shows that the rate of return using actuarial values falls from 2.5 percent in the no-tax-increase scenario to 2.3 percent. The return using insurance values fall from 3.2 percent to 2.8 percent. It is worth noting that this return is still competitive with returns available in the private sector and is considerably better than the 2.0 percent breakeven level. While a very large segment of the workforce will probably fit into the category of two-earner couples, with medium and low earnings histories, the reduction in the returns calculated in this scenario should give a reasonable approximation of the magnitude of the reductions that would apply to other types of workers. A 0.4 to 0.5 percentage point reduction in the rate of return would still leave the vast majority of workers receiving a rate of return that was in excess of 2.0 percent. Since the tax increase modeled here is larger and more immediate than any likely to be approved, the impact for most workers of any effort to solve the shortfall primarily on the tax side will almost certainly be considerably less than the calculation here indicates. It is also worth noting that returns should improve through time, after any particular change has been fully implemented. The reason that returns will improve is that life expectancies increase through time. Therefore, for any fixed schedule of benefits and taxes, later generations will always get a better return.

REALISTIC EARNINGS HISTORIES

As was noted earlier, the calculations above assume that workers work every year from age twenty-one until retirement, and that they always earn the same amount relative to the average wage. Neither of these assumptions is very realistic. Most workers will have spent at least some time out of the labor force during this period. For example, they may have been out of the labor force for one or several years because they were raising children, getting additional education, traveling, or simply because they were unemployed. The size of the Social Security benefit would not be affected by reducing the number of years worked over this period. It depends on the best thirty-five years of earnings between ages twenty-one and sixty. Up to four years of zero earnings in this stretch would not reduce the worker's benefit at all.[21]

Also, a more realistic earnings path would show relatively low earnings early in life, when a worker has little experience. Workers in their twenties tend to change jobs frequently and be near the bottom of the wage ladder. In their late thirties or forties they reach their peak earnings potential. Earnings may decline somewhat as workers get into their fifties, as they develop health problems or opt to work fewer hours.

If the calculations were adjusted to allow either some number of years outside the labor force or a more realistic earnings path, it would result in a higher rate of return. The calculations in Table 6 incorporate both these effects with a medium-income man. The calculations assume zero earnings for the years from age twenty-one to age twenty-four, and then a gradual rise in earnings from age twenty-five to age forty. (The exact schedule of earnings is described in the appendix.) For purposes of calculating Social Security benefits, average lifetime earnings in this situation are exactly the same as in the case of the medium-earnings male discussed earlier; the only difference is the number of years in which taxes are paid and the timing of the tax payments.

The returns in this situation are substantially higher than in the case discussed earlier. The rate of return in the case in which benefits are assessed at their actuarial value rises from 1.8 percent to 2.2 percent. In the case in which benefits are assessed at their insurance value, the rate of return rises from 2.2 percent to 3.1 percent. Since benefits have not changed, this increase is entirely the result of a lower tax burden.[22] The fact that four years of taxes have

TABLE 6. MALE WORKERS WITH WAGES RISING THROUGH TIME

	Medium Earners
OASI taxes	196,015
DI taxes	21002
Retirement benefit actuarial value	190,302
Retirement benefit insurance value	228,362
DI benefit actuarial value	40,187
DI benefit insurance value	47,421
Total taxes	217,017
Total benefits actuarial value	230,489
Total benefits insurance value	275,783
Rate of return—OASDI actuarial value	2.2
Rate of return—OASDI insurance value	3.1

All numbers are in 1995 dollars. Taxes and benefits were calculated assuming a 2.0 percent real discount rate. See the appendix for a full explanation of the methodology.

been eliminated and that the tax payments have been shifted to later in life, so the 2.0 percent implicit interest is not compounded over a long period of time, leads to a substantial decline in the cumulative value of taxes paid, from $269,622 in the earlier scenario to $217,017 after these adjustments are incorporated in the calculation.

The adjustments made in this section probably understate earnings for most workers in their early years, and therefore overstate returns, but they should provide a useful approximation of the impact on returns of having a pattern of earnings that more closely approximates actual wage patterns. Some studies have examined the rate of return to Social Security based on actual earnings patterns.[23] While this calculation simply substitutes one stylized earnings pattern for another, it does point out that the timing of earnings can make a large difference in the rate of return.

RETURNS IN A PRIVATIZED SYSTEM

Several studies have grossly exaggerated the returns that would be obtainable in a privatized system by seriously overestimating the returns that will be available in equity markets, and by underestimating or ignoring the administrative costs associated with private retirement accounts.[24] The exaggeration of returns in equity markets results from projecting into the future based on the market's past performance. An earlier study[25] showed that projections based on historic rates of return in the stock market are inconsistent with the economic growth projections in the Social Security Trustees Report. This study indicated that if the Trustees' growth projections prove accurate, given current price-to-earnings ratios, the real rate of return in the stock market would average less than 4.0 percent over the next seventy-five years. Since a typical portfolio is roughly split between stocks and bonds over a worker's life, the yield will be the average of the two. The Trustees currently project a real yield of 2.9 percent on bonds, which means that a mixed portfolio would have a yield of 3.45 percent. The President's Advisory Council estimated that the administrative costs in a system of private accounts would be approximately 1.0 percent annually. This fee would lower the net yield to 2.45 percent.

Even this return would be higher than that received by many workers in a privatized system. The estimated return on stocks is an average: Some workers will do considerably better than the average, while some will do considerably worse. Depending on timing or luck, it is entirely possible that many workers will receive extremely poor returns from investments in the stock market. This is particularly likely to be the case if a privatized system is loosely regulated so that workers are allowed to place money with funds that either charge very high administrative costs or engage in speculative investment strategies. Limits can be placed on the extent to which workers engage in excessive speculation with their accounts. Strict limits can also be placed on the fees that financial institutions are allowed to charge, but these measures would require a much greater level of government involvement in the management of the financial markets than is currently the case.

When the returns to private accounts are examined in a serious way, they do not stack up very well against the Social Security program. The Employee Benefit Research Institute (EBRI) constructed a model in which they ran simulations comparing the returns from a mixed system with private accounts and with the existing program, including the tax increases or benefit cuts that would be needed to maintain a balance in the system.[26] They also incorporated the cost of the transition to a privatized system. Unlike the calculations presented above, the EBRI model included realistic age-earnings profiles for workers. The simulations showed that most workers in the 1976 age cohort would have a higher payback ratio with the Social Security program than with the system of private accounts.[27]

This result is striking because the EBRI model included several assumptions that may be seen as biasing the result in favor of the system with private accounts. For example, it assumed that the premium associated with the purchase of a real valued annuity in the private system was only 5.0 percent. As was noted earlier, research indicates that the premium associated with purchasing a nominal valued annuity is 15 to 20 percent.[28] The additional cost of purchasing an annuity that provides protection against inflation should push the premium to at least the top end of this range. The EBRI analysis also assumed that the administrative expenses in private accounts would be only 0.5 percent. This is half the 1.0 percent assumed by the President's Advisory Council in its projections of the returns from private accounts. The EBRI study also assumed that equity returns would average more than 7.0 percent in real terms over the period of its analysis, instead of the 4.0 percent that would be consistent with the Social Security Trustees' projection for the growth rate of profits. Finally, it deliberately separated out the survivor and disability aspects of the program, modeling only the benefits received by retired workers and their spouses.

Even with these assumptions built into the analysis, only high-earning men from the 1976 age cohort received a better payback ratio in the system with private accounts than with the existing Social Security system. Assuming that these workers have some level of risk aversion would make them losers under the privatized system as well. If the model incorporated assumptions that were more accurate in the other areas noted and included the full insurance value of the Social Security program, the superiority of the existing system to a privatized system would appear even greater.

CONCLUSION

This study has calculated the rates of return that the Social Security program can be expected to provide for a variety of types of workers. Unlike most assessments of the rates of return provided by Social Security, this study included all the benefits provided by the program. It also assessed the value of these benefits as insurance, rather than using only their actuarial value.

It found that the inclusion of the disability portion of the program significantly increases the rate of return above what is calculated when only the retirement benefit is examined. This is especially the case with men, for whom the disability benefits increased the calculated rate of return by 0.4 to 0.7 percentage points. Assessing benefits at their insurance value rather than their actuarial value also significantly increased rates of return, in most cases adding 0.5 percentage points to the rate of return.

The calculations here indicate that when all the benefits of the Social Security program are included, and assessed at their insurance value, the rate of return provided by the program to most workers appears comparable to returns that might otherwise be available in the private sector. Only the highest-income workers will fail to receive a return in excess of the 2.0 percent discount rate that is often treated as a breakeven point. This would be the case even if the payroll tax was raised enough to bring the program into long-term actuarial balance. In short, when all aspects of the Social Security program are factored into the equation, these calculations suggest it provides a quite reasonable rate of return to the vast majority of workers.

APPENDIX

The calculations in this study are modeled on the ones that appear in the studies by C. E. Steuerle and J. M. Bakija.[29] The low-wage earner is assumed to earn $12,000 in 1995 in 1995 dollars. The medium-wage earner is assumed to earn $25,000 in 1995 in 1995 dollars. The high-wage earner is assumed to earn $40,000 in 1995 in 1995 dollars. In each case, wages are assumed to grow at the rate of real wage growth projected by the Social Security Trustees. The projected annual rate of real wage growth of 0.9 percent that appears in the 1998 Trustees Report was increased to 1.1 percent to reflect the changes that will be made in the consumer price index (CPI) in January of 1999. According to the Bureau of Labor Statistics, these changes should reduce the rate of inflation measured by the CPI by 0.2 percentage points annually. This means that an annual rate of wage growth that showed a 0.9 percent increase in real wages using the current CPI would show a 1.1 percent annual increase in real wages with the new CPI.

The mortality probabilities for the 1975 birth cohort were constructed by taking mortality probabilities for 1994 from the *1997 Annual Statistical Supplement to the Social Security Bulletin*[30] and adjusting them in accordance with the intermediate projection from the 1998 Social Security Trustees Report. This projection assumes that the age-adjusted death rate declines at the rate of 0.6 percent annually. The disability probabilities also rely on data from the Social Security Administration, which can be found in the studies by C. E. Steuerle and J. M. Bakija.[31] This data (which is for the 1965 birth cohort) was applied directly to the 1975 birth cohort, since the Trustees do not assume any clear trend in disability rates. It is assumed that, prior to retirement, a worker pays taxes in every year that he or she is alive and not disabled.

The retirement benefits were calculated directly by using the formula relating average annual earnings to benefits. The basic annual benefit in 1995 dollars was $11,171 for low-earnings workers, $18,279 for medium-earnings workers, and $23,646 for high-earnings workers. Following the studies by Steuerle and Bakija, the benefits for spouses and dependents were divided into three types. The first type is the benefit to a spouse over age sixty-seven when the worker lives past age sixty-five. This is either the 50 percent additional benefit paid to a spouse who has no earnings or the survivor benefit to a spouse who had a lower earnings history. For purposes of this calculation, the Type I benefit counts only the incremental benefit that a working spouse receives above the benefit she would have been entitled to based on her own earnings history (the woman is also assumed to be the spouse with the lower earnings history in this set of calculations).

Type II benefits are the benefits paid to a spouse after age sixty-seven in the situation where the worker died before age sixty-seven. This benefit will vary depending on the exact age at which the worker died. To simplify the calculation it was assumed that the worker has a 25 percent probability of dying before age sixty-seven. (The actual probability from the Social Security mortality projections is 24.6 percent for men. By assumption, the worker in a one-earner couple is male.) The average benefit used was based on the assumption that the worker died at age fifty-seven after thirty-six years of work. (According to Social Security mortality tables, 11.6 percent of male workers will have died by age fifty-seven.) This produced an annual Type II benefit of $10,013 for a low-earnings worker, $13,951 for a medium-earnings worker, and $22,070 for a high-earnings worker, all in 1995 dollars.

A similar simplification was used to calculate Type III benefits. These are the benefits that go to the surviving spouses, under age sixty-five, and to the children of workers who die before age sixty-five. The annual benefit was calculated under the assumption that the worker died after twenty years of work. This led to a benefit of $8,405 for low-wage earners, $13,951 for medium-wage earners, and $17,887 for high-wage earners. The probability that the worker dies was taken from the mortality tables. As in the studies by Steuerle and Bakija, it is assumed that all couples have two children, one born when the parents are twenty-five and one born when the parents are thirty. All calculations assume that the spouses are the same age.

The calculation of disability benefits relies directly on the calculations produced by Steuerle and Bakija. The present values that appear in their appendix tables were converted back into nominal values. These were adjusted upward by 17.4 percent to account for the wage growth between 1986 and 1995 and the inflation between 1992 and 1995. Since the high-wage earner in the Steuerle and Bakija calculations had an income of $62,700 in 1995, while the high-wage earner in these calculations had an income of $40,000, the benefits were adjusted downward. It was assumed that the disability benefits for a worker with an income of $40,000 were equal to the disability benefits of the medium-wage earner plus 75 percent of the difference between the benefits of the medium-wage earner and the high-wage earner.

The simplifications used to calculate survivors benefits and disability benefits in the case of high-income workers do not appear to have had any significant effect on the rates of return found in this study. While the numbers do differ somewhat from those that appear in the Steuerle and Bakija studies, they vary in both directions. Furthermore, these benefits are small compared to the size of the core retirement benefits, so it is unlikely that any inaccuracy in the procedure applied here would have changed the calculation of the rate of return by more than 0.1 percentage points.

IV

IS THE MARKET THE CURE?

10

PRIVATIZATION

HENRY J. AARON and ROBERT D. REISCHAUER

As the twentieth century comes to a close, private enterprises operating in a competitive market stand triumphant around the world. Free markets have proven themselves the most efficient way to produce and distribute almost all goods and services. In virtually all countries, state-run monopolies and nationalized industries have been marked by inefficiency, high costs, shoddy quality, and a lack of innovation. Against this backdrop, almost any call to convert to private management a government activity that the private sector has successfully performed should command a serious and sympathetic hearing. Since many elements of Social Security, such as pension management and insurance, resemble services that the private sector delivers successfully, the strengths and weaknesses of privatizing Social Security are well worth examining.

Other than a few hardcore "libertarians"—who believe that government should make no laws restricting individual behavior and should impose no taxes other than those necessary to provide for national defense and ensure public safety—almost no one favors complete privatization of pension saving and disability and survivor's insurance. Such a step would involve not only repealing Social Security but also abandoning the notion that government should require people

From Henry J. Aaron and Robert D. Reischauer, *Countdown to Reform: The Great Social Security Debate* (New York: The Century Foundation Press, 1998), Chapter 5.

to save for their retirement. Most people recognize that without some requirements or powerful incentives, many of us would save too little to prepare adequately for retirement and carry too little disability and life insurance. Accordingly, virtually all who favor privatization of Social Security—"privatizers" for short—acknowledge the need for measures to compel or encourage people to save for old age and protect against the risks that they or a principal earner will become disabled or die, leaving their families with inadequate means of support.

WHAT IS PRIVATIZATION?

Privatizing Social Security entails two fundamental steps: first, establishing a defined-contribution pension system with individually owned personal retirement accounts, and second, gradually scaling back or eliminating current Social Security retirement benefits. Contributions to personal retirement accounts, like the payroll tax payments made to support Social Security, would be mandatory. Instead of supporting defined-benefit pensions for current and future workers, these payments would be deposited in individually owned, defined-contribution accounts. The funds in these accounts would be managed by private financial institutions selected by either individuals or the government. The total balances in these accounts—the contributions plus the investment returns—would be available to support a pension for the account's owner.

The balance in each worker's account would depend on how much was contributed, the account's investment returns, and administrative costs. Workers who made identical contributions throughout their working years but invested in different assets or were charged different administrative fees could end up with very different balances when they retired. Similarly, workers who invested in the same assets managed by the same financial institution could end up with very different pensions if some retired when asset prices were high and others when asset prices were low.

Privatization plans differ in several key areas: how much of Social Security the personal accounts would replace; what rules would govern investments; how benefits would be distributed; and how the transition to the new system would be handled.

SCOPE AND DISTRIBUTION

Some privatization plans would scale back Social Security and supplement these reduced benefits with pensions financed from mandatory saving in personal retirement accounts. Other plans would replace the entire old-age insurance benefit with a new defined-contribution system. Almost all privatization plans retain the disability and survivor's insurance programs, which account for about 30 percent of the total cost of Social Security, although most cut these programs' benefits. Balances in defined-contribution accounts would usually be insufficient to provide adequate survivor's or disability benefits for workers who died or became disabled in their 30s, 40s, or even 50s. Privatization plans could require that workers buy private life and disability insurance policies of a certain minimum size. However, supplementary assistance would be necessary for low earners and large families if the social assistance functions of Social Security were to be sustained. In the end, private disability and survivor's programs that contained regulations to ensure that insurance carriers did not discriminate against workers with high risks would probably look very much like the current government programs, but without the administrative efficiencies of a centrally managed program.

Most, but not all, privatization plans would provide larger retirement benefits in relation to earnings and contributions to low earners than to high earners. Some would do this by retaining a scaled-back Social Security program. Others would create a new flat benefit to accompany the defined-contribution pension system. And one would supplement the contributions of low earners to the defined-contribution plan.

INVESTMENT RULES

Some privatization plans would be individually managed. They would permit workers to invest their retirement accounts in any approved financial asset, much as owners of existing Individual Retirement Accounts (IRAs) now can do. Others would permit investments only through financial organizations that were government certified through yet-to-be-specified procedures. Still other plans would be government managed. They would limit investments to a few publicly managed stock, bond, or money market index funds, similar to those currently available to federal employees under the Thrift Savings Plan (TSP). Restrictions curtail individual control over their accounts, but reduce the likelihood that the returns of some participants fall far short of broad market rates of return.

POSTRETIREMENT REGULATION

Under some plans individuals could do what they want with their account balances once they retire—withdraw funds gradually or all at once, buy an annuity, or hold their funds for their heirs. To prevent retirees from squandering their savings, becoming impoverished, and ending up on welfare, other plans would require retirees to make phased withdrawals over a number of years or buy an annuity with all or part of the retirement account balances.

TRANSITION

The transition from Social Security to a privatized system would create a knotty financial problem. Under current arrangements, most payroll taxes support pensions for *previous* generations of workers who are now retired. Under a privatized system, workers would contribute to *their own* personal retirement accounts. However, unless contributions were increased sharply, it would take a full working life to build a fund sufficient, on the average, to provide an adequate pension. Consequently, a new defined-contribution system could fully replace current Social Security benefits only for younger workers— say, those under about age 35. Since current retirees and workers over the age of 50 or 55 would have little or no accumulation in private accounts, most privatization plans continue to rely entirely on the current Social Security system for these age groups. Workers of intermediate age would receive benefits partly under the new system and partly under the old.

With all or a portion of the contributions of current workers going to personal retirement accounts, extra revenues would be needed to pay for the benefits of current retirees and those older workers still under the current system. Some privatization plans permanently or temporarily raise payroll taxes. One would redirect payroll taxes to individual accounts and pay for Social Security

benefits with a new 10 percent national sales tax that would gradually phase out as the benefit promises for current retirees and older
workers were fulfilled.

Supporters of privatization realize that it is difficult to win support for a new policy if workers think they will have to pay significantly higher taxes. Accordingly, some plans have developed ways to
soften the blow. One such solution is to impose a tax sufficient to
cover the transition costs averaged over many years. The revenue
generated by such a tax would not cover the initial costs of benefits
for workers retired under the old system, and the government would
have to borrow to meet the shortfall. Later on, when retirees would
need smaller and smaller supplements to their growing individual
accounts, the revenue from the new tax would be more than is needed to pay benefits to retirees still under the old or hybrid systems.
The excess would be used to retire the debt issued during the early
years of the transition. While borrowing reduces the additional taxes
that have to be paid in the early years, higher taxes must be imposed
for more years to cover interest on the early loans and eventually to
pay them off.

When projections of significant and sustained budget surpluses
first appeared in mid-1998, some advocates of privatization developed plans that tapped these surpluses to pay for transition costs.
This use of the surpluses would preclude devoting them to debt reduction, tax cuts, or spending increases.

However it is handled, the transition to a privatized system
would take a long time. Exactly how long depends on whether taxes
are increased immediately to cover the full annual costs of Social
Security benefits or borrowed funds are used to cover part of the
early transition costs. If all workers age 55 or older remained entirely under the current system, Social Security benefits would be undi-
minished for at least seven years—that is, until the first workers who
would receive a portion of their benefits under the new system
reached age 62. If every worker under age 30 had to rely solely on the
new privatized system, the transition would not be complete until
the last person who is now over age 30, and that person's spouse,
died. Even after twenty-five years, the transition period would be less
than half complete.

If funds are borrowed, the transition will take even longer. One plan
would raise the payroll tax by 1.52 percentage points—far less than
necessary to maintain Social Security for retirees and older workers while

building up private account balances. To fill in the gap, this plan would require the government to borrow approximately $2 trillion (in 1998 dollars) over the first thirty-four years of the plan. The payroll tax increase would remain in force approximately seventy years to pay off the loan. This "transition" tax would last nearly as long as the modern personal income tax, which was first imposed in 1913, has been in place.

A decision to privatize Social Security would mean that, for several decades, workers would have to pay not only to build up personal account balances, but also to support pensions for older workers and retirees who were not part of the new system. This consequence is unavoidable because Social Security has an "unfunded liability"—the excess of benefit obligations to retirees and current workers over accumulated reserves. It will be necessary to pay this unfunded liability whether Social Security is privatized or the current system is retained.[1]

ADVANTAGES OF PRIVATIZATION

Advocates of privatization claim benefits both for individuals and for society. Since plans differ, so do the advantages claimed for them. We gloss over some of these differences to facilitate consideration of the advantages of the privatization approach in general, but it is important to keep in mind that some forms of privatization are demonstrably superior to others.[2]

INCREASED RETIREMENT INCOMES

The primary attraction of privatization to individuals is the claim that it would significantly increase retirement incomes. Privatizers point out that annual real returns on investments in common stocks have averaged 8.2 percent over the *past* forty years and 11.4 percent over the past twenty years, far in excess of the projected returns on Social Security over the *next* thirty-five years of only about 1 percent.[3]

These comparisons are misleading for three reasons. First, most Social Security contributions are devoted to paying benefits to current retirees rather than to building investable balances. Workers, or tax-payers more generally, would have to meet these obligations under a privatized system just as they now must do. These payments generate no return for taxpayers, dragging down the overall yield. Second, abstracting from the contributions needed to meet current benefit obligations, the higher yield on additional funds invested in individual accounts has nothing to do with privatization. Rather, it arises from the requirement that Social Security reserves be invested in relatively low-yielding government securities. If Social Security reserves were invested in assets similar to those used to estimate the returns on personal retirement accounts, the average returns of Social Security and a privatized system would be similar. Third, one should include differences in administrative costs, which we examine later in this chapter.

INDIVIDUAL CONTROL AND SELF-RELIANCE

Most people like to have a hand in making important decisions that personally affect them, reflecting the American emphasis on self-reliance, individual freedom, and responsibility. Privatization clearly would represent a move to empower individuals.

From its earliest days, critics worried that Social Security would undermine self-reliance by protecting people from the full consequences of imprudence. Others simply deplored government interference in an activity—saving and insuring to provide protection against income loss—that they believed individuals could and should perform for themselves. Few now argue that Social Security has caused moral decay, but many believe that it has reduced personal saving.

Supporters of privatization claim that people should exercise increased control over and responsibility for their well-being during retirement. Millions already manage investments made through their company-sponsored, defined-contribution retirement plans. Everyone has complete discretion about how much to save voluntarily and how to invest it. Supporters of privatization think it is now appropriate for individuals to exercise more control over the investment of the mandatory saving that is the bedrock of their retirement income.

Even though individuals should control their own lives as much as possible, some limits are necessary. The gains from individual control must be weighed against other goals, such as keeping administrative costs reasonable and ensuring pension adequacy. Administrative costs and the variability of returns rise when people invest in diverse assets. Because record keeping and mailings cost the same for large and small accounts, overhead costs are proportionately larger when the average account is small than when it is large. Costs are minimized if account administration is centralized in a single entity. They are somewhat higher if participants can choose among a few financial institutions and much higher if many fund managers are competing for accounts and workers can shift their accounts from manager to manager. Similarly, administrative costs are low if workers are limited to a few indexed funds and increase steadily as investment choice is broadened. The annual costs of a completely decentralized system like that of current IRAs might exceed those of a centralized system like Social Security by as much as 1 to 2 percent of funds held on deposit, a difference that lowers lifetime accumulations 20 to 40 percent.

Allowing individuals wide latitude over the investment of their mandatory retirement savings has risks as well as benefits. Even the sophisticated sometimes fall prey to scams or exercise bad judgment. But most Americans have little experience managing investment funds. Less than half of the U.S. population has a tax-sheltered, individually managed retirement account. Only one-fifth directly own mutual fund shares or common stocks. Fewer than one in five has accumulated liquid assets equal to the income they earn in one year.[4]

These facts do not mean that private accounts are a bad idea—the long-run growth of U.S. financial markets testifies to their potential. Rather, administrative costs and the limited investment experience of the average worker suggest that relying exclusively on loosely regulated personal retirement accounts is risky. Some investors would take excessive risks in the search for high returns. Others would be excessively cautious, choosing low-yielding assets that would produce inadequate retirement benefits. Unless sales practices of financial institutions authorized to manage personal retirement accounts were tightly regulated, some investors would succumb to sharp sales practices, and marketing costs would eat up a substantial portion of the returns. Experience in the United Kingdom supports such concerns.[5] Even with extensive protections, individuals would be exposed to the risks of fluctuations in interest rates and asset prices that can undermine the adequacy of what once looked like a sufficient nest egg.

LABOR MARKET EFFICIENCY

Advocates of personal accounts claim that a privatized system would distort workers' decisions about how much to work less than Social Security does. They argue that workers are well aware of the payroll taxes they must pay, but have little understanding of, and therefore place little value on, the benefits they will ultimately receive in return for these payments. Thus, the system as a whole is perceived primarily as a tax that, like other taxes on earnings, distorts labor supply by reducing the returns workers receive for additional work effort. Distortions under a privatized system, they feel, would be smaller because workers would better understand, and feel more secure about, the benefits that contributions to their retirement accounts finance.

This argument is somewhat oversimplified. The same myopia that makes mandatory saving desirable will cause workers to undervalue future benefits from individual accounts just as they do Social Security benefits. Nevertheless, it is possible that labor supply could be affected differently if workers have a greater appreciation of the benefits they hope to receive from their personal accounts versus those they will receive from Social Security. To the extent that misunderstanding is the problem, education is the answer.

The principal difference in work incentives between a privatized system and Social Security arises from variations in the social assistance each system might provide. On average, the benefits per dollar of taxes paid would be the same under the two systems, if reserves are similarly invested (apart from administrative costs). But income redistribution necessarily entails taxing some people to provide assistance to others. The labor supply distortions that arise from taxes and transfers are an inescapable price of social assistance. The more social assistance—for low earners, large families, nonworking spouses, and widows and widowers—the more the distortions. If the effects on labor supply of Social Security vary from those of a privatized system, the differences arise either from lack of information or from differences in real social assistance.

INCREASED NATIONAL SAVING

The primary benefit claimed for privatization is that it would boost national saving. The case for raising national saving is strong (see Chapter 3, "Will the Baby Boomers Break the Bank," of this volume). Increased saving, and the higher rate of capital formation that this saving would generate, would boost the growth of output per worker and help the nation shoulder the costs of a gradually increasing dependent population. Replacing a pay-as-you-go Social Security system with fully funded private accounts would probably boost national saving. But so too would a buildup of Social Security reserves.

Which approach would raise saving more? The answer, alas, is a resounding: "Nobody knows!" To explain why this is the case, we must examine the three conditions that determine how much new saving would result from a dollar added to the Social Security trust funds' reserves and a dollar deposited in a personal retirement account—the yield on the two balances, budget offsets, and private offsets.

Yields. If the choice is between contributions to personal retirement accounts and equal additions to Social Security reserves, the one that has the higher yield will grow fastest and tend to add more to saving since all the contributions and investment returns accumulated in the two are held until paid out as pensions.[6] Current law requires Social Security to invest its reserves only in securities guaranteed as to principal and interest by the government.[7] These securities tend to yield less than the assets held by private pension funds—corporate bonds, stocks, and real estate. In other words, yield differences arise from restrictions imposed on the trust funds' managers, and have nothing to do with privatization. If Social Security could invest its additional reserves in the same assets private fund managers normally select, it would earn similar returns and generate as much saving.

Budget Offsets. The buildup of Social Security reserves may tempt elected officials to raise government spending or cut taxes, thereby reducing the effect of accumulation of the trust funds on national saving (see Box 1). To the extent that buildup in the trust funds does not trigger tax cuts or spending increases, additions to Social Security reserves boost national saving by raising unified budget surpluses or reducing deficits. Keeping the operations of

Box 1
The ABCs of National Saving

National saving is the difference between what the nation produces and what it consumes, publicly and privately. It consists of real resources that are available for investment in new office buildings and stores, industrial plants, warehouses, equipment, inventories, and residential structures. It is this real capital that adds to national productivity. Certificates of ownership—common stocks, bonds, mortgages, mutual fund shares, royalty contracts—are the counterparts of this real capital, but do not themselves add a scintilla to economic capacity. It is *real* capital that counts, not the value of *paper* capital.

To understand how an increase in funding of pensions can raise national saving, it helps to divide total national saving (NS) into four components: private saving for retirement (P_{RS}), private saving for other purposes (P_O), government saving under Social Security (G_{SS}), and government saving in the rest of its operations (G_O).

$$NS = P_{RS} + P_O + G_{SS} + G_O$$

Social Security surpluses increase trust fund reserves and raise G_{SS}. This will not raise national saving, however, if elected officials use Social Security reserves to underwrite equal increases in deficits (or reductions in surpluses) on other operations of government, which would show up as a decline in G_O. Mandatory private retirement saving will boost P_{RS}, but this will not raise national saving if people cut back on other forms of saving, P_O, equally. The effect on national saving of adding the same amount to P_{RS} or to G_{SS} will be identical as long as the offsets to P_O and G_O are the same.

The central question in the debate about whether accumulating reserves in Social Security (that is, adding to G_{SS}) or in personal retirement accounts (that is, adding to P_{RS}) will add more to national saving boils down to whether the offsets in P_O or in G_O will be larger.

Social Security separate in financial presentations and in policy debate involving other tax and expenditure decisions would make it more likely that any reserve accumulation will boost saving.*

Private Offsets. The creation of personal retirement accounts could either raise or lower other household saving. Personal retirement accounts might advertise the virtues of saving and thereby increase it. Business-sponsored programs to explain their 401(k) pension plans have raised saving.[8] They heighten people's awareness of the advantages of saving, showing that repeated deposits, even small ones,

---

*See Chapter 6 of *Countdown to Reform* for a description of the ways to effect such a separation.

can grow to significant balances over time, and create a workplace climate in which saving is respected and valued. Periodic statements of personal account balances could also demonstrate the power of compound investment returns. Such reports, together with reminders about the dangers of saving too little, can teach frugality and lead workers to save more outside their personal retirement accounts. Of course, one does not need to privatize Social Security to undertake private and public campaigns to educate workers on the virtues of saving.

While this "consciousness-raising" argument carries some force, the bulk of economic research suggests that growing balances in private accounts would tend to raise consumption—that is, lower saving—because asset owners feel wealthier. Most people now express great skepticism that they will receive all the Social Security benefits current law promises. If they receive a periodic statement showing that their very own personal retirement account balances are large and rising, they are likely to feel more secure about their retirement incomes, raise consumption, and reduce other saving.

Thus, creating private retirement accounts would *probably* reduce other saving. How much is unclear. Experience with tax provisions designed to encourage retirement saving is worrisome. After Congress created tax incentives, like IRAs, to promote individual retirement saving, saving in tax-sheltered individual accounts rose from nothing to 1.4 percent of national product during the 1986–93 period. Unfortunately, voluntary saving, apart from retirement saving and life insurance, vanished entirely, dropping from 3 percent of national product in the 1970s to net *borrowing* of 0.2 percent of national product.[9] While many factors other than the advent of tax-sheltered saving influenced private saving during this period, one cannot escape the troubling possibility that many people may have just shifted assets and saving from taxable accounts to the new tax-sheltered vehicles. This episode serves as a warning: If people are forced to save in one form they may cut back in another.

It is impossible to forecast reliably the net effect of these various incentives and offsets. Replacement of the government's largest program, one that provides most retirees with most of their income, is bound to have unforeseen consequences. But one effect is likely—accumulating pension reserves should raise national saving somewhat, whether reserves are held in Social Security trust funds or personal retirement accounts. Which form of reserve accumulation will raise saving most is impossible to predict because the results depend sensitively on plan details and on behaviors—of private individuals and elected officials—that no one can estimate with any degree of certainty.

POLITICAL CONFLICT

The specter of intergenerational conflict has been much in the news in recent years. Some people fear an ugly political scrum between greedy geezers struggling to hold on to their benefits and beleaguered workers fighting to protect themselves and their families from onerous taxes. It is hard to know how seriously to take such apprehensions. Opinion polls report that young and middle-aged adults strongly support Social Security and Medicare, even as they voice concern over whether these programs will actually deliver benefits promised to them. The young are almost as likely as the elderly to feel that these programs should be enriched rather than cut back.[10] This situation is unlikely to change, as elderly and disabled beneficiaries are always the parents and grandparents of active workers who care not only about their taxes but also about the continued financial security of their elderly relatives.

Privatization could eventually end the potential for intergenerational conflict over Social Security taxes and benefits because each generation would pay fully for its own retirement. This advantage, however, would be slow in coming. For several decades, in fact, privatization could intensify intergenerational conflict, as young workers would have to support previous generations of workers who would be receiving diminished Social Security benefits at the same time as they were contributing to their own retirement accounts. This extra burden might well provoke resentment among younger workers. Some would consider it "unfair" to force them to pay the retirement costs of two generations, especially when some of the benefits for retirees would be going to people with significant private pensions and asset income.

Updating Contribution Rates. Privatization would raise new and potentially divisive issues for public discussion. Instead of debating whether to impose added taxes on workers or to cut benefits, people would argue over how much each person should be required to contribute to his or her own account. If contribution rates were held constant, changes in wage growth, in asset values, and in interest rates could produce large changes in replacement rates.* To prevent such large fluctuations, sizable adjustments would have to be made periodically in the required individual contribution rate. And when asset prices fell, Congress would come under pressure to compensate those who were about to retire (see Box 2 for a past example of such pressures).

The problem can be illustrated by examining the changes in contribution rates that would have been required under a hypothetical defined-contribution retirement plan that started operations in 1953 and was designed to provide pensions that replaced half of preretirement earnings. If the contribution rate was adjusted once each decade to keep the plan headed for that 50 percent replacement rate, contributions would have varied from a low of 5.2 percent to a high of 39 percent of earnings.[11] With less frequent adjustments, pensions would have fallen well short of or greatly exceeded the target replacement rate. This analysis does not reflect the sharp variations in asset values that occur within and between years which would have caused replacement rates for workers reaching retirement age just a few months or years apart to differ greatly if personal retirement account assets were invested exclusively in common stocks.* Of course, most people would choose to invest their personal account balances in a portfolio containing different kinds of assets. But the historical record shows that the value of a balanced portfolio also varies a good deal from year to year. Therefore, pensions for workers with similar contribution records and investment patterns would vary depending on asset levels when they retire or become disabled.

Government guarantees of minimum returns on their investments or minimum benefits could protect defined-contribution pensioners from drops in asset values or imprudent investments. Such a safety net would probably be subject to a means test to limit costs, to concentrate assistance on the truly needy, and to minimize the incentive for workers to pursue excessively risky investment strategies, safe in the knowledge that they could keep high returns while the government, in effect, insured them against loss. Means tests increase complexity and administrative costs. In addition, a guarantee would have to be financed by raising taxes or cutting other government spending, measures that would raise intergenerational tensions similar to those allegedly facing Social Security.

---

*See Chapter 3 of *Countdown to Reform* for a discussion of this issue.

Box 2
The Peculiar Politics of "Notch Babies"

Before 1975, Social Security benefits were not automatically adjusted for inflation. Instead, Congress periodically passed legislation to offset the effects of inflation. Doing so took time and bother, but it had its reward—voters were grateful. Not surprisingly, bills to raise Social Security benefits were enacted mostly just before congressional elections. Democrats controlled Congress and got most of the credit. Republicans steamed. Partly to eliminate this opportunity for political advantage, Republicans urged that benefits be automatically adjusted for inflation. The proposal was clearly a good idea on substantive grounds. By the 1970s, inflation was becoming more of a problem than it had been since World War II. Why make the retired and disabled wait until Congress got around to acting? With bipartisan support, legislation was passed in 1972 that raised benefits by a whopping 20 percent and called for automatic "indexation" of Social Security starting in 1975.

Unfortunately, the adjustment formula Congress adopted was flawed. Congress was not at fault. The formula was the same one the actuaries had used in the past to design ad hoc legislated increases. It worked well enough when inflation was low, but provided excessive adjustments when inflation was high. When inflation was more than 1 to 2 percent, as it was with disturbing consistency during the 1970s, replacement rates—the ratio of benefits to average wages—rose relentlessly. For the average earner, replacement rates rose from 34 percent in 1970 to a peak of 54 percent for those who turned 62 in 1978. But payroll tax receipts rose no faster than average wages, and deficits began to develop.

Something had to be done. The Carter administration proposed a formula that adjusted benefits correctly for inflation and called on Congress to reduce replacement rates for people who reached retirement age *after* 1977 to what they would have been if the inflation adjustment had been made correctly all along. But it did not propose, and Congress did not enact, any change in benefits for those who had reached retirement age *between* 1972 and 1977 and had benefited from the flawed indexation mechanism.

This decision spared Congress one problem—the need to take benefits away from people who already had reached retirement age. But it created another—a "notch." Benefits were approximately 10 percent smaller on the average for people who reached retirement age just after 1977 than for those who reached retirement just before. Those affected adversely came to be known as the "notch babies." The exact differential between their benefits and those of people who became eligible just before 1977 depended on individual circumstances. But, whatever the differential, those on the short end felt shortchanged. They formed protest clubs. They filled congressional mailbags with letters venting outrage. Commissions were established to analyze the problem. Congressional committees held hearings. Members introduced "corrective" legislation. Not surprisingly, only two of the 113 "corrective" bills would have lowered the erroneous excess benefits paid to those born before 1917. The others would have raised the correctly calculated benefits of those born after 1916.

Continued on the next page

BOX 2 (CONTINUED)
THE PECULIAR POLITICS OF "NOTCH BABIES"

In the end, Congress resisted the protests of the notch babies. Privately, many members understood that the case for raising benefits for the notch babies was insubstantial. Outside organizations, including a blue-ribbon panel created by the National Academy of Social Insurance, made clear that the claims of the notch babies were unjustified. And budget pressures made any expenditure increases hard to justify. In the end, Congress left the 1977 legislation alone. But the furor created over the 10 percent benefit differential that arose from the flawed adjustment formula serves as a warning of the problems that might arise if price fluctuations in financial markets cause even larger benefit differentials under a privatized system.

Social Adequacy. Income redistribution is likely to become a more divisive issue under a privatized system than it is today. The Social Security benefit formula simultaneously provides pensions for all beneficiaries and additional social assistance for low earners. Some privatization plans maintain benefits for low earners through a separate component in a dual system. For example, under one plan, retired workers who had been employed a minimum number of years would receive a flat benefit financed by payroll taxes, in addition to a pension derived from personal retirement accounts that were financed by mandatory individual deposits. The combination could approximate the distribution of benefits under the current system. However, all the redistribution would be concentrated in the flat benefit component, and as the ratio of retirees to active workers increases, the payroll tax rate required to support the flat benefit would increase, raising pressures similar to those that some feel will lead to generational warfare if the current Social Security system is maintained. Creating a dual system does nothing to reduce this source of potential intergenerational conflict. It would simply focus this tension on the component of the new system that disproportionately serves low earners.

To sum up, replacing Social Security with a system of individual accounts would change, but not necessarily cool, debate about retirement policy. Pensions are so costly to society and so important to the elderly, disabled, and survivors that political debate on retirement policy will always be a hot political issue. Privatization would eventually end debates over how to close the projected deficits in the partially funded Social Security system because the benefit obligations of defined-contribution plans are limited to accumulated reserves in personal retirement accounts. Nevertheless, other contentious issues would remain to inflame political passions. One would be whether to compensate retirees who end up with inadequate pensions because of bad investment decisions or downturns in financial markets. Others include how to manage the transition and how to sustain the retirement incomes of low-wage workers whose personal security accounts provide insufficient benefits.

RISKS OF PRIVATIZATION

A switch from Social Security to privatized personal retirement accounts carries a number of risks. We have already described several. Variability of investment returns could leave some workers with inadequate pensions and would assuredly produce large variations in pensions among people who had made similar contributions. Unanticipated inflation could erode the value of pensions of older retirees. Political support for the crucial antipoverty role that Social Security has played for more than a half-century could atrophy. Two other problems associated with privatization deserve more attention—administrative costs and individual ignorance about financial markets.

ADMINISTRATIVE COSTS

All pension plans, public or private, must collect and keep track of individual workers' contributions, distribute information to participants, manage assets, determine eligibility for benefits, and pay retirement benefits. Expenditures to perform these tasks unavoidably reduce the growth of account balances and should therefore be kept as low as possible, consistent with adequate service.

The Social Security Administration (SSA) sets a high standard for administrative efficiency and customer service. The total cost of administering Social Security retirement and survivor's insurance averages only about 0.7 percent of benefit payments.[12] SSA enjoys economies of scale that private plans cannot match. Practically all of SSA's costs go for clerical functions—keeping track of individuals' earnings, distributing reports to participants, and paying benefits.[13] A small amount represents the costs the Treasury Department incurs collecting payroll taxes. Private employers also incur few extra costs collecting and remitting the Social Security payroll taxes because they must keep track of workers' earnings anyway to compute business and personal income, Medicare, and unemployment compensation taxes.

Running a system of personal retirement accounts would be more expensive than running Social Security. How much more expensive depends on the type of plan. The principal extra administrative costs of privatized alternatives arise from selling expenses, fees for managing assets, and costs for verifying the accuracy of records. Social Security incurs no selling costs because the plan is universal and mandatory. The cost of managing the trust funds' reserves is also trivial because the balances in the Social Security trust funds are invested centrally only in securities guaranteed as to principal and interest by the U.S. government. And verification costs are limited because earnings credits are linked to wages reported for income tax purposes. In addition, because Social Security benefits depend only on average earnings, which are calculated once at age 60, errors are relatively easy to correct. In contrast, personal account balances would have to be verified repeatedly because miscredited amounts would compound over time.

The 1997 Advisory Council on Social Security estimated that costs for individually managed plans that would permit people to invest freely in stocks, bonds, or mutual funds, as well as in investment products offered by insurance companies or brokerage houses, would average 1 percent of funds managed per year—*this would be equal to a front-end loading charge of 20 percent*. This IRA-type of privatized system would also cost employers substantially more than Social Security does if they were required to remit funds directly to a number of different financial intermediaries rather than send payroll tax contributions to the Treasury, along with other taxes that would have to be paid anyway. Small businesses and firms employing low-wage workers would be especially burdened. The 5.4 million employers that do not use computerized payroll systems would find it costly to make timely deposits into their workers' various investment accounts. Moreover, many of these deposits would be small. If 2 percent of earnings were designated for personal retirement accounts and each worker maintained only one account, half of the deposits employers would make each month would be less than $31 and one-fifth would be less than $9. Relative to the amounts involved, employer and financial institution administrative costs would be high. Finally, if workers in such a plan could choose whether to convert fund balances into annuities, they would face an additional charge that is estimated to average between 10 and 20 percent of the price of the annuity.[14]

Not all privatization plans would involve such high administrative costs. The Advisory Council estimated that government-managed plans modeled after the federal employees' Thrift Savings Plan (TSP) would have annual costs close to those of the TSP—that is, about 0.105 percent of funds managed. Several factors suggest that this estimate may be too low. The TSP deals with only federal agencies, all of which are computerized, not with millions of small and large employers. These agencies, not TSP, provide many account services and education. Furthermore, job turnover in the federal government is low, and wages, and thus contribution amounts, are relatively high. In addition, federal personnel records contain family information that a pension plan would need if a worker got divorced.[15] Taking account of all these factors, one analyst has estimated that total administrative costs for a TSP-type plan would be equivalent to a front-end loading charge of 6 to 9 percent.

Nonetheless, costs for this type of plan would be substantially lower than those for the IRA-type plan for several reasons. The TSP-type plan limits investment choice to a small number of passively managed, no-load index funds—such as a stock market index fund, a corporate bond index fund, and a government bond fund. A few financial institutions would be selected through competitive bids to manage the stock and corporate bond funds. The government would prohibit the management firms from attempting to influence investors' choices through aggressive selling or advertising, and account balances would have to be paid as indexed annuities upon retirement. Such a centralized system of individual accounts would capture many of the economies of scale in administration enjoyed by Social Security today.

A system of individually managed accounts could bring huge revenues to the financial services industry. The initial annual flow of investment funds into a privatized system that channeled 2 percent of earnings into private accounts would be about $75 billion. If administrative costs average 1 percent of accumulated funds, the annual revenue from managing these funds would reach $14 billion after ten years and rise steadily thereafter. Nonetheless, it is unclear whether this business would be profitable. Small accounts are costly to administer. Any whiff of scandal would bring congressional hearings and federal regulation that may well affect the other operations of the financial industry.

Any comparison of administrative costs should encompass the whole system. Social Security's administrative structure handles three categories of benefits—retirement pensions, survivor's benefits, and disability payments. This arrangement provides economies of scope—one agency for three programs—and of scale—176 million insured workers and 44 million beneficiaries. Privatization plans would unavoidably require duplicate administrative structures and costs because most privatization plans would retain Social Security retirement benefits for at least several decades and continue survivor's and disability insurance permanently.

PERSONAL CONTROL OVER ACCOUNTS

Advocates of privatization lay particular stress on the value of individual control of personal retirement accounts, both before and after retirement. With individual control, however, come important economic and political problems. If individuals own identified personal accounts and are free to determine how these funds are invested, they are likely to regard these accounts as personal property similar to other personal saving. Pressure will build to allow withdrawals before retirement. The experience with IRAs is instructive. Originally, nearly all IRA withdrawals made before age 59 1/2 were subject both to regular income tax and to a 10 percent penalty tax. In 1996, the law was changed to permit penalty-free withdrawals to meet large medical expenses and to buy health insurance if the account holder was unemployed. The Taxpayers Relief Act of 1997 liberalized the law further by permitting penalty-free withdrawals to cover expenses associated with the purchase of a first home and for postsecondary educational expenses of a family member. Under a privatized system, similar arguments will be made—that account holders should be allowed to withdraw funds from their retirement accounts to pay for personal health care expenses if they or a family member is seriously ill, to pay educational expenses, and for other purposes. As restrictions are relaxed, it becomes more likely that personal account balances will be drawn down before retirement, defeating the very purpose of the accounts and exposing the government to larger future welfare payments for those who have depleted their accounts.

The discretion that people are given over the use of their personal accounts at retirement also is problematic in a program to assure a basic retirement income. While some privatization schemes would require workers to convert account balances into annuities at retirement, others would permit people to withdraw funds in a lump sum when they retire or in a series of payments spread over several years. Still other plans would allow those who can support themselves in retirement through other income sources to leave their fund balances on deposit and bequeath them to their heirs at death. Because of adverse selection, giving people an option *not* to annuitize boosts costs for those who want annuities. To combat this risk, insurers must offer smaller annuities to everyone than would be possible if annuitization were mandatory.[16]

If annuitization were optional, some people would exhaust their savings and become public charges. In addition, people whose annuities would approximate the aggregate benefits from Supplemental Security Income benefits, food stamps, and other means-tested programs would face a perverse incentive not to annuitize. Instead, they could withdraw their savings over a few years, during which they could enjoy an elevated standard of living. After their savings were exhausted, they could fall back on welfare, where they would enjoy about the same income an annuity would have provided.

If people could hold their personal accounts until they die, so-called retirement accounts would become little more than devices people could use to escape taxes on investment income and to build their estates for their heirs. This feature would help only the wealthy.

Privatization—A Summing Up

Converting Social Security retirement benefits to personal retirement accounts means replacing a defined-benefit pension system with a defined-contribution pension system. This shift would place on individual retirees a variety of financial market risks that Social Security now diffuses broadly across workers and taxpayers, both current and future. We believe that individuals are poorly equipped to handle these risks and that a defined-benefit pension should continue to serve as the source of the nation's basic retirement pensions.

On the other hand, reserve accumulation in private accounts or in expanded Social Security trust funds could increase U.S. saving rates. Forcing the baby-boom generation, now in its prime working years, to shoulder a part of the burden of building these reserves would enrich the nation's capital stock, raise worker productivity, and offset some of the costs future workers will bear to support the baby boomers.

A system of supplementary personal retirement saving could also be used to build up reserves. If such a course were followed, the new program should be additional to a basic defined-benefit pension, such as Social Security. We can see no compelling case for scaling back Social Security benefits to "make room" for a supplementary system.* Such "carve-out" plans would cut assured benefits that are by no means generous to make room for supplementary benefits that force more risk on workers and pensioners and raise administrative costs. Whatever the size of a new program of mandatory personal saving, rules should restrict investments to no-load index funds managed in a manner similar to the Thrift Savings Plan of federal employees. The average returns on funds as large as those any mandatory saving program would generate cannot deviate much from the market-wide average rate of return. Since nothing can significantly boost this return, anything spent on administration, beyond the bare minimum necessary for speedy investment, is pure waste and should be avoided. Enriching pensioners, not financial institutions, should be the objective of pension reform.

---

*For a more detailed discussion of this conclusion, see *Countdown to Reform*, Chapter 6.

11

THREE NEW IDEAS FOR "PRIVATIZING" SOCIAL SECURITY, ONE CONCLUSION: BAD IDEA

JOHN MUELLER

F or most of the past decade, I have made my living as a principal in a market forecasting firm that deals not only with U.S. stocks and bonds but also with commodities, currencies, and foreign securities. Our typical clients are Wall Street money managers—though nowadays "Wall Street" is as likely to mean Parsippany, New Jersey, or Menomonee Falls, Wisconsin, as lower or mid-Manhattan.

Before that, from 1979 through 1988, I worked for Jack Kemp in the House of Representatives, mostly as economic counsel to the House Republican Caucus, of which Kemp was chairman. You could accurately

This chapter by John Mueller, senior vice president and chief economist at Lehrman Bell Mueller Cannon, Inc., is from a speech given at the National Committee to Preserve Social Security and Medicare, Washington, D.C., National Press Club, October 14, 1997. It is reprinted here with permission.

describe me as a conservative, Reagan Republican, and I am proud to have played a small role (as one of a cast of thousands, obviously) in the 1981 tax cuts, the 1986 tax reform, and in laying groundwork for initiatives enacted only much later, like regional free trade agreements and welfare reform.

In the mid-to-late 1980s, I had to do a lot of analysis of proposals to "privatize" Social Security, which were reaching political mass in anticipation of the 1988 presidential primaries. To tell the truth, I had never doubted the wisdom of phasing out Social Security until I had to sift the arguments in favor of doing so. To my great surprise and consternation, they didn't make sense. The arguments in favor of ending pay-as-you-go Social Security are, on the whole, a curious mix of horse-and-buggy economic theories with a remarkable ignorance of financial markets. The more I looked into the question, the more obvious it became that pay-as-you-go Social Security is one of those genuine cases, like national defense, in which the government is necessary to perform a role that the private markets alone cannot—in this case, providing the "foundation layer" of retirement income.

The issue of "privatizing" Social Security went away for several years, after the stock market crash of October 1987. And as a private forecaster I had no opportunity or time to do anything more on the subject. But last year, I was asked if I would be willing to do a series of papers for the National Committee to Preserve Social Security and Medicare. The following summarizes three of those efforts.

AN OVERVIEW OF THE DEBATE ABOUT "PRIVATIZING" SOCIAL SECURITY

Since retirees began collecting Social Security benefits in 1941, the average real return on payroll taxes paid has been about 9%—far above the average returns in the stock market, and financial assets in general.

Until the late 1970s, most economists believed that, while future returns could not remain so high, the average return on pay-as-you-go Social Security in the long run would equal the rate of economic growth—and that this rate of return would exceed the average return on financial investments of comparable risk. (Pay-as-you-go means that each generation pays the benefits for its parents.)

About 25 years ago, Martin Feldstein and some other economists began to question this conclusion. Feldstein agreed that the long-term return on Social Security would equal the rate of economic growth. But the return on Social Security, according to Feldstein, must be compared not with a low-risk investment like Treasury bills but with the total pretax return on business investment in plant and equipment. In fact, Feldstein proposed abolishing all Federal, state, and local taxes on the business investment financed by retirement saving, while raising taxes on labor compensation. This, he argued, would reduce consumption, increasing saving and economic growth, and pay for the large transition cost of ending pay-as-you-go retirement benefits.

But most "privatizers" do not go so far in their proposals. They argue that, even without such major changes in taxation, ending pay-as-you-go Social Security makes sense because the future average return on financial assets like stocks and bonds will exceed the return on pay-as-you-go Social Security.

For example, they point out, the average annual real return on common stocks since 1926 has been about 7%—about 5% on a mix of stocks and bonds—while real economic growth averaged about 3%.

Usually, the "privatizers" push their comparisons further, comparing past returns on financial assets with projected economic growth—and projected returns on Social Security—of 1% to 2%.

All of these arguments depend on three (invalid) assumptions:

1. that investors ignore the difference in risk between Social Security and financial assets;

2. that the future return on Social Security will be reduced, by slower economic growth and changing demographic trends, but the future return on financial assets will not; and

3. that there is no such thing as investing in "human capital"—the costs of child rearing, education, and so forth, that yield a return in the form of higher future wages.

To deal with one fallacy at a time, I examine different aspects of the "privatizers'" argument in three separate papers.

1. CAN FINANCIAL ASSETS BEAT SOCIAL SECURITY? NOT IN THE REAL WORLD

In the first paper, I pose the question, "Can financial assets beat Social Security?" And the conclusion is, "Not in the real world."

We all know that the stock market is a volatile place, even ignoring the Great Depression. The past 25 years have included 12-month periods in which the real value of stocks dropped as much as 40% (1974), and rose as much as 50% (1983).

But the "privatizers" assume that over any longer periods—one or two decades—the return on financial assets dependably approximates its long-term average. This shows a remarkable lack of familiarity with the behavior of the financial markets.

The typical family has an average of about 20 years to save for retirement. (Someone who begins saving at age 25, saves an equal amount each year for 40 years, and retires at age 65, will earn a return on those savings for an average of 20 years. For most families, the saving is bunched between the ages of 45 and 65, which shortens the average, but part of the saving earns a return after age 65, before it is spent.)

Since 1900, the 20-year average real total return on the stock market fell to about zero three times—from 1901 to 1921, from 1928 to 1948, and from 1962 to 1982 (see Graph 1). Of course, the returns were substantially negative after paying taxes on interest and dividends. In between were periods in which 20-year average stock market returns peaked at rates ranging from 6% to 10%.

GRAPH 1
REAL STOCK MARKET TOTAL RETURN: 20–YEAR ANNUAL AVERAGE

Net of Management Fees

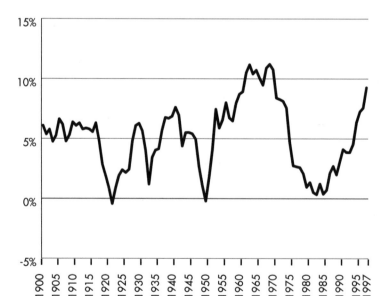

Source: Standard & Poor's 500 index (Cowles Commission Index before 1926), deflated by CPI: geometric annual mean. Lehrman Bell Mueller Cannon, Inc.

This meant that some people earned a negative real return from investing in the stock market, while others received a real pretax return as high as 10%.

In most cases, it was not possible to avoid below-average performance of the stock market by investing in other financial assets. Since 1945, the 20-year average real total return on long-term government bonds was negative almost exactly two-thirds of the time—in fact, for 33 years straight—including the worst periods for the stock market (see Graph 2).

The "privatizers" assume that investors are indifferent to these variations in the returns on investment.

But in fact, investors as a group are "risk-averse." Most of us don't use the term, but we all know exactly what it means. The idea of risk aversion is captured exactly in the adage, "a bird in hand is worth two in the bush." For the typical investor, in fact, a dollar in hand is literally worth two in the stock market.

Just as investors adjust nominal returns for differences in inflation, they adjust real returns for differences in risk. Both theory and the evidence show that

GRAPH 2
REAL GOVERNMENT BOND RETURN: 20–YEAR ANNUAL AVERAGE

Net of Management Fees

Source: Financial data, Ibbotson Associates; fees, Morningstar, Inc. CPI-adjusted long-term government bond total return, 20–year annual geometric average.

investors do not seek the highest possible average return but rather the highest risk-adjusted return. They make this adjustment by subtracting a "risk premium" which varies with the degree of risk involved (see Graph 3).

The first paper explains how to calculate these risk premiums, and shows that the risk-adjusted returns on all classes of financial assets—including the stock market—were significantly lower than the rate of economic growth. This means that financial asset returns, under the same economic conditions, are lower than the average return on a "mature" or "steady-state" pay-as-you-go Social Security system. The difference is still larger when the returns are measured net of management fees, which are roughly 25 times as large for financial portfolios as the administrative costs of Social Security.

Viewed as an investment, therefore, Social Security has some extraordinary characteristics. Its volatility risk is little higher than for Treasury bills—and only one-quarter the risk of common stocks—but its long-term real return is about halfway between Treasury bills and common stocks. As a result, its risk-adjusted return is much higher than on any class or mixture of financial assets.

This means that the risk-adjusted return of a portfolio including Social Security systematically exceeds the return on a portfolio limited to financial assets alone. I illustrate this point by showing that not a single one of the model portfolios recommended by the "privatizers"—who seek to write them into law—can match the risk-adjusted returns on "steady-state" Social Security (see Graph 4).

GRAPH 3
RISK PREMIA FOR DIFFERENT INVESTORS
Risk-return Tradeoffs Equivalent to 0% Risk-free Return

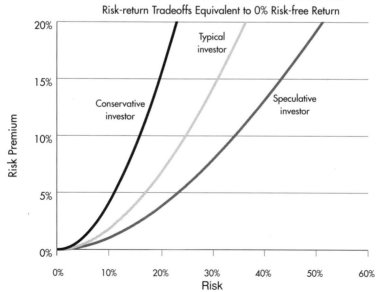

Risk = standard deviation of returns
Source: Lehrman Bell Mueller Cannon, Inc.

The conclusion is that the total return on retirement saving is higher with pay-as-you-go Social Security than without it.

2. IF ECONOMIC GROWTH FALLS TO 1.4%, WHAT HAPPENS TO THE STOCK MARKET?

While the first paper looks at the past, the second paper looks forward and asks, "If economic growth falls to 1.4%, what happens to the stock market?"

Using past financial asset returns to forecast future returns makes sense if we think the future will resemble the past (apart from random differences). In that case, we would have to conclude that Social Security will outperform financial assets in the future, because it always did so in the past.

GRAPH 4
"PRIVATIZERS'" MODEL PORTFOLIOS VS. SOCIAL SECURITY

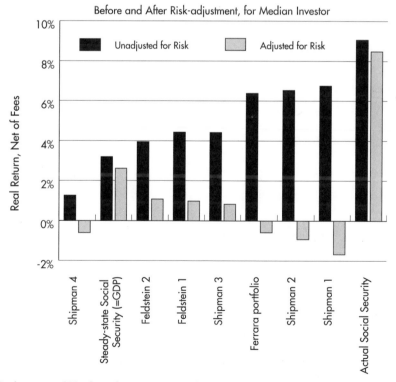

Before and After Risk-adjustment, for Median Investor

Real return = CPI-adjusted geometric annual return, 1926–96.
Source: Financial, Roger G. Ibbotson and Rex A. Sinquefield, *Stocks Bonds Bills and Inflation: 1997 Yearbook* (Chicago, Ill.: Ibbotson Associates, 1997); portfolio and risk calculations, Lehrman Bell Mueller Cannon, Inc.

But the "privatizers" warn us that the future will be very different from the past. In particular, according to the projections of the Social Security administration, future growth of the economy will be slower, and the number of retirees will rise compared with the number of workers.

However, this means that future financial asset returns will also be lower. Instead, the "privatizers" make two rather extreme assumptions: 1) that Social Security is affected by economic growth, but the stock market is not; and 2) that Social Security is affected by demographic changes, but the stock market is not.

The second paper shows that, apart from random variation, the return on the stock market is systematically determined by three factors: the rate of economic growth, the varying size of generations, and the market's volatility risk. The paper shows how to construct a projection for financial asset returns consistent with the Social Security actuaries' economic and demographic projections.

The actuaries' projections imply that the same economic and demographic factors that drove average annual real stock market returns up to 10% in the past 20 years will drive returns down to about 1.5% in the next 20 years—almost exactly like the periods from 1901 to 1921, from 1928 to 1948, and from 1962 to 1982. The main factor will be a sharp decline in the ratio of middle-aged savers to young workers setting up households (see Graph 5).

GRAPH 5
REAL STOCK MARKET TOTAL RETURN: 20–YEAR ANNUAL AVERAGE

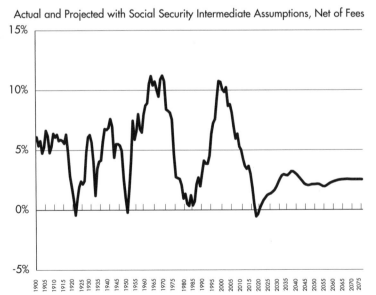

Actual and Projected with Social Security Intermediate Assumptions, Net of Fees

Source: Standard & Poor's 500 index (Cowles Commission Index before 1926), deflated by CPI: geometric annual mean. Lehrman Bell Mueller Cannon, Inc.

The projections also imply an average annual real return on the stock market over the next 75 years of 3.2%—or about 2.2% after subtracting management fees but before paying taxes.

Conclusion: if the Social Security actuaries' projections are correct, the United States is about to enter a 75-year economic Ice Age. Financial assets will perform very poorly in such an environment. This will make pay-as-you-go Social Security more, not less, attractive than investments in financial assets.

3. THE ECONOMICS OF PAY-AS-YOU-GO SOCIAL SECURITY AND THE ECONOMIC COST OF ENDING IT

In the third paper, I examine the economics of pay-as-you-go Social Security and the economic cost of ending it.

Economists like Martin Feldstein, who seek to "privatize" Social Security, rely on what's called the "neoclassical" theory of economic growth. But this theory was challenged by Nobel laureate Theodore W. Schultz nearly 40 years ago, and disproven by the research of John W. Kendrick and others more than 20 years ago.

The third paper recounts the neoclassical theory's shortcomings as an explanation of economic growth and a guide to policy. The neoclassical theory ignores the existence of "human capital"—those costs of child rearing and education, training, safety and mobility that increase future income (see Graph 6, page 198).

Kendrick's research shows that business investment in plant and equipment has contributed about one-quarter of the growth in national output and income, but investment in human capital has contributed between two-thirds and three-quarters of that growth (see Graph 7, page 198).

Pay-as-you-go Social Security did have an enormous impact on the saving habits of American households. But far from encouraging more consumption, as Feldstein has argued, pay-as-you-go Social Security financed more investment—especially the massive investment in "human capital" associated with the baby boom—and more economic growth than could otherwise have occurred (see Graphs 8 and 9, page 199). Moreover, the real rate of return on this investment in human capital was much higher than the return on nonhuman capital.

Ending pay-as-you-go Social Security—particularly by raising taxes on labor compensation and cutting taxes on property income, as Feldstein proposes—would throw the same process into reverse. The necessary result is lower investment, slower growth, and a smaller economy.

The paper concludes by calculating the economic cost of ending pay-as-you-go Social Security. After 75 years, the U.S. economy would be about 4%

GRAPH 6
REAL GROSS INVESTMENT: SHARE OF REAL GDP

U.S. Domestic Economy (peak years, 1929–90)

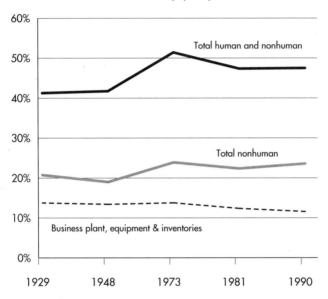

Source: John W. Kendrick, "Total Capital and Economic Growth," *Atlantic Economic Journal* 22, no. 1, March 1994, p. 3.

GRAPH 7
SOURCES OF REAL GDP GROWTH

U.S. Domestic Business Economy, 1929–90

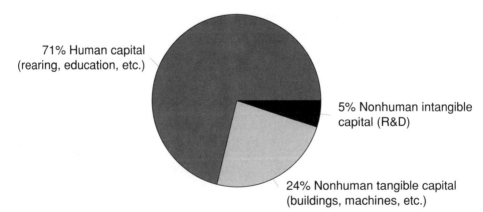

Source: Kendrick, "Total Capital and Economic Growth," p. 15.

GRAPH 8
SOCIAL SECURITY INTERGENERATIONAL
TRANSFER VS. TOTAL FERTILITY RATE

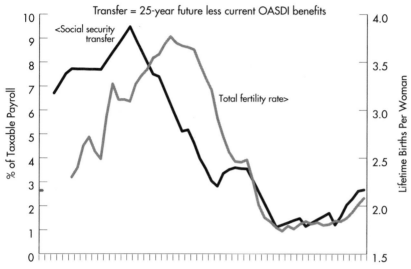

Source: Lehrman Bell Mueller Cannon, Inc.

GRAPH 9
TOTAL FERTILITY RATE VS. REAL BUSINESS GDP GROWTH

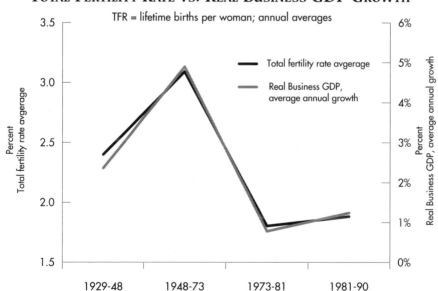

Source: Census Bureau; real business GDP growth: John W. Kendrick, "Total Capital and Economic Growth," *Atlantic Economic Journal* 22, no. 1, March 1994, p. 8.

smaller—not 8% larger, as Martin Feldstein predicts. The present value of the economic loss is about $3 trillion.

SUMMARY OF CONCLUSIONS

Replacing Social Security with private savings accounts is one of those issues that are more attractive the less you know about them. In my own opinion, the political movement to "privatize" Social Security will abruptly collapse as soon as the public begins to learn what's actually being proposed: a big tax increase and a permanently lower standard of living for most American families.

The evidence presented by all three papers points to the same conclusion: It would be a costly mistake to end pay-as-you-go Social Security. The result would be a lower real return on retirement saving, a tax increase on working families, and a smaller economy. Instead of "privatizing" Social Security, we should maintain Social Security on a pay-as-you-go basis.

12

SAVING SOCIAL SECURITY WITH STOCKS: THE PROMISES DON'T ADD UP

DEAN BAKER

EXECUTIVE SUMMARY

The headlines following the release of the report of the Advisory Council on Social Security trumpeted the group's agreement that investing some of the system's money in stocks might save it from an anticipated shortfall in the next century. Although the council split into three factions that supported widely divergent proposals, any change in Social Security involving investment in equities would constitute a fundamental transformation of the program.

This paper analyzes whether the claims in the Advisory Council report about the benefits to the Social Security system of investing in the stock market are consistent with the economic forecasts by the program's Trustees. Any

This report, which was a joint project of The Century Foundation and the Economic Policy Institute, originally appeared as a white paper published by The Century Foundation press.

significant inconsistencies between the Trustees' projections of economic growth and the Advisory Council's assumptions about future stock market performance would call into question the wisdom of their recommendations.

The central conclusion of this paper is that there are serious inconsistencies between the forecasts for the economy and stocks. If the projections for the stock market turn out to be right, the economy will have to grow much more rapidly than the Trustees predict. In this case, there would be no reason to change Social Security at all because payroll tax receipts would be sufficient to finance benefits. On the other hand, if the projections for the economy turn out to be right, the council's forecasts for the stock market are vastly overstated. In that case, diverting Social Security funds into stocks might leave most retirees worse off.

The main challenge facing Social Security is the increasing life expectancy of the population. Even though the system now accumulates surplus payroll taxes from workers well in excess of the benefits paid to today's retirees, and will continue to do so until the year 2012, the Social Security Trust Fund financed by those surpluses is projected to be depleted by 2029 because Trust Fund assets would be used to make up the shortfall between taxes and benefits as the ratio of retirees to workers increases. Thus, if the economic projections are correct, and if there are no changes in the program, the system would be unable to pay all retirees their benefits in full.

The mandate of the thirteen-member Advisory Council was to develop ideas for warding off that unthinkable scenario. A plurality of six members recommended incremental changes similar to those made in the past, and suggested that the possibility of investing some of the Trust Fund's assets (now entirely in U.S. Treasury securities) in the stock market should at least be considered. Five members proposed replacing a portion of Social Security with government-mandated but privately managed Personal Security Accounts (PSAs) that individual workers would invest in a range of financial instruments. They also recommended a significant increase in the payroll tax to finance the new accounts while maintaining benefits for today's retirees. The other two members favored an alternative to PSAs that would offer workers a small selection of investment options managed by the government.

The attraction of equities as a partial solution to Social Security's future shortfall rests on a basic premise: stock market returns to investors have significantly exceeded those of alternatives in the past, and they can be expected to do so in the future.

But is that premise valid? This paper shows that it is not, if one accepts the economic forecasts of the Trustees.

THE MAIN CONCLUSIONS

◆   The claim that stock market returns will match past performance is inconsistent with the decline in economic growth predicted by Social Security's Trustees. The Advisory Council and others extrapolate from the past and project continuing 7 percent annual returns from stocks. But applying the past to the future is incompatible with the Trustees' forecast that annual economic growth will be more than 2 percentage points slower over the next seventy-five years than it has been during the past seventy-five years. If the Trustees' projections about the economy hold true, annual stock returns are more likely to decline to 4 percent than to continue at 7 percent.

◆   In order for stocks to continue to generate a 7 percent annual return under the Trustees' assumptions of economic growth, price-to-earnings ratios, now averaging an unprecedently high 20 to 1, would have to soar to an unheard of 34 to 1 in 2015, and an absurd level of 485 to 1 by 2070. If wages do not decline relative to profits, the forecasts of the Trustees and the assumptions of the Advisory Council depend upon sustaining nonsensical price-earnings relationships. On the other hand, if price-earnings ratios remain near their historical averages, wages would have to plummet to ridiculous levels: to just 18 percent of their currently projected level for the year 2055, and they would have to turn negative by 2070.

◆   The transaction and administrative costs of the new accounts could actually be more than twice as high as estimated by proponents of mandated savings accounts. The Advisory Council estimates that these costs would average 1 percent annually of the values of equities held in an account. But the cost of holding equity-based mutual funds in 401(k) plans currently averages about 2 percent a year. It is likely that greater regulation, insurance, and smaller average account sizes would raise costs further. Combine the lower estimates of stock returns with higher estimates of administrative costs, and the returns from mandated savings accounts plunge dramatically.

The greater life expectancy of workers retiring in 2040 means they will enjoy on average nineteen years in retirement. If mandatory savings accounts play a major role in Social Security, those years will be anything but golden. Such accounts would provide these retirees with less than 20 percent and at worst only 14 percent of their salaries at retirement, while Social Security

currently promises low-income workers 56.7 percent of their salary at retirement for as long as they live.

In sum, realistic estimates of stock returns and administrative costs show
that government-mandated savings accounts are not likely to offer workers
better returns, on average, than the current Social Security system. And they
would subject workers to enormous risk, making their retirement prospects
far less—rather than more—secure.

INTRODUCTION

In recent years there has been growing interest in public policy circles in
replacing partially or completely the existing Social Security system with a
"privatized" system of government-mandated savings.[1] This interest was
reflected in the disparate recommendations of the January 1997 report of
the Advisory Council on Social Security. Under these proposals, the federal government would require workers to divert a portion of what they now
pay as Social Security taxes into private savings accounts. These proposals
have been promoted as a way of dealing with the stress that an aging population will place on the Social Security system in the next century.
Proponents argue that retirees would receive a much higher rate of return on
such accounts than they could expect to receive from the Social Security system as it is currently structured. But many of the claims about rates of return
are highly unrealistic and exaggerate the benefits of government-mandated
savings.

> Many of the claims about rates of return are highly unrealistic
> and exaggerate the benefits of government-mandated savings.

This paper provides a range of estimates of the rate of return that can be
expected from private savings accounts. It is divided into four sections. The
first establishes a framework for evaluating the merits of such government-
mandated savings plans. The second provides a set of estimates of stock market returns that are consistent with the rates of economic growth projected by
the Social Security Trustees. The third estimates a range for the transaction-
al and administrative costs likely to be incurred by government-mandated
savings accounts. The fourth combines the estimates in the second and third
sections to project the retirement income such accounts would generate.

The analysis in this paper loosely follows the outline of the Schieber-Weaver plan, one of the three proposals for reforming or transforming the Social Security system put forth by the divided Advisory Council. Sylvester J. Schieber, a benefits consultant, and Carolyn L. Weaver, director of Social Security and pension studies at the American Enterprise Institute, are both members of the council. While there are some differences among the various plans for mandated savings programs, the analysis in this paper has clear implications for all of them.

1. WHY GOVERNMENT-MANDATED SAVINGS WON'T SPARK ECONOMIC GROWTH

When workers retire, they continue to require goods and services from the economy. Those goods and services must be subtracted from the amount available to the rest of the population regardless of how retirees pay for them. If, for example, retirees consume $600 billion of goods and services in a given year (which is roughly how much they consume today), it makes no difference whether they pay for them with Social Security checks from the government or with stock dividends or interest from their private savings accounts: the drain on the economy will be the same. Piling up paper assets by itself will not help the country cope with the retirement of the baby-boom generation. The only way the United States can provide for our future is by building up its productive capacities so the economy as a whole grows more rapidly. (The sole exception to this rule is if the nation accumulates foreign assets, in which case goods and services would be provided by other countries' economies.) This increase in productive capacities can only be achieved by investing in public and private capital, and by creating a better-educated, more productive work force. This point must be kept in mind when evaluating the merits of any government-mandated savings proposal. Unless the plan will actually increase the productive capacities of the economy, it can only redistribute assets within or between generations—it cannot make everyone, or Americans as a whole, better off.

> Unless the plan will actually increase the productive capacities of the economy, it can only redistribute assets within or between generations—it cannot make everyone, or Americans as a whole, better off.

For example, if a plan allows future retirees to benefit from stock market returns exceeding the projected benefits that Social Security would provide under the current system, but does not in any way increase economic growth, the plan must make those who are still working worse off. The most obvious way this could happen is if the loss of Social Security tax revenue, diverted to private savings accounts, led to an increase in the annual federal budget deficit, and therefore to a larger debt burden. Eventually this would raise interest rates as well as taxes for future generations, because not only would the national debt be greater, but higher interest rates also would be necessary to entice investors to purchase that additional debt. Thus, the working population would have to pay more to the government in taxes and more to private lenders in interest on their mortgages and car loans. Those increased costs to workers would roughly equal the additional returns that retirees would obtain by investing in the stock market rather than Social Security.

It is possible that a shift to government-mandated savings could be accompanied by other policies that would promote more rapid economic growth. For example, if the switch were coupled with a tax increase, as in the Schieber-Weaver plan, the result could be a lower budget deficit, and therefore an increase in national savings. (National savings are the sum of corporate and personal savings minus the budget deficit, assuming the government runs one.) To the extent that a falling deficit and rising savings encouraged businesses to make bigger capital investments in plants, equipment, and research and development, this could lead to a somewhat higher rate of economic growth. However, the acceleration in the growth rate would be attributable to the tax increase, not to a government-mandated savings system. The same increase in savings and acceleration in growth would occur if the tax increase were instituted without switching to a government-mandated savings system. The switch might provide the political justification for a tax increase, but the tax increase, not the switch, would actually have the impact on growth. (Remember, investing in the stock market may increase the return on an individual's savings, but it does not necessarily encourage companies to invest in productive assets.)

Although it is possible that switching to government-mandated savings accounts might affect workers' incentives to save,[2] there is little evidence that such a change would be substantial, or even in what direction it would go.[3] It is entirely possible that mandatory accounts would encourage workers to reduce the amount they save in other forms.

It is also important to recognize the limited impact such policy changes can have. The Congressional Budget Office (CBO) has estimated that moving from a budget path that projects deficits equal to approximately 3 percent of gross domestic product (GDP) to a path toward a balanced budget would increase the growth rate by approximately 0.1 percent a year.[4] The deficit reduction envisioned by the Schieber-Weaver plan would be less than half as large as the CBO balanced budget scenario, and could therefore be expected to have an effect on growth of less than 0.05 percent a year. By the year 2030, this would increase the size of the economy negligibly—by less than 2 percent compared with the current growth path projected by the CBO.[5] The links between deficit reduction, investment, and productivity growth are sufficiently tenuous that even this figure may be overstated, particularly if the deficit is reduced by cutting back public investment in physical and human capital.

It may still be desirable to adopt a system of government-mandated savings even if it has no positive impact on growth. If a system of mandated savings allows retirees to benefit from higher rates of return in private capital markets, it can finance their retirement. However, if the gains for retirees are not accompanied by an acceleration in the economy's rate of growth, those gains will be at the expense of the working population. And a system of mandated savings might well have a negative impact on growth, because in all likelihood it would be much more expensive to operate than the current Social Security system. The operating expenses of private life insurance companies are approximately 27 percent of benefits.[6] By comparison, Social Security's administrative expenses are less than 0.8 percent of benefits.[7] The increase in costs would be pure waste from the standpoint of the economy as a whole, and insofar as a system of mandated savings led to higher administrative costs, it would dampen economic growth. If the main concern of proponents of mandated savings plans is the well-being of younger generations, simply increasing returns for retirees is a move in the opposite direction.

> If the main concern of proponents of mandated savings plans is the well-being of younger generations, simply increasing returns for retirees is a move in the opposite direction.

2. Why the Stock Market Can't Outpace Growth Forever

The return on holding a share of stock consists of two parts: the dividend payout and the rise in the price of the stock. Both sources of return depend ultimately on the profits per share. The relationship between the dividend payout and profits per share is fairly direct. The amount of dividends a corporation can pay out to shareholders, after meeting its needs for investment capital, will depend largely on its profits. If profits rise, firms can afford to pay out larger dividends. (When profits fall, on the other hand, many firms are more reluctant to reduce dividends than to cut back on investment.)

The relationship of the rise in the share price to earnings is somewhat less direct. In principle, the current share price should reflect the value placed by the shareholder on the stream of future earnings expected from the share. However, research has shown that share prices fluctuate far more than actual earnings.[8] This means that the ratio of a stock's price to its earnings per share can change considerably over time; a stock's price does not necessarily rise at exactly the same rate as an increase in earnings per share. However, this research has also found that divergences between the growth rate in earnings and the growth rate of the share price tend over time to even out. For example, if the share price rises 50 percent in a year while the company's earnings rise by only 5 percent, it is likely that in subsequent years the share price will rise less rapidly than earnings. Similarly, a period in which the rise in a share's price lags behind the growth rate of earnings is likely to be followed by a rapid increase in the stock's price. This tendency for rapid growth in stock prices relative to earnings to be followed by slow growth, and for bursts in earnings relative to stock price to be followed by lulls, means that, over the long run, the rate of growth of a stock's price can be crudely predicted by the rate of growth of earnings.

Applying this logic to the stock market as a whole, it should be possible roughly to estimate the rise in the market over time based on projections of growth in corporate earnings. Because the 1995 report of the Social Security Trustees implicitly assumes that profits will grow at the same rate as the economy as a whole, its projections for GDP growth provide a basis for estimating the growth in corporate profits. (In estimating the future growth of wages, the Trustees assume that labor's share of output does not change, and therefore the corporate share of output also remains constant.)[9]

Table 1 shows the projected rates of economic growth in the Trustees' intermediate scenario, the consensus basis for policy projections. The growth rates are calculated in *real* terms, ignoring increases in nominal value that result from inflation. The growth rate through 2005 is projected to average 2.0 percent a

Table 1
Social Security Trustees Projections of Annual GDP Growth

1997–2006	2.00%
2007–2016	1.80%
2017–2026	1.30%
2027–2036	1.40%
2037–2046	1.40%
2047–2056	1.20%
2057–2066	1.20%
2067–2071	1.20%
Average	1.49%

Source: Social Security Trustees, OASDI, *Annual Report of the Board of Trustees of the Old-Age and Survivors Insurance and Disabilities Insurance Trust Funds* (Washington, D.C.: U.S. Government Printing Office, 1995).

year.[10] It slows considerably over the next fifteen years, declining to just 1.3 percent by the year 2020. Growth is projected to remain slow for the rest of the seventy-five-year planning horizon, settling down at 1.2 percent by 2050. The average for the whole period is just under 1.5 percent. Using the Trustees' assumption that the profit share of income will remain constant, it is possible to take the GDP growth rates in Table 1 as proxies for growth rates for stock prices over the next seventy-five years.

To estimate the total return that shareholders can anticipate, it is necessary to add the annual dividends paid out to shareholders. At present, the average price-to-dividend ratio is 34.8 to 1.[11] (The price-to-dividend ratio is the ratio of the average price of a share of stock to its annual dividend payout.) This implies a return in dividend payouts that is equal to 2.87 percent of an average stock's price. The total return for holding a share of stock is simply the sum of the dividend yield and the growth in the stock's price. If the portion of profits paid out in dividends remains constant (an assumption that will be considered below), then the total return can be calculated by adding 2.87 percent to the GDP growth rates in Table 1. The implied average rates of return appear in Table 2 (see page 210).

The rates of return shown in Table 2 start at 4.87 percent and fall over the course of seventy-five years to 4.07 percent, following exactly the slowdown in growth projected in the Trustees' report. The average return over the entire planning horizon is 4.36 percent.

This is not an economic model, of course, or an elaborate projection. It is a series of back-of-the-envelope calculations based on the Social Security Trustees' own assumptions and figures. But these numbers are far below the rates of return for stock holdings that are widely assumed by people working with the same Social Security data and projections. For example, the Advisory Council used an inflation-adjusted return of 7 percent as the central estimate in constructing its projections. This difference is extremely important because of the effect of compounding. If the stock market yields an average return of 7

TABLE 2
Projected Stock Returns

1997–2006	4.87%
2007–2016	4.67%
2017–2026	4.17%
2027–2036	4.27%
2037–2046	4.27%
2047–2056	4.07%
2057–2066	4.07%
2067–2071	4.07%
Average	4.36%

Source: Author's calculations using data from Social Security Trustees, OASDI, *Annual Report of the Board of Trustees of the Old-Age and Survivors Insurance and Disabilities Insurance Trust Funds*; Federal Reserve Board web site, www.bog.frb.fed.us, Flow of Funds table; Bureau of Economic Analysis web site, www.bea.doc.gov, National Income Products Account table.

percent, $1000 will grow to nearly $15,000 after forty years. If, on the other hand, the expected return is 4.37 percent, in forty years the same sum will grow to only $5,530. Differences of this magnitude will be quite important to someone trying to plan for retirement.

The reasons for the large differences in these projections are very simple. The returns projected by the Advisory Council and in most other calculations are extrapolations from the past. Over the past seventy-five years, the average real return to stockholders has been close to 7.0 percent. The Advisory Council has simply projected the same return into the future. However, over the past seventy-five years the average annual rate of economic growth has been approximately 3.5 percent. As noted earlier, in their intermediate scenario the Trustees project that the average rate of growth over the next seventy-five years will be less than 1.5 percent. If profits grow at the same rate as the economy (which has been roughly the case over the past seventy-five years), then the economy's growth rate over the past seventy-five years has supported an annual rate of growth in stock prices more than 2 percentage points higher than we can expect during the next seventy-five years.

> If profits grow at the same rate as the economy (which has been roughly the case over the past seventy-five years), then the economy's growth rate over the past seventy-five years has supported an annual rate of growth in stock prices more than 2 percentage points higher than we can expect during the next seventy-five years.

The other reason the returns shown in Table 2 are lower than the historic rate of return is the recent run-up in stock prices relative to earnings. Over the past eighteen years, the price of an average share of stock has risen from just nine times annual earnings to more than twenty times annual earnings.[12] Current stock prices are at record highs in relation to corporate earnings.[13] This rise in the price-to-earnings ratio has two effects. It raises the historic rate of return by adding to the growth in share prices, and it lowers the current dividend-to-price ratio. The current dividend-to-price ratio of 2.87 percent is nearly a full percentage point below the average of 3.65 percent from 1959 to 1995. This difference in dividend-to-price ratios is the other major factor explaining the lower rate of return projected for the next seventy-five years compared with the past seventy-five. Until and unless stock prices fall relative to dividends, the 2.87 percent dividend return will be 0.87 percentage points less than the average dividend return over the past forty years.

If the projections in the Trustees' report are accurate, the only way the stock market can generate higher returns than those shown in Table 2 is if the price-to-earnings ratio continually rises. Figure 1 (see page 212) shows the price-to-earnings ratios that would be necessary at various points in the future if the stock market were to yield real annual returns of 6 percent, 7 percent, and

8 percent. These calculations assume that corporate profits and dividend pay-outs both grow at the same rate as the economy as a whole. In the 7 percent scenario, the price-to-earnings ratio hits 34 to 1 in 2015, and 485 to 1 by 2070. The 8 percent scenario, which is suggested by some proponents of mandated

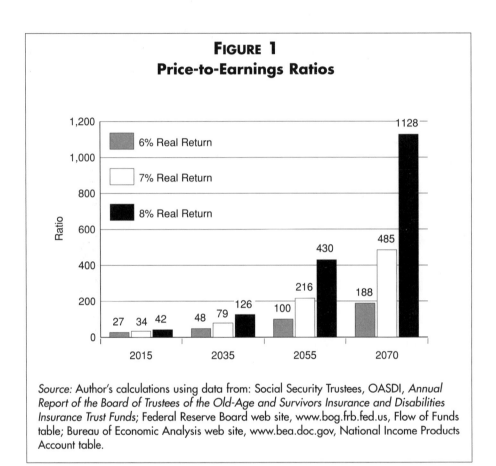

FIGURE 1
Price-to-Earnings Ratios

Source: Author's calculations using data from: Social Security Trustees, OASDI, *Annual Report of the Board of Trustees of the Old-Age and Survivors Insurance and Disabilities Insurance Trust Funds;* Federal Reserve Board web site, www.bog.frb.fed.us, Flow of Funds table; Bureau of Economic Analysis web site, www.bea.doc.gov, National Income Products Account table.

savings, hits 126 to 1 by 2035. Even the 6 percent scenario hits an astronomical 188 to 1 by 2070.[14]

The assumption that average rates of return will exceed the sum of the growth rate and the dividend-to-price ratio (the projected returns in Table 2) requires that the price-to-earnings ratio rise continually, and at an accelerating rate. This can happen for a period of time. The history of capitalism is marked by speculative bubbles of this sort, dating from the tulip bulb mania in seventeenth-century Holland and the South Sea bubble in eighteenth-century England. The run-up of stock prices in the United States in the 1920s and in Japan during the 1980s are more recent examples. At some point such bubbles inevitably burst, and prices come crashing down to the point where they reflect underlying values.

As an alternative to soaring price-to-earnings ratios, let us consider the possibility that profits could rise enough to support returns of 6 percent, 7 percent, or 8 percent by some other means. But if we adhere to the growth projections of the Social Security Trustees, such increases in corporate profits could be achieved only by reducing wages. Figure 2 shows the percentage of decline in wages, from their baseline growth path, that

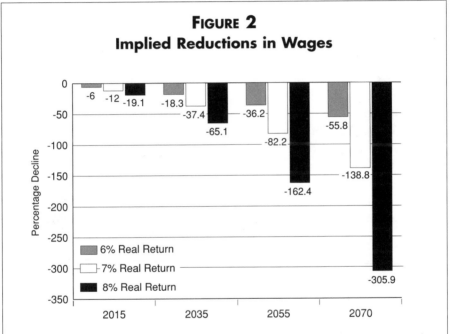

FIGURE 2
Implied Reductions in Wages

Source: Author's calculations using data from: Social Security Trustees, OASDI, *Annual Report of the Board of Trustees of the Old-Age and Survivors Insurance and Disabilities Insurance Trust Funds*; Federal Reserve Board web site, www.bog.frb.fed.us, Flow of Funds table; Bureau of Economic Analysis web site, www.bea.doc.gov, National Income Products Account table.

would be required to support each rate of return, assuming that the price-to-earnings ratio does not change.[15] Under these assumptions, in order to generate 7 percent returns to shareholders, wages would have to fall to just 63 percent of their currently projected level for the year 2035. By 2055, real wages would have to fall to just 18 percent of the levels projected in the Trustees' report, and by 2070 they would actually turn negative. Even a 6 percent return would imply an 18 percent reduction in wages by the year 2035. This decline in wages, of course, would create a major shortfall in anticipated collections from the Social Security payroll tax.

> Wages would have to fall to just 63 percent of their currently projected level for the year 2035. By 2055, real wages would have to fall to just 18 percent of the levels projected in the Trustees' report, and by 2070 they would actually turn negative.

It is possible to construct a mixed scenario in which high rates of return in the stock market are obtained by a combination of record-high price-to-earnings ratios and declining wages, but that is neither a very pretty nor a plausible picture of the future. The rates of return to stockholders that are assumed by the Advisory Council's proponents of government-mandated savings plans are simply inconsistent with the Social Security Trustees' growth projections. Yet those proponents and others use the Trustees' projections to argue that the Social Security system must be replaced.[16]

> The rates of return to stockholders that are assumed by the Advisory Council's proponents of government-mandated savings plans are simply inconsistent with the Social Security Trustees' growth projections. Yet those proponents and others use the Trustees' projections to argue that the Social Security system must be replaced.

In fact, even the 4.36 percent average return shown in Table 2 is optimistic, given the growth assumptions in the Trustees' report. As noted before, the current price-to-earnings ratio of 20.3 to 1 is the highest since World War II. Stock prices have seldom been so high relative to corporate earnings. The price-to-earnings ratio since 1959 has averaged 15.1 to 1. It was only because stocks maintained a lower price-to-earnings ratio in the past that they were able to sustain such high real rates of return. The cheaper the stock, the greater the potential return on investment. Low price-to-earnings ratios allowed for high dividend-to-price ratios. These higher dividends, coupled with the economy's 3.5 percent annual growth rate, made possible an average 7.0 percent annual return over the past seventy-five years. In order to sustain a comparable rate of return in a future with slower growth, it would be necessary for the price-to-earnings ratio to *fall*, not rise.

In the past, investors choosing stocks rather than bonds have sought a substantial premium. This has been partly to compensate them for the risk associated with holding stocks and partly for other reasons that have long puzzled many economists.[17] Current high stock values combined with growth projections for profits will almost certainly not allow for such premiums. The nominal yield on long-term Treasury bonds was approximately 7.0 percent at the end of the second quarter of 1996. The annual rate of inflation was approximately 2.7 percent, meaning that the real return was approximately 4.3 percent. This is only about 0.5 percentage points less than the yields that can be expected from stocks, assuming current economic growth projections and a constant price-to-earnings ratio. This compares with a historic premium of 6.0 percentage points. Unless investors have radically reassessed the relative risks associated with owning stocks and government bonds, the current price-to-earnings ratios are not sustainable. Stock prices will have to fall to restore some of the premium that existed historically.

In addition to the possibility that the price-to-earnings ratio may fall back toward its historic average, two other statistical relationships that deviate from the past also suggest that the returns shown in Table 2 may be overly optimistic. One, the capital share of corporate GDP—that is, the profits and interest earned by incorporated private businesses—is now 15.3 percent, its highest level since 1969. Since 1959, the capital share of corporate GDP has averaged 14.4 percent. Two, the 36.2 percent share of profits paid out in taxes is only slightly above the 34.2 percent low of the postwar period, and well below the 41.2 percent average since 1959. If any or all of these numbers revert to their averages since 1959, annual returns to stockholders will be even lower than the 4.36 percent shown in Table 2.

Table 3 (see pages 216–17) estimates annual returns in the stock market if any or all of these possibilities actually occur over the next forty-five years, a period that corresponds roughly to a working lifetime. The numbers in the first column show the annual returns based on the assumptions in Table 2—that is, if the price-to-earnings ratio, the capital share of GDP, and the tax share of profits all remain constant. The second column shows annual returns under all the same assumptions except that the capital share gradually falls back to its average over the past thirty-six years. The third column assumes that the capital share falls back to its average since 1959 *and* that the tax share of profits rises back to its average over the same period, while the dividend-to-price ratio remains the same. The fourth column assumes that the price-to-earnings ratio and the capital share of income gradually fall back to their average over the past thirty-six years, while the tax share and the dividend-to-price ratio gradually *rise* to their average levels.[18]

TABLE 3
Expected Annual Stock Returns

	1	2	3	4	5	6
1997	4.87%	4.73%	4.57%	3.92%	2.55%	4.17%
1998	4.87%	4.73%	4.57%	3.94%	2.59%	4.17%
1999	4.87%	4.73%	4.57%	3.95%	2.62%	4.17%
2000	4.87%	4.73%	4.57%	3.97%	2.66%	4.17%
2001	4.87%	4.73%	4.57%	3.98%	2.69%	4.17%
2002	4.87%	4.73%	4.57%	4.00%	2.73%	4.17%
2003	4.87%	4.73%	4.57%	4.01%	2.76%	4.17%
2004	4.87%	4.73%	4.57%	4.03%	2.80%	4.17%
2005	4.87%	4.73%	4.57%	4.05%	2.83%	4.17%
2006	4.87%	4.73%	4.57%	4.06%	2.87%	4.17%
2007	4.67%	4.53%	4.37%	3.88%	2.71%	4.17%
2008	4.67%	4.53%	4.37%	3.90%	2.75%	4.17%
2009	4.67%	4.53%	4.37%	3.91%	2.79%	4.17%
2010	4.67%	4.53%	4.37%	3.93%	2.83%	4.17%
2011	4.67%	4.53%	4.37%	3.94%	2.87%	4.12%
2012	4.67%	4.53%	4.37%	3.96%	2.91%	4.07%
2013	4.67%	4.53%	4.37%	3.98%	2.95%	4.02%
2014	4.67%	4.53%	4.37%	3.99%	2.99%	3.97%
2015	4.67%	4.53%	4.37%	4.01%	3.03%	3.92%
2016	4.67%	4.53%	4.37%	4.03%	3.07%	3.87%
2017	4.17%	4.03%	3.88%	3.55%	2.62%	3.82%
2018	4.17%	4.03%	3.88%	3.57%	2.66%	3.77%
2019	4.17%	4.03%	3.88%	3.58%	2.71%	3.72%
2020	4.17%	4.03%	3.88%	3.60%	2.75%	3.67%
2021	4.17%	4.03%	3.88%	3.62%	2.79%	3.66%
2022	4.17%	4.03%	3.88%	3.64%	2.84%	3.65%
2023	4.17%	4.03%	3.88%	3.65%	2.88%	3.64%
2024	4.17%	4.03%	3.88%	3.67%	2.93%	3.63%
2025	4.17%	4.03%	3.88%	3.69%	2.97%	3.62%
2026	4.17%	4.03%	3.88%	3.71%	3.02%	3.61%

TABLE 3
Expected Annual Stock Returns (Continued)

	1	2	3	4	5	6
2027	4.27%	4.13%	3.98%	3.82%	3.16%	3.60%
2028	4.27%	4.13%	3.98%	3.84%	3.21%	3.59%
2029	4.27%	4.13%	3.98%	3.86%	3.26%	3.58%
2030	4.27%	4.13%	3.98%	3.88%	3.31%	3.57%
2031	4.27%	4.13%	3.98%	3.89%	3.36%	3.56%
2032	4.27%	4.13%	3.98%	3.91%	3.41%	3.55%
2033	4.27%	4.13%	3.98%	3.93%	3.46%	3.54%
2034	4.27%	4.13%	3.98%	3.95%	3.51%	3.53%
2035	4.27%	4.13%	3.98%	3.97%	3.56%	3.52%
2036	4.27%	4.13%	3.98%	3.99%	3.61%	3.51%
2037	4.27%	4.13%	3.98%	4.01%	3.67%	3.50%
2038	4.27%	4.13%	3.98%	4.03%	3.72%	3.49%
2039	4.27%	4.13%	3.98%	4.04%	3.77%	3.48%
2040	4.27%	4.13%	3.98%	4.06%	3.83%	3.47%
2041	4.27%	4.13%	3.98%	4.08%	3.88%	3.44%
Average	4.47%	4.33%	4.17%	3.89%	3.04%	3.82%

Column 1 assumes constant price-to-earnings ratio and capital share
Column 2 assumes constant price-to-earning ratio and falling capital share
Column 3 assumes constant price-to-earnings ratio and rising tax share
Column 4 assumes falling price-to-earnings ratio and capital share and rising tax share
Column 5 assumes 1978 price-to-earnings ratio and capital and tax shares
Column 6 assumes Social Security Trustees' low-growth projections (see text for full
    explanation)

Source: Author's calculations using data from: Social Security Trustees, OASDI, *Annual Report of the Board of Trustees of the Old-Age and Survivors Insurance and Disabilities Insurance Trust Funds*; Federal Reserve Board web site, www.bog.frb.fed.us, Flow of Funds table; Bureau of Economic Analysis web site, www.bea.doc.gov, National Income Products Account table.

Think of the returns in the first column as a realistic, optimistic scenario, and of the returns in the fourth column as an intermediate scenario. To round out the picture, it is necessary to add a pessimistic scenario. Two possibilities appear in columns five and six. Column five shows rates of return if the price-to-earnings ratio and capital share of corporate GDP both gradually fall to their 1978 levels (8.8 to 1, and 14.2 percent, respectively), after the first oil shock and rising inflation sent the market reeling. This scenario assumes that the tax share of profits also returns to its 1978 level (43.6 percent), while the dividend-to-price ratio rises to its average since 1959 (3.65 percent). The returns shown in column six are based on the same assumptions as the calculations in column one, except they use the growth projections from the Social Security Trustees' pessimistic scenario. As noted before, the projections of economic growth in the intermediate scenario are already quite pessimistic, but many critics of Social Security, such as Concord Coalition founder Pete Peterson, have suggested that the pessimistic scenario may be more accurate. If this scenario is accepted as a basis for making policy decisions about Social Security, its implications must also be accepted in evaluating the benefits of mandated savings proposals.

The returns shown in Table 3 indicate that most calculations significantly overstate the retirement income that government-mandated savings would generate. Such calculations have generally assumed annual returns of 7 percent or more, but even the most optimistic scenario in Table 3 (column 1) projects returns averaging just 4.47 percent. And when all values—profit and tax shares, price- and dividend-to-earnings ratios—revert to their average over the previous thirty-six years in column 4, the returns average 3.89 percent. This scenario will be used as the intermediate scenario in subsequent calculations. In the scenario where values fall to their 1978 level, column 5, the average return is 3.04 percent. This scenario will be used as the pessimistic scenario in later calculations. These more realistic projections of returns to stockholders radically reduce the estimates of retirement income that private savings plans can generate.

> Realistic projections of returns to stockholders radically reduce the estimates of retirement income that private savings plans can generate.

It is also important to remember that all the scenarios in Table 3 are averages, not the actual returns a particular individual might receive. Actual returns will vary because in any particular year, or set of years, the stock market will not produce its *average* return but one that is somewhat higher or lower. Moreover, the returns on the actual stocks any particular individual holds will differ from the overall market average.

Inevitably, some people will retire and have to sell some or all of their stock at a point when the market has just taken a sharp downturn. From 1968 to 1978, for example, the stock market fell by 44.9 percent in real terms. If a person had been forced to sell stock to support his or her retirement at the low point of this market, the return would have been well below the market's historic average. Other people, as a result of bad judgment or bad luck, will end up with stocks that significantly underperform the market. These are risks associated with owning stock, and risks are the reason stocks offer higher *average* returns than other assets. While some winners do substantially better than the market average, it is equally certain there always will be some big losers.

> While some winners do substantially better than the market average, it is equally certain there always will be some big losers.

Before leaving the issue of estimated stock returns, it is worth considering one last possibility. Suppose projections of 7 percent real average annual stock market returns turn out to be accurate after all, and that the Social Security Trustees' projections of declining economic growth prove dead wrong. What would happen if—mirabile dictu—the economy actually grew fast enough to enable the stock market to provide 7 percent returns without price-to-earnings ratios soaring or wage growth falling to zero or worse? The Social Security Trust Fund would bulge almost beyond belief. Figure 3 (see page 220) shows how it would swell if the economy grew fast enough to allow 7 percent returns while price-to-earnings ratios and the profit share of income remained constant. Instead of dipping below zero in 2029, the Fund would reach $24.6 trillion, and by 2045 it would exceed $100 trillion. In short, if the Advisory Council's stock market projections are accurate, there is no need to fix Social Security. The system will be solvent for at least another century.[19]

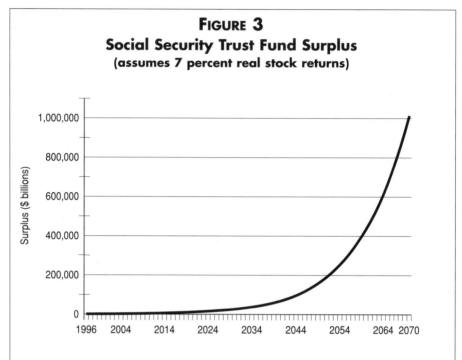

FIGURE 3
Social Security Trust Fund Surplus
(assumes 7 percent real stock returns)

Source: Author's calculations using data from: Social Security Trustees, OASDI, *Annual Report of the Board of Trustees of the Old-Age and Survivors Insurance and Disabilities Insurance Trust Funds;* Federal Reserve Board web site, www.bog.frb.fed.us, Flow of Funds table; Bureau of Economic Analysis web site, www.bea.doc.gov, National Income Products Account table.

3. THE HIDDEN COSTS OF PRIVATE ACCOUNTS

The returns in Table 3 could be used directly to project retirement income from mandated savings programs—if funds could be invested in the stock market free of charges and workers invested all their money in stocks. But maintaining individual accounts entails considerable costs, and most people will find it too risky to keep all their savings in the stock market throughout their working lives. These factors must be taken into account before estimating retirement income.

> Trading securities and commodities drains more than $100 billion in transaction costs from investors' returns each year.

Trading securities and commodities drains more than $100 billion in transaction costs from investors' returns each year. These costs are borne by holders of stock and other financial assets, and must be subtracted from their earnings to determine their actual return. The Advisory Council on Social Security estimates that these costs will average 1.0 percent of the value of equities held in personal savings accounts. This may significantly understate the true costs.

The average management fee of forty no-load mutual funds listed among "the best" in the growth and growth-and-income categories by *Fortune* magazine in 1996 was 0.98 percent.[20] But this figure includes only the cost of operating a fund, not the costs of trading stock. The average share of stock is traded every two years. Many funds trade far more actively, often turning over more than 100 percent of their portfolios in any given year. When a share is traded, the agent executing the trade charges a brokerage fee, and the specialty trader who runs the market charges another fee. A recent estimate pegs these costs at approximately 0.50 percent of the transaction price for institutional traders.[21] However, since the sale of one stock is usually accompanied by the purchase of another, the fees per trade would come to 1.0 percent of the amount traded. If a fund turns over 50 percent of its stocks each year, the transaction costs would be equal to 0.5 percent of the fund's value. This makes the total cost of administering an equity fund approximately 1.5 percent annually.

Mandated savings accounts would require far more oversight and regulation than mutual funds, however. Existing 401(k) accounts, which receive special tax treatment, may provide the best approximation; however, since these are voluntary, they should not require as much regulation as mandatory savings accounts. *Plan Sponsor* reports that the expense ratios for 401(k) plans holding mutual funds concentrated on equities average 1.44 percent a year.[22] Adding in the cost of trading stock pushes total administrative expenses to 1.94 percent a year.

The new accounts will also be considerably smaller, on average, than existing accounts. Many of the expenses for handling an account are fixed independently of the size of the account. This means that expenses may constitute a far greater percentage of the value of the newly created accounts for lower- and moderate-income workers than they do for the comparatively high-income individuals who own most accounts today.[23]

> Expenses may constitute a far greater percentage of the value of the newly created accounts for lower- and moderate-income workers than they do for the comparatively high-income individuals who own most accounts today.

It is also likely that many of the additional workers forced into the market for the first time will be less savvy in their choice of funds than experienced investors are. Many funds charge fees that are well above the average, including substantial up-front loads or redemption fees. This could cause the average expense ratio to rise.

Another factor to consider in estimating the fees associated with the proposed mandated accounts is insurance. If the accounts are guaranteed in some manner, as many proponents of mandated savings accounts advocate, an additional fee will have to cover this expense. Bodie and Merton estimated that the cost of the pension insurance provided by the Pension Benefit Guarantee Corporation is 0.15 percent of the assets for a fully funded program.[24] This guarantee covers only 70 percent of the specified level of benefits.

> If the accounts are guaranteed in some manner, as many proponents of mandated savings accounts advocate, an additional fee will have to cover this expense.

Clearly, there is considerable uncertainty about the fees that mandated savings accounts would entail, but it is possible to estimate these expenses within a range. At the low end, let us assume that expenses fall about 0.5 percentage points below the current average for 401(k) plans to 1.5 percent a year (including trading costs). A middle estimate assumes that the cost would remain about the same as the average cost of operating a 401(k) plan currently, 2.0 percent annually. The high-end estimate assumes that costs rise by 0.5 percentage points to 2.5 percent a year. Unless the government imposes regulations on fees, it is likely that lower-income workers will often end up near the top of this range because the cost of administering their accounts will be higher in percentage terms. For purposes of this analysis, let us assume that the annual fees will be 2.5 percent for a low-wage worker (making $12,000 a year),

2.0 percent for a middle-income worker ($25,000 per year), and 1.5 percent for a high-income worker ($50,000 per year).[25]

The last factor that needs to be considered in assessing the retirement income that mandated savings accounts could generate is the distribution of holdings among stocks and other assets. The calculations prepared for the Advisory Council assume that 50 percent of the holdings would be in stocks and 50 percent in bonds—roughly the mix today for people who have 401(k) retirement accounts. This is probably a reasonable assumption for projecting average returns, but it is important to note that many workers at present opt for much more conservative allocations and hold little or no stock.[26] This reduces risk but also lowers the expected return. Workers who follow this path will receive very low returns on their accounts and will not be able to accumulate much for retirement beyond the money they have actually set aside.

According to the Trustees' (and Advisory Council's) intermediate projections, the expected annual return from holding bonds is 2.3 percent. But holding bonds through a bond fund also entails expenses. The eight no-load bond funds listed by *Fortune* in 1996 averaged annual expenses of 0.72 percent. Although the commissions and spreads associated with bond trading are quite low, the turnover is enormous. Turnover in these bond funds averages more than 200 percent yearly. Let us estimate, very conservatively, that trading fees average 0.08 percent annually, raising total fees for bonds held in mandated savings accounts to an average of 0.8 percent a year.[27] The average fees associated with 401(k) plans holding bonds are actually somewhat higher. *Plan Sponsor* reported an average expense ratio, not counting trading costs, of 1.0.[28] For the analysis in the next section, let us assume that low-income workers pay total annual fees averaging 1.2 percent of their bond holdings, middle-income workers pay fees averaging 1.0 percent, and high-income workers pay fees averaging 0.8 percent.

3. Retiring with a Whimper, Not a Bang

Now the estimates of returns and holding costs for stocks and bonds can be combined to make back-of-the-envelope projections of the retirement income that mandated savings accounts could generate. The projections use the high-, middle-, and low-range scenarios for stock returns described in the second section of this paper. The return on bonds is the 2.3 percent projected by the Social Security Trustees. The annual holding costs for stocks and bonds follow the pattern described in the third section. The mix of assets is the same 50 percent in stocks and 50 percent in bonds assumed in the calculations prepared for the Advisory Council. The projections assume that workers' real wages will grow at the rate of overall wage growth projected in the Trustees' intermediate scenario, and also that a worker will be continuously employed during a working career of forty-six years. In every one of those years, workers will place 5 percent of their wages, as specified in the Schieber-Weaver proposal, in a mandated savings account.

Table 4 shows what a low-income worker now making $12,000 a year, a middle-income worker with an annual wage of $25,000, and a high-income worker with a salary of $50,000 might expect to accumulate by the end of their working careers, and the average rate of return on their holdings in the low-, middle-, and high-range scenarios. It also shows the wage each worker can expect to be making in the last year of his or her career. All calculations are in 1996 dollars. The returns range from 2.2 percent for high-income workers in the optimistic scenario to just 0.8 percent for low-income workers in the pessimistic scenario.

TABLE 4
Lifetime Accumulations

	Final Wage	Low Return	Mid Return	High Return
Low Income	18,778	42,393	45,767	48,356
Middle Income	39,120	95,754	103,621	109,661
High Income	78,240	208,006	225,630	239,162

Average Net Returns

	Low Return	Mid Return	High Return
Low Income	0.79%	1.21%	1.50%
Middle Income	1.14%	1.56%	1.95%
High Income	1.49%	1.91%	2.20%

Source: calculations using data from Social Security Trustees, OASDI, *Annual Report of the Board of Trustees of the Old-Age and Survivors Insurance and Disabilities Insurance Trust Funds.*

Table 5 shows the number of years that these sums could support retirees with incomes that would be 30 percent, 50 percent, and 70 percent, respectively, of their last working year's wages.

The calculations in Table 5 assume that workers receive a real interest rate of 2 percent on their accumulations after they retire.[29] In the high-return scenario, the accumulation will be sufficient to support a low-income worker at 30 percent of final pay for 9.5 years. It will support a high-income worker at a 30 percent level for 11.5 years. At a 50 percent replacement ratio, a low-income worker would be supported for 5.5 years and a high-income worker for 6.6 years. In the low-return scenario, a low-income worker would be supported at a mere 30 percent of final wages for just 8.2 years, and a high-income worker for 9.8 years.

TABLE 5
Years of Retirement Income

LOW RETURN

Percentage of Final Wage	30%	50%	70%
Low Income	8.20	4.80	3.40
Middle Income	9.00	5.20	3.70
High Income	9.80	5.70	4.00

MIDDLE RETURN

Percentage of Final Wage	30%	50%	70%
Low Income	8.90	5.20	3.60
Middle Income	9.80	5.60	4.00
High Income	10.70	6.20	4.30

HIGH RETURN

Percentage of Final Wage	30%	50%	70%
Low Income	9.50	5.50	3.80
Middle Income	10.40	6.00	4.20
High Income	11.50	6.60	4.60

Table assumes 2 percent real return after retirement

Source: Calculations using data from Social Security Trustees, OASDI, *Annual Report of the Board of Trustees of the Old-Age and Survivors Insurance and Disabilities Insurance Trust Funds.*

But the Social Security Trustees estimate that the life expectancy of Americans who turn 65 in 2040 will be an another 17.2 years for men, and 20.9 years for women. That is an average retirement of 19 years. Over that long a period of time, mandated savings plans could provide 19.0 percent annually of a high-income retiree's final salary in the optimistic scenario, and just 14.0 percent of a low-income retiree's wages in the pessimistic scenario. In the optimistic scenario, a worker earning $50,000 a year at retirement would have an income of $9,500 a year. In the pessimistic scenario, workers earning $12,000 at retirement would receive $1,680 annually from their accumulations.

Social Security as currently structured promises to pay these low-income workers an annual income equal to 56.7 percent of their final wages, regardless of the scenario for return on investments or whether they live for nine, nineteen, or thirty more years. The middle-income worker will receive 43.9 percent of final salary, and the high-income worker 31.4 percent.[30] These numbers cannot provide a direct or fair comparison between mandated savings and Social Security, of course, because the Social Security program will require some combination of tax increases and benefit reductions to remain solvent. Also, most mandated savings proposals, like the Schieber-Weaver plan, provide for a poverty-level benefit of approximately $5000 a year in addition to whatever money is accumulated privately. On the other hand, the tax increases specified by the Schieber-Weaver plan and some other mandated savings proposals are of approximately the same magnitude as the tax increases, accompanied by some benefit reductions, that would be needed to keep Social Security in its current form solvent.

> The tax increases specified by the Schieber-Weaver plan and some other mandated savings proposals are of approximately the same magnitude as the tax increases, accompanied by some benefit reductions, that would be needed to keep Social Security in its current form solvent.

Another important factor in evaluating alternatives is that Social Security provides its payout in the form of an annuity that continues for the life of the worker and is not diminished by inflation. Annuities are very costly in the private market, and insurance against inflation is generally unobtainable.[31] Therefore, the dollar sums provided by Social Security significantly understate the true value of the benefit for workers seeking a secure retirement.

That a system of government-mandated savings cannot, by itself, increase savings and economic growth is well known among economists. However, many economists have accepted the view that such a system can generate higher incomes for retirees by investing funds in the stock market. By now it should be clear that this view is false. Its advocates on the Advisory Council are hoist on the petard of the Social Security Trustees' own projections. The projected returns for stockholders are demonstrably inconsistent with projections for growth in the economy, and stock market returns that are consistent with projected economic growth will not provide current workers with a prosperous retirement.

V

ASSESSING PROPOSALS TO SAVE SOCIAL SECURITY

13

RESTORING SOCIAL SECURITY TO LONG-TERM BALANCE: WHAT SHOULD BE DONE?

ROBERT M. BALL
with THOMAS N. BETHELL

As has been the pattern for the past several years, the Social Security Trustees in their 1997 report, looking ahead for 75 years, anticipate a long-term deficit, which they estimate at an average of 2.23 percent of payroll.[1] If we act promptly, we can substantially reduce this projected deficit without having to make major tax increases or benefit cuts and without sacrificing or compromising the basic principles and traditional advantages of the program. There is no need to turn to a system of individual accounts, which in themselves do nothing to help the long-range balance of Social Security.* A large part of the job of restoring the program to long-term balance can be done by making several relatively minor changes.

---

*See Chapter 4 of *Straight Talk about Social Security* for a discussion of this issue.

From Robert M. Ball with Thomas N. Bethell, *Straight Talk about Social Security: An Analysis of the Issues in the Current Debate* (New York: The Century Foundation Press, 1998), Chapter 2.

Minor Changes Similar to
Those Made in the Past

To begin with, the options available include several that are entirely within the tradition of the present Social Security program:

◆   extending coverage in order to make the program truly universal;

◆   increasing taxation of benefits in line with taxation of other defined-benefit contributory plans;

◆   improving the accuracy of cost-of-living adjustments in accordance with anticipated changes to the Consumer Price Index;

◆   moderately increasing future taxes; and

◆   moderately reducing future benefits.

The first three of these changes would be desirable in any case from an equity standpoint. Whether or not all of them are politically feasible right now is a matter for discussion.

1.   Make the Program Truly Universal

Over time, almost all occupational groups have been incorporated into the Social Security program, and coverage is now nearly universal, including most full-time state and local government employees. But about 25 percent of these state and local employees are not covered. This is the last large group of excluded workers. Phasing them into the program would be beneficial to Social Security's financing largely because, as with other groups when newly covered, revenues accrue for many years before benefits must be paid out. The effect of this change is to reduce the long-term 2.23 percent-of-payroll deficit by about 10 percent or 0.25 percent of payroll.

It would be advantageous to these workers and their families to be part of the universal system while retaining supplementary protection under their own plans. They would have greater freedom to change jobs without forfeiting protection; improved protection against inflation; better survivor and disability protection in most cases; and reliable coverage for spouses (which is not required under some state and local government pension plans). And in any case, it is only fair for all state and local employees to be contributing to the nation's social insurance system, which protects them as taxpayers against what could otherwise be the very substantial tax burden of supporting much larger welfare and relief programs.

The best approach would be to phase in Social Security coverage by covering only new hires, as was done when coverage was extended to federal employees. This gives the employing entity time to adapt to any increases in cost, and if provision is made for implementing this change a year or two after enactment, there will also be time to work out the integration of Social Security with state and local retirement systems in order to ensure that employees have optimal protection. There will be opposition in particular states, but it should be possible to get agreement for this change.

2. Increase the Taxation of Benefits

It is reasonable to ask present beneficiaries to help bring Social Security into long-term balance, as long as the burden is fairly distributed. The most equitable way to do this is to apply the progressive income tax rules to Social Security benefits in the same way they apply to other contributory defined-benefit plans, so that Social Security benefits are taxed to the extent that they exceed what the worker paid in. This change would reduce the projected long-term deficit by about 0.13 percent of payroll.

In connection with this change, as a matter of fairness Social Security beneficiaries should not be given the special exemption from income taxes that they now have solely because of being beneficiaries, whereas other people with the same level of income are taxed. Accordingly, the current exemption for beneficiaries with annual incomes below $25,000 for single persons and $32,000 for couples should be repealed. Beneficiaries at the lower end of the income scale (about 30 percent of all beneficiaries) would be unaffected by this change because their benefits would remain untaxed under general income tax rules protecting low-income people. This change would save Social Security another 10 percent or about 0.23 percent of payroll.[2]

3. IMPROVE THE ACCURACY OF SOCIAL SECURITY COST-OF-LIVING ADJUSTMENTS

The Bureau of Labor Statistics (BLS) is currently considering changes to the Consumer Price Index (CPI) in order to improve its accuracy in measuring inflation. There seems to be general agreement that any correction of the CPI should be reflected in Social Security Cost-of-Living Adjustments (COLA). Although occasionally the argument is made that there should be a separate CPI for the elderly, this line of reasoning is probably not a major barrier to translating a BLS reduction in the CPI into reduced COLA increases. (The 1994-96 Advisory Council agreed that it would be an unwise precedent to change the CPI measure by legislation without BLS support, believing that adjustment should be based on technical considerations rather than introduce political competition, as would inevitably accompany any effort to change the CPI by legislation in the absence of a BLS recommendation.)

It is now reasonable to anticipate a downward adjustment in the expected CPI growth rate of 0.20 percentage points as a result of BLS's stated intent to correct the "lower level substitution bias" by 1999. BLS now proposes to substitute a geometric weighting in the formula for the present arithmetic weighting in a major proportion of the some 9,000 categories in the CPI market basket. Additional reduction would result if the market basket were brought up to date more often than the present 10-year timetable. If done every year, which seems reasonable given the importance of this measure, the reduction would be another 0.10 percentage point or so. For the purpose of these cost estimates, the assumption is that there will be a total reduction of 0.30 percentage points in the CPI—0.20 percentage points from the introduction of geometric weighting and 0.10 from updating the market basket annually. This results in reducing the long-range deficit by nearly 19 percent, or 0.42 percent of payroll.

The combined effect of these three changes that improve the equity and accuracy of the system is to reduce the projected deficit from 2.23 percent of payroll to 1.34 percent. Small increases in taxes and cuts in benefits reduce the deficit further.

4. Increase the Maximum Earnings Base

At one time, the maximum earnings base—the level of annual earnings above which earnings are neither taxed nor credited for the purpose of computing benefits—represented 90 percent of all wages in covered employment. Today, however, the base ($68,400 in 1998) is covering a smaller and smaller proportion of earnings; this is a result of the fact that wages are increasing faster for the higher-paid than for others. By 2006 the base is expected to cover only 84.5 percent of earnings. Under present law, the base is scheduled to increase automatically each year with increases in average wages. It would take an additional 4 percent each year between the years 2000 and 2009 in order to bring the proportion of earnings covered back up to 90 percent. But with the base now considerably below that target, increases of the magnitude necessary to entirely close the gap may be ill-advised. Higher-income earners would be required to contribute substantially more but without being able to expect anything like a commensurate increase in benefits. Accordingly, I would propose closing only half of the gap—that is, going from 84.5 to 87.3 percent over 10 years—by increasing the maximum earnings base 2 percent each year above the automatic increase. The effect in any given year would ordinarily be modest as compared to the automatic increase taking place anyway. This change reduces the projected long-term deficit by about 0.27 percent of payroll.

5. Increase the Length of the Averaging Period

The wage averaging period, which for decades now has started for almost all workers with 1951, has been gradually increasing as wages have been posted for more and more years. In 1991, wages were being posted for 40 years and, as has always been the case when averaging, retired workers were allowed to drop the five years of lowest earnings, resulting in 1991 in basing benefits on the average of the highest 35 years. This is the maximum number required in the basic law, so the averaging period has remained at 35 years since 1991. Setting the basic limit at 35 years is entirely arbitrary. The objective is to relate the benefit to the worker's career earnings, indexed to the present and with some leeway for periods of illness, unemployment, or special family obligations. With additional years of earnings since 1991, it is now feasible to relate the benefit to a somewhat longer career average while maintaining the five-year forgiveness period. Since most people work more than 35 years, counting more years would cause benefits to reflect average career earnings more accurately than they now do. But lengthening the averaging period also lowers benefits because earnings for currently excluded years are necessarily lower than the 35 highest years now used in computing benefits. Doing so reduces benefits somewhat for those with fewer years under the program and those who have less than full-year earnings. Raising the end point to 38 years would reduce benefits an average of 3 percent and reduce the Social Security deficit by 0.27 percent of payroll. The comparable figures for 39 and 40 years are 4 percent and 0.48 percent and 5 percent and 0.59, respectively (without adjusting for interaction with any other changes).

A good case can be made for this method of trimming benefits, but the proposal does arouse controversy. It reduces benefits somewhat more for workers with intermittent rather than steady wage records. Since women are more likely than men to go in and out of the workforce, the argument is made that this proposal is disadvantageous to more women than men. This is true to a limited extent, but because of Social Security's weighted benefit formula, which favors those with intermittent wage records, and because of the continuance of the five-year forgiveness period, workers going in and out of the workforce would continue to receive very favorable treatment. The issue is whether to favor the intermittent worker slightly less than under present law.

The net effect of these five proposals, as shown in Table 1, is to reduce the projected long-term deficit from 2.23 percent of payroll to 0.72 percent.

This brings the deficit well within the customary definition of "close actuarial balance"—that is, with expenditures within 5 percent of income over the long run—and postpones the estimated date of trust fund exhaustion by more than 20 years, pushing it back from 2030 to beyond 2050.

One could argue that this would be enough for a first step toward long-term balance, and that additional options could then be explored over the next few years. After all, the 1977 amendments aimed at achieving a 50-year rather than a 75-year balance, and 50 years is a

TABLE 1
RESTORING SOCIAL SECURITY TO LONG-TERM BALANCE: AN INITIAL PACKAGE OF OPTIONS TO REDUCE THE DEFICIT*

Proposal	Comment	Reduces Deficit
1. Make the program universal, gradually extending coverage to all full-time state and local government workers by covering workers hired after 2000.	Most state and local government workers are already covered by Social Security. The 3.7 million who are not are the last major group in the labor force not covered.	-0.25
2. Increase the taxation of benefits and drop the special income tax exemption that applies only to Social Security beneficiaries.	Benefits should be taxed to the extent they exceed what the worker has paid in, as in other contributory defined-benefit plans, and dropping the special exemption would improve income tax equity (the lowest income beneficiaries, about 30% of the total, would still be untaxed).	-0.36
3. Change the Social Security cost-of-living adjustment (COLA) to reflect corrections to the Consumer Price Index (CPI).	With the CPI presently believed to overstate inflation, changes contemplated by BLS plus annual pricing of the market basket should result in a more accurate CPI and smaller COLAs.	-0.42
4. Increase the maximum earnings base an additional 2% each year during the 2000–2009 period.	At one time 90% of wages in covered employment were under the base, above which earnings are neither taxed nor credited for benefit computation purposes. The base will soon cover only 84.5% of wages; this change moves halfway back to the 90% standard, increasing coverage to 87.3%.	-0.27
5. Increase the length of the wage-averaging period for benefit computation purposes from 35 to 38 years.	Current 35-year averaging period is arbitrary. As the longevity of the program increases, it is feasible to extend the averaging period. Increasing it from 35 to 38 years, and thus more closely relating benefits to the worker's career-long earnings, reduces benefits for those becoming eligible in the future by 3% on average.	-0.27
Balance after implementing above changes (*adjusted for interaction of proposals*):		-0.72%

*Assumes an average long-term (75-year) deficit of 2.23% of payroll as estimated by the Social Security Trustees.

long time indeed compared to the much shorter periods over which other nations view their social insurance systems. I would prefer, however, to recommend changes now that will eliminate the entire 75-year deficit.

This could be done by providing for a modest increase in the contribution rate and a modest reduction in replacement rates beyond the benefit cut that results from lengthening the averaging period and increasing the taxation of benefits.

6. INCREASE THE CONTRIBUTION RATE

Increasing the contribution rate by 0.20 percentage points for workers, matched by employers, assures that wage-earners will be making at least a modest contribution to closing the long-range deficit. This proposal would increase what they pay by $20 per $10,000 of annual earnings (see Table 2). This change would reduce the remaining long-term deficit by 0.37 percent of payroll—leaving 0.35 percent of payroll to be met by a benefit cut. Since the benefits

TABLE 2
RESTORING SOCIAL SECURITY TO LONG-TERM BALANCE:
PACKAGE 2 OF OPTIONS TO CONSIDER
(In combination with the first five proposals summarized in Table 1)

Option	Comment	Reduces Deficit
6. Increase the contribution rate by 0.20 percentage points.	Amounts to deducting $20 per $10,000 of annual earnings.	-0.37
7. Reduce benefits by modifying the benefit formula gradually so as to maintain 1997 real benefit levels but cut replacement rates 5% by 2029.	Assumes that future beneficiaries should share in sacrifices needed to reach long-term balance. Reduces replacement rates but ensures that beneficiaries in the future get at least the benefit amounts going currently to new beneficiaries.	-0.35
Balance after implementing above changes (*adjusted for interaction of proposals*):		-0.04%

payable in the future under present law are not by any means too high, benefit cuts beyond those resulting from the suggested increase in the tax on benefits and the lengthening of the averaging period, as discussed above, are undesirable, but modifying the benefit formula to produce a moderate cut should be considered if other options, discussed later, are rejected.

7. MODIFY THE PRESENT BENEFIT FORMULA

An additional way to reduce benefits is to change the benefit formula. This can be done, of course, without changing the relative positions of intermittent and steady workers or the positions of the low-paid. On the other hand, when such a change is made the positions of low-paid and intermittent workers could be improved at the expense of the higher-paid.

Since the formula is already skewed substantially in favor of those who are worse off, I would urge that any cuts from a benefit-formula change be evenhanded across the range of covered wages. It is important to retain the support of higher-paid workers for Social Security, and it is a matter of delicate balance to determine just how far it is wise to go in pursuing income redistribution through this program. It seems to me that we now have it about right.

If a benefit cut is deemed necessary, it should not affect those already retired, and should be phased in so that the benefits for those retiring in the future are not cut below the amounts being paid to those retiring today. This can be done because, while present law maintains benefits at approximately a fixed percentage of past earnings (the replacement rate), new benefit amounts rise for future retirees as wages rise (wages are assumed to rise 0.9 percent per year faster than the CPI). If benefits are reduced, the timing should be such that future beneficiaries get lower replacement rates but not lower real benefits. This principle requires timing the reductions in the replacement rate to take into account the provision of present law that, beginning in the year 2000, gradually raises the normal retirement age from 65 to 67.

The benefit formula for 1998 is 90 percent of the first $477 of average indexed monthly earnings (AIME), 32 percent of the next $2,875 of AIME, and 15 percent for any AIME above that. A 3 percent cut in average benefits could be achieved by changes in the three factors. This cut could be made gradually beginning with beneficiaries becoming eligible in 2020 and reaching 3 percent (87.3, 31.04, and 14.55) for those becoming eligible in 2029 and later. A 5 percent reduction could be reached by changing the three factors to 85.5, 30.4, and 14.25. These cuts would save 0.21 percent of payroll for the 3 percent cut (see Table 2) and 0.35 percent of payroll for the 5 percent cut. Under this approach and with these effective dates, real benefits for future retirees would never be less than benefits being paid to new retirees today.

ADDITIONAL OPTIONS

There are other options—alternatives to the above proposals—that would also bring the program into long-range balance. Two in particular deserve attention here because, whatever their merit, they will certainly be considered as part of the legislative process.

8.   INCREASE THE NORMAL RETIREMENT AGE BEYOND THE PROVISIONS OF CURRENT LAW

The normal retirement age (NRA), the age of first eligibility for full benefits, is now 65. Under present law it is scheduled to increase gradually to age 67 in 2022. Benefits could be reduced by providing for further increases. Accelerating the scheduled change and raising the NRA automatically as longevity increases is an approach that has attracted considerable support, and one that was endorsed by eight members of the 1994–96 Advisory Council. I am opposed to any such change, particularly in the near term, for the reasons discussed in the council report.[3] But if anything along this line is done, the least harmful approach would be to let present law stand until the NRA reaches 67 in 2022, and *then* begin indexing it to life expectancy. This would allow sufficient time before the change becomes effective to see whether in fact the present-law change to 67 is working out and whether workers both want to and are able to work later into their lives. If the necessary societal adjustments are slow in coming, the indexing timetable could be adjusted. This change would reduce the projected long-term deficit by another 14 percent or 0.30 percent of payroll.

9. APPLY THE SOCIAL SECURITY TAX ON EMPLOYERS TO THE ENTIRE PAYROLL

The amount of wages on which workers pay Social Security taxes is the same amount used for benefit credits. This is an important principle that follows from the concept of Social Security benefits making up for wage loss because of the old age, disability, or death of a family breadwinner. The principle preserves the contributory nature of the system and limits the amount of redistribution from higher-paid to lower-paid wage-earners in a way that seems reasonable to most Social Security participants. If, on the other hand, workers were required to pay on all earnings without limit, the relationship of benefits to contributions would be greatly weakened, and with this weakening would come the possibility of a very different attitude toward Social Security on the part of the higher-paid.

The tax on the employer, however, can be thought of as going to the Social Security system in general rather than being linked to each individual employee, and a case can be made that, as a tax on payrolls, it should be applied to the entire payroll. This would reduce the deficit by well over half, or 1.20 percent of payroll. (The reduction is as large as it is because there are no offsetting benefit increases, as would be the case with an increase in the maximum earnings base governing both taxes and benefit credits.)[4]

10. INVEST PART OF SOCIAL SECURITY'S BUILDUP IN STOCKS

Another change that would eliminate the need for either the benefit cuts or the contribution rate increases discussed above as items 6 and 7 would be to invest a portion of the Social Security trust fund in private equities. Under present law the traditionally pay-as-you-go Social Security system moves in the direction of partial advance funding with a trust fund buildup until about 2020, but then dissipates the trust fund over the following 10 years and does not rebuild it. However, various combinations of the proposals discussed above designed to bring the program into long-range balance have the effect of building the fund indefinitely into the future and explicitly shifting the system to partial advance funding. (This would substantially reduce the contribution rates needed to support the system as compared to pay-as-you-go rates; see Tables 4, page 250, and 5, page 251, later in this discussion.)

Building a fund of considerable size, as would now happen, raises sharply for the first time the issue of trust fund investment. As long as the system followed a pay-as-you-go plan, with reserves at a contingency level equal to only about one to one-and-a-half times the following year's outgo, the investment returns had little effect on long-range financing. But with the fund building because of partial advance funding, the rate of return on investment becomes important. A policy of investing part of the fund buildup in stocks—rather than exclusively in lower-yielding long-term government bonds, as required by present law—could make a major contribution to reducing the long-term deficit and make benefit cuts or contribution-rate increases as described above unnecessary. Investing 40 percent of Social Security's accumulating funds in equities would reduce the deficit by approximately 0.92 percent of payroll. (Interaction with other proposals could reduce this effect by as much as 10 percent but would still be enough to eliminate the 0.72 deficit left after adopting universal coverage, additional taxation of benefits, taking account of BLS changes in the CPI, increasing the earnings base, and lengthening the averaging period [see Table 1].)

Just about all other public and private pension plans invest in stocks, and Social Security contributors should have the same advantages that are available to participants in other plans. Improving investment returns for Social Security would not only help eliminate its projected deficit but would also improve the benefit/contribution ratio for younger workers and future generations. In fact, if the problem presented for solution is not solely the elimination of the long-term deficit but also the improvement in the Social Security rate of return for young workers, there is an additional important reason for interest in direct equity investment.

The problem of the relatively low rate of return in Social Security for those now young as compared to the rate of return experienced by earlier participants in Social Security arises because, when the Social Security program began, it was decided to pay retirement benefits to the first generation of workers even though their contributions to the system fell far short of paying for their own benefits. This started the system down the road of pay-as-you-go rather than reserve financing.

It would have been possible to have had a fund buildup in addition to paying benefits from the beginning, but in practice this was never done. For decades the Social Security Act provided for future contribution-rate levels that would have done just that, giving us a system of partial-advance funding, as is now so widely advocated. (Virtually no one advocated the sacrifices that would have been necessary to produce full funding and full current payments.) But these rates were never allowed to go into effect, and the system has operated close to pay-as-you-go. Now, unless the system is changed, there is little financial help to be expected from earnings on the present Social Security fund, as there would be in the case of a system of private or, for that matter, public investment. Thus, in comparing future rates of return from a funded system and Social Security, Social Security is at a disadvantage equal, in the first instance, to what the earnings would have been on the accumulation of a full reserve.

On the other hand, our national system of Social Security has much lower administrative costs than would be the case under most of the current proposals to shift the system toward relying on individual investment accounts. The costs of managing the accounts plus the added costs (in some proposals) of converting the accumulated funds to annuities at market rates upon retirement would greatly reduce the real rates of return, to the point where they would compare very unfavorably with the rate of return from a Social Security system centrally investing in equities.

For example, under the Personal Security Accounts (PSA) plan proposed by five members of the 1994–96 Advisory Council, workers would contribute 5 percent of earnings annually to private accounts. Over 40 years, the annual cost of managing the accounts (estimated by the PSA plan's sponsors at one percent of the accumulating funds) would reduce the benefits by 20 percent or more. On top of that, the cost of converting the account balances into annuities (an option under the PSA plan rather than compulsory as in some other proposals) would reduce the benefit by another 20 percent or so—in part because of the cost of adverse selection (the risk that annuities, which guarantee an income until death, will be disproportionately purchased by those most likely to live long into retirement). Benefits under the PSA approach are thus reduced over the long term by 40 percent or more. Clearly, whatever financial advantage is obtainable by partial funding in a private accounts system is obtainable by the same degree of funding in a central Social Security system, without the administrative costs of individual accounts.

Not all of the partial privatization plans have the administrative drawbacks of the PSA plan. For example, the Individual Accounts (IA) plan proposed by 1994–96 Advisory Council chairman Edward Gramlich avoids the market costs of buying annuities by making conversion of funds to annuities compulsory and thus universal. And because the IA plan would channel individual investments into a limited number of government-managed funds, its administrative costs would be much lower than the PSA plan with its essentially unlimited choice of investment vehicles. (But the IA plan has many drawbacks of its own.*

Nevertheless it is highly desirable to improve the rate of return under Social Security for young workers and future generations who see themselves as disadvantaged compared to recipients who came before, and as the 1994–96 Advisory Council recognized, any solutions to the long-term deficit problem requiring benefit cuts or increased contributions make future rates of return for Social Security lower. In this context, investment in equities is especially attractive. This would improve the rate of return for workers now young and for future generations, while at the same time greatly reducing the Social Security deficit.

The rate of return is, of course, only one criterion among many for determining what is the best retirement system for the long run. But even if the rate of return were given great emphasis and there was a desire to move very substantially toward a funded system for the future, there is a large transition cost that would have to be paid by the generation of workers just now beginning work and perhaps by the next one as well. Whether the accumulating funds arise through private accounts or through a change in the government plan, the transition generation(s) would have to pay twice: once to pay for the benefits of those who have accumulated rights under the present system and once for their own at least partially funded benefits.

The six of us on the Advisory Council who pressed for consideration of trust fund investment in equities developed the outline of a model[5] designed to protect the neutrality of investment policy by indexing investments to practically the entire market. The selection of indexes and portfolio managers would be under the general direction of a Federal Reserve-type board with members appointed for long and staggered terms. Portfolio managers would be selected by

---

*See Chapter 4 of *Straight Talk about Social Security* for a detailed discussion of the plan's drawbacks.

bid from organizations qualified by long experience with very large, indexed private funds.[6]

Relying on the market for retirement income is risky for the individual—in part because the dates of investing are more or less fixed by the time of first going to work and the time of retiring. Although the individual would have the choice of moving investments between equities and bonds, investors could hardly anticipate when such shifts would be desirable except for the general pattern of emphasis on equities when young, with increasing amounts in bonds as retirement approaches. In contrast, direct investment by Social Security would be very long term, and consequently the volatility of the market would have little effect in the long run on the income from stocks held by Social Security.

Without regard to how it is invested, a sizable increase in national savings would result from shifting Social Security from pay-as-you-go to partial reserve financing. As the fund builds up so do national savings, but the key point is that growth in national savings comes principally from a shift to partial reserve financing, not from how the accumulating fund is invested.[7] In considering whether to allow Social Security investment in stocks, the most important consideration would be equity, not national savings. It is only equitable for Social Security contributors to get an equal return for what they pay in, as do contributors to other types of retirement plans, since both forms of saving make the same contribution to the broad economy. Equal treatment for Social Security participants is a matter of particular importance from the standpoint of income distribution, given that Social Security covers just about all workers, including the low-paid, while private pensions provide supplements for only about half of the workforce, and predominantly for the higher-paid at that.

Such a change in investment policy is not necessary to bring the system into long-term balance, which can be accomplished entirely by selecting from the more traditional proposals discussed earlier. But this method of giving workers' contributions to Social Security more financial power offers an attractive alternative to benefit cuts and contribution rate increases, and over the long run greatly improves the ratio of contributions to benefits for long-term contributors. And there is another positive by-product from having a substantial part of the trust fund buildup invested in equities. To the extent that this is done and funds are not lent to the government in return for government bonds, public confusion is avoided. Today, with the trust fund investing solely in government bonds, this is widely misinterpreted as "Social Security funds are being spent for other purposes" and "Social Security funds are not really contributing to savings."

One way or another, eliminating Social Security's long-range deficit requires generating more income or less outgo. But the methods chosen may affect Social Security participants—including both current beneficiaries and wage-earners and future beneficiaries and wage-earners—very differently. Three of the changes discussed earlier—extending coverage to those state and local employees now excluded (thus increasing income), increasing the taxation of benefits and eliminating the special tax exemption applying only to Social Security beneficiaries, and making the CPI more accurate (thus reducing outgo)—would contribute to restoring long-range balance as a by-product of making the program more equitable. And allowing Social Security to invest directly in equities would result in properly allocating income from the economic contributions made by Social Security and private investments, such as private pensions, and in providing for a fairer distribution of the returns from retirement saving. The remaining proposals discussed above are simply benefit cuts or tax increases. They require sacrifices—but sacrifices that can be broadly shared so that no one group has to sacrifice very much.

Table 3 (see pages 248–49) summarizes the major options and their impact on the deficit.

Although I believe it has major disadvantages, another way to eliminate the deficit is to explicitly turn to pay-as-you-go as the long-range plan and institute a schedule of pay-as-you-go tax rate increases in the law. Table 4 (see page 250) shows the contribution rates that would be needed based on present benefit and financing provisions (that is, without any of the proposed changes summarized in Table 3).

Still another possibility would be a hybrid of partial advance funding and pay-as-you-go, resulting from selecting some of the changes described in Table 3 and later, when necessary, introducing a pay-as-you-go contribution rate.

If the changes selected for near-term enactment were those summarized in Table 1, reducing the long-range deficit to 0.72 percent of payroll, the contribution rate would need to climb to 7.4 percent of earnings in about 2040 and to 8.1 percent in 2070 (see Table 5, page 251). But the contribution-rate increases required under pay-as-you-go financing, even though long postponed under this hybrid approach, share with any tax increase or benefit cut the undesirable effect of worsening the benefit/contribution ratio for younger work-ers, and the rates are of course higher than needed under partial advance funding.

In March 1998, Senator Daniel Patrick Moynihan of New York, the ranking Democrat on the Senate Finance Committee, proposed modifying Social Security to keep it quite literally and strictly on a pay-as-you-go basis (as he had previously recommended in 1989). He would cut the contribution rate for the employer and for the employ-ee from the current rate of 6.2 percent of earnings to 5.2 percent for the next 30 years,[8] thus preventing any substantial buildup in the fund. Senator Robert Kerrey (D., Neb.) joined in this proposal.

The effect of reducing income to the program over the next 30 years is, of course, to increase the long-range Social Security deficit, bringing it up from the estimated 2.23 percent of payroll under present law to nearly 3 percent. Under a pay-as-you-go approach, this change, by itself, would necessitate very large contribution-rate increases after 2030, rising to over 9 percent by 2070, as shown in Table 4.

To avoid such major tax increases over the long run, a strict pay-as-you-go plan would have to make major cuts in benefits. In Senator Moynihan's proposal, the cuts reach 30 percent. To make up for these cuts—at least in part—he proposes to create a voluntary savings plan to be financed by the reduction in Social Security taxes. The worker, whose Social Security tax is reduced by one percentage point under the plan, can choose to put this 1 percent of earnings in a savings plan to be matched by the employer, who also has had a one per-centage point reduction in the tax. The employer does not have to pay this 1 percent unless the employee makes the election.

Under a voluntary approach, of course, there is no way of know-ing to what extent workers would elect to save rather than spend the 1 percent and thus attract the employer match. Perhaps most of the higher-paid would do so, although many would certainly offset at least part of the 1 percent against saving they are already making. For those who choose to save, the deductions from the worker's earn-ings plus the employer contribution would, over the next 30 years, equal the 6.2 percent of payroll required under present law for Social Security. But beginning in 2030 the percent of earnings per worker for the two proposals combined would reach 7.2 percent; later, 7.7 per-cent would be required, with the employer paying a like amount.

Workers who did not elect to save the 1 percent reduction—probably a high percentage of the lower-paid—would suffer the full

TABLE 3

OPTIONS TO BRING SOCIAL SECURITY INTO LONG-TERM BALANCE*

Option	Comment	Reduces Deficit**
1. Make the program universal, gradually extending coverage to all full-time state and local government workers hired after 2000.	Most state and local government employees are already covered. The 3.7 million who are not are the last major group in labor force not covered	-0.25
2. Increase the taxation of benefits and drop the special income tax exemption applying only to Social Security beneficiaries.	Benefits should be taxed to the extent they exceed what worker has paid in, as in other contributory defined-benefit plans, and dropping the special exemption would improve income tax equity (lowest-income beneficiaries, about 30% of total, would still be untaxed).	-0.36
3. Change the Social Security Cost of Living Adjustment (COLA) to reflect corrections to the Consumer Price Index (CPI).	With the CPI presently believed to overstate inflation, changes announced by BLS plus annual pricing of the market basket should result in more accurate CPI and smaller COLAs.	-0.42
4. Raise maximum earnings base an additional 2% each year from 2000 to 2009.	At one time, 90% of wages in covered employment were under this base, above which earnings are neither taxed nor credited for benefit-computation purposes. Under present law the base is expected to cover only 84.5% of wages by 2006. This change goes halfway toward the 90% standard, increasing coverage to 87.3%.	-0.27
5. Increase the length of the wage-averaging period for benefit computation purposes from 35 to 38 years.	Current 35-year averaging period is arbitrary and has not been increased since 1991 despite increased longevity of program. Extending it to 38 to 40 years is feasible; extending it to 38 reduces benefits for those becoming eligible in the future by 3% on average.	-0.27
5a. Increase the wage-averaging period from 35 to 40 years.	Reduces future benefits by an average of 5%.	-0.46

Option	Comment	Reduces Deficit**
6. Increase contribution rates by 0.20 percentage points for workers and employers alike and comparably for the self-employed.	It is reasonable to ask workers in the future to contribute modestly to bringing the program into balance. Increase equals deduction of $20 per $10,000 of annual earnings.	-0.37
6a. Increase contribution rates by 0.40 percentage points.	Equals deduction of $40 per $10,000 of annual earnings.	-0.75
7. Modify the benefit formula gradually so as to maintain 1997 real benefit levels at a minimum but cut replacement rates 3% by 2029.	Future beneficiaries should share in sacrifice needed to reach long-term balance by reducing replacement rate, but benefits on into the future should equal or exceed those now being paid to new beneficiaries.	-0.21
7a. Modify formula to cut replacement rates 5%.	As above.	-0.35
8. Increase normal retirement age (NRA) by indexing it to longevity after NRA reaches 67 as scheduled under present law.	If NRA is to be increased at all (see text), this is the most cautious and least harmful approach.	-0.30
9. Apply the Social Security tax on employers to the entire payroll.	There is no good reason to limit the payroll tax on employers to a match with what individual workers are required to pay, since the employer tax can be thought of as going to the support of the entire system.	-1.20
10. Invest part of trust fund in stocks beginning in 2000, reaching 40% of assets in stocks in 2015 and thereafter (assumes ultimate 7% real yield in stocks).	Produces higher return on trust fund investments, giving Social Security participants same advantages as those participating in other pension funds and improving benefit/contribution ratio for younger workers.	-0.92

*There are, of course, other options, such as meeting the entire imbalance with benefit cuts or contribution-rate increases, but the options shown can, in various combinations, accomplish the same purpose with less modification of present-law provisions.

**Assumes an average long-term deficit of 2.23% of payroll as estimated by the Social Security Trustees.

TABLE 4
PAY-AS-YOU-GO FINANCING: CONTRIBUTION RATES* REQUIRED TO MAINTAIN SOCIAL SECURITY IN LONG-TERM BALANCE WITHOUT OTHER CHANGES

Years	Rate
1996–2024	6.20**
2025–2029	8.00
2030–2049	8.45
2050–2059	8.65
2060–2069	8.90
2070–2079	9.15***

   * Rates shown are for deductions from workers' earnings, to be matched by the employer.
  ** This is the present rate.
 *** The rate will continue to rise in following years.

Source: Based on *1997 Annual Report of the Board of Trustees of the Federal Old-Age and Survivors Insurance and Disability Insurance Trust Funds* (Washington, D.C.: Government Printing Office, 1997).

30 percent cut in retirement income. For those who did save, the ultimate level of their Social Security-related retirement income would depend on their investment returns. Some might have retirement income greater than promised under the current Social Security system. Others would have less—much less if they had bad luck with their investments. There are no guarantees.

The Moynihan plan would also make several changes that have wide support among Social Security experts and that are essentially the same as those summarized in Table 1 and that appear later in my preferred plan (see Table 6, page 254, Package 7). With regard to the Cost-of-Living Adjustment, however, the Moynihan plan would go far beyond the anticipated BLS changes to the Consumer Price Index (shown in Table 3, Option 3), cutting the CPI rate by a full 1 percent.[9]

There is much dispute over how much the Consumer Price Index needs to be reduced to make cost-of-living adjustments and automatic adjustments in income tax brackets as accurate as possible. The 1 percent reduction in the Moynihan plan has the support of a study made for the Senate Finance Committee by a group of economists led by Michael Boskin, who chaired the Council of Economic Advisers

TABLE 5

MODIFIED PAY-AS-YOU-GO FINANCING: CONTRIBUTION RATES* REQUIRED TO
MAINTAIN SOCIAL SECURITY IN LONG-TERM BALANCE UNDER AN APPROACH
COMBINING PARTIAL ADVANCE FUNDING AND PAY-AS-YOU-GO

Years	Rate
1996–2039	6.20**
2040–2059	7.40
2060–2069	7.80
2070–	8.10***

* Rates shown are for deductions from workers' earnings, to be matched by the employer.

** This is the present rate (plus any increase selected from Table 3).

*** The rate will continue to rise in following years.

Source: Based on *1997 Annual Report of the Board of Trustees of the Federal Old-Age and Survivors Insurance and Disability Insurance Trust Funds* (Washington, D.C.: Government Printing Office, 1997).

during the Bush administration. The Bureau of Labor Statistics, which is responsible for the CPI, has improved the measure's accuracy in several ways over the past few years and has announced further changes, but these changes are not nearly as great as that recommended by the Boskin group. Table 3, Option 3 reflects the BLS changes and adds a 0.1 percent reduction from more frequent pricing of the CPI market basket.

Social Security's effectiveness in providing a dependable income in retirement is very dependent upon the COLA. Over the course of time, retirees may use up other savings, and the value of private pensions declines because of not being protected against inflation, with the result that low income and impoverishment rise with longevity. Aging widows are particularly at risk of impoverishment. Thus the crucial importance of proceeding with great caution in making any changes to the CPI, which determines the COLA. The CPI is similarly important in determining income tax brackets. For both of these reasons, a strong case can be made that any changes to the CPI should have the support of the experts at BLS or, at the very least, of a strong consensus of non-BLS experts. That kind of support does not exist for any changes beyond the 0.42 percent of payroll change shown in Table 3, Option 3. The differences are significant. While a reduction of the CPI to the extent shown in Table 3 has the effect of reducing Social Security benefits (as compared to present law) about 8 percent by age 85, a reduction to the CPI of 1 percent would reduce benefits about 21 percent by age 85. And this is not exclusively a problem for the elderly: Benefits for a worker disabled at age 25 would be reduced 26 percent over 30 years.

The other major way in which the Moynihan plan cuts benefits is to raise the age of first eligibility for full benefits beyond the age (67) provided for in present law. (The Moynihan plan is similar in this respect to Option 8 in Table 3, but with a somewhat speeded-up schedule.)

Those who advocate going to a strict pay-as-you-go plan—by cutting back on the Social Security contribution rate in order to eliminate the buildup of funds that would otherwise take place—usually do so because they fear that the buildup would not be preserved for Social Security but instead would probably be used to support an expansion of other government spending, thus negating the increase in Social Security funds.

Whether government would actually preserve a buildup in Social Security is arguable. Little can be proven one way or another from looking at the past. For example, would general taxes have been higher in recent years if Congress had not had Social Security funds to borrow from? That is an unknown. If Congress did everything it was going to do in any case, then Social Security's buildup kept the national debt from rising even faster and further than it did—in effect saving the Social Security surplus.

Now that Congress has balanced total government income and expenditures, the prospect of exercising the discipline to save any Social Security surplus seems brighter than at any time in the recent past. It would greatly help to clarify the issue, however, if Social Security could not only be declared legally off-budget, as is the case now, but could stand truly apart in the same way that state retirement systems are typically separated from state budgets. This now seems a quite reasonable goal since under present law the non-Social Security budget is predicted by the Office of Management and Budget to come into balance within the next 10 years or so.

In any case, there is broad agreement among Social Security experts that partial advance funding—paying today for some of tomorrow's costs—is highly desirable. With partial advance funding, bringing the program into long-range balance is not very difficult. Senator Moynihan could have easily done so if he had not proposed to increase the long-range imbalance by cutting the contribution rate for the next 30 years. The options in Table 1 that have near-consensus support (and that are also included in the Moynihan plan) reduce the estimated long-range deficit from 2.23 percent of payroll to about 0.72 percent of payroll. The remaining imbalance can be brought to zero by making the additional changes shown in Table 2 or by various combinations of the proposals shown in Table 3. Or, best of all, it can be eliminated simply by combining the consensus items with investing part of the fund buildup in equities (see Table 6, pages 254–55, Package 7). Any of these approaches would do the job.

Table 6 shows four different packages in addition to the one in Table 1 (which would bring the deficit within "close actuarial balance" but not eliminate it) and the one in Table 2, Package 2.

There are advantages and disadvantages in each of these groupings (and in the many others that could be developed from Table 3). To illustrate: Table 2, Package 2 or Table 6, Package 3 may be the most attractive of those building on past practices, but Package 4 avoids some of the proposals that would be most likely to draw particular opposition, such as taxing more of the benefit, eliminating the special tax exemption for low-income Social Security beneficiaries, and extending the period over which average wages are computed. On the other hand, it includes further increases in the NRA, which many oppose. Package 5 has no increases in the taxation of benefits or tax increases on employees but will run into major employer objection. Package 6 can avoid taxation of benefits, retain the special income tax exemption for low-income beneficiaries, avoid a benefit cut, and provide for only a small increase in the contribution rate, because it invests part of the accumulating surplus in stocks. Finally, there is the package that I prefer over the others—Package 7.

In addition to eliminating the deficit, all seven packages would increase national savings, just as individual account plans are expected to, and Package 7 by 2015 would be saving about two-thirds as much as the IA plan proposed by Advisory Council chairman Edward Gramlich. If policymakers feel that increasing national savings is a more important goal than holding down deductions from workers' earnings and maintaining benefit levels close to those provided in present law,

TABLE 6
RESTORING SOCIAL SECURITY TO LONG-TERM BALANCE:
FIVE ADDITIONAL PACKAGES OF OPTIONS THAT WOULD DO THE JOB
(In addition to those shown in Tables 1 and 2)

Package 3

Proposal	Number in Table 3	Reduces deficit
Adjust COLA to reflect corrections to CPI.	3	-0.42
Extend coverage.	1	-0.25
Increase maximum taxable earnings base.	4	-0.27
Increase contribution rate by 0.40 percentage points.	6a	-0.75
Increase taxation of benefits.	2	-0.36
Change benefit formula to reduce replacement rate by 3%.	7	-0.21

Balance after implementing above changes (*adjusted for interaction of proposals*): -0.03%

Package 4

Proposal	Number in Table 3	Reduces deficit
Adjust COLA to reflect corrections to CPI.	3	-0.42
Extend coverage.	1	-0.25
Increase maximum taxable earnings base.	4	-0.27
Increase contribution rate by 0.40 percentage points.	6a	-0.75
Change benefit formula to reduce replacement rate by 5%.	7a	-0.35
Index NRA to life expectancy after age-67 NRA is reached under present law (not recommended, but has broad support).	8	-0.30

Balance after implementing above changes (*adjusted for interaction of proposals*): +0.50%

Package 5

Proposal	Number in Table 3	Reduces deficit
Adjust COLA to reflect corrections to CPI.	3	-0.42
Extend coverage.	1	-0.25
Change benefit formula to reduce replacement rate by 5%.	7a	-0.35
Apply tax on employers to entire payroll.	9	-1.20

Balance after implementing above changes (*adjusted for interaction of proposals*): -0.11%

Package 6

Proposal	Number in Table 3	Reduces deficit
Adjust COLA to reflect corrections to CPI.	3	-0.42
Extend coverage.	1	-0.25
Increase maximum taxable earnings base.	4	-0.27
Increase contribution rate by 0.20 percentage points.	6	-0.37
Invest part of the trust fund in stocks.	10	-0.92

Balance after implementing above changes (*adjusted for interaction of proposals*): -0.03%

TABLE 6 CONT.		
Package 7 **(Recommended Proposal)**	**Number in** **Table 3**	**Reduces** **deficit**
Adjust COLA to reflect corrections to CPI.	3	-0.42
Extend coverage.	1	-0.25
Increase taxation of benefits.	2	-0.36
Increase wage-averaging period from 35 to 38 years.	5	-0.27
Increase maximum earnings base.	4	-0.27
Invest part of the trust fund in stocks.	10	-0.92
Balance after implementing above changes (*adjusted for interaction of proposals*): +0.10%		

Social Security can do the job: The buildup in the trust fund can be accelerated by raising contribution rates or reducing benefits more than called for by any of the proposals in Table 3. The IA plan achieves greater national savings not by setting up individual accounts but by requiring greater deductions from workers' earnings (in order to fund the new IAs while at the same time continuing to fund Social Security's ongoing albeit reduced obligations). Equivalent deductions from workers' earnings or reductions in benefit amounts within the traditional program would produce the same result in terms of national savings. Personally, I would prefer to seek additional national savings elsewhere, but the point is simply that a decision about higher contribution rates and greater national savings can be arrived at independently of a decision on whether to recommend individual accounts.

Among the important conclusions to be drawn from this discussion are these: (1) substituting partial advance funding for pay-as-you-go keeps down the ultimate contribution rate, improves the benefit/contribution ratio for younger workers, and improves national savings; (2) there are several ways to bring the program into long-range balance while maintaining it as a fully defined-benefit program continuing to follow the same basic principles as in the past; (3) the system can be brought into balance for the next 50 years and trust fund exhaustion postponed from 2030 to 2050 largely by program changes that are desirable in any case from the standpoint of improving equity; (4) a future benefit cut of 5 percent (in addition to taxing benefits as other defined-benefit contributory plans are taxed) is the most that needs to be considered under any acceptable plan, and much less of a cut is all that is required under several plans; (5) a contribution rate increase of

0.4 percentage points on both employers and employees is the most that needs to be considered, and much less is all that is required under several acceptable plans; and, finally, (6) investing part of Social Security's trust fund accumulations could avoid tax increases on earnings and all but a small cut in benefits.

In summary, it can be stated categorically that there are many acceptable ways of bringing the present Social Security system into long-range balance without departing from the major principles that have been responsible for the program's great success. It is not at all necessary to turn to compulsory saving and private accounts because of the deficit in the existing system. In fact, there are major problems in cutting back on the basic government program and substituting compulsory saving for part of the basic protection now furnished by the traditional Social Security system.*

---

*See Chapter 4 of *Straight Talk about Social Security* for a detailed discussion of this issue.

14

SOCIAL SECURITY REFORM CHECKLISTS

SOCIAL SECURITY REFORM PROPOSALS: HOW THEY STACK UP AGAINST PRINCIPLES FOR PRUDENT CHANGE

Members of Congress, private organizations, academics, and others have put forward widely differing plans for reforming Social Security. Many of the details of those proposals are complicated, and the extent to which they address the primary problem confronting the program—a projected shortfall beginning in the year 2032—varies considerably.

To help those who care about the future of Social Security understand the most prominent proposals under consideration, The Century Foundation has been publishing a series of Social Security Reform Checklists. Each summarizes the main provisions of a particular plan and then assesses whether it adheres to seven principles for prudent reform that were developed by a panel of leading Social Security experts.

The checklists are reprinted from a series of Century Foundation issue briefs.

THE SEVEN SOCIAL SECURITY REFORM PRINCIPLES

1. Social Security should continue to provide a guaranteed lifetime benefit that is related to past earnings and kept up-to-date as the general standard of living increases.

2. American workers who have the same earnings history and marital status, and who retire at the same time, should receive the same retirement benefit from Social Security.

3. Social Security benefits should continue to be fully protected against inflation, and beneficiaries should continue to rest assured that they will not outlive their monthly Social Security checks.

4. Retirees who earned higher wages during their careers should continue to receive a larger check from Social Security than those with lower incomes, but the system should also continue to replace a larger share of the past earnings of low-income workers.

5. Social Security's insurance protections for American families, including disability insurance, should be fully sustained.

6. Social Security's long-term financing problem should not be aggravated by diverting the program's revenues to private accounts, and benefits should not be reduced to make room for private accounts; any such accounts should be supplementary to Social Security, treated entirely as an add-on.

7. In addition to securing Social Security as the foundation of income support for retirees, their dependents, the disabled, and survivors, more needs to be done to encourage private savings and pensions.

CHECKLIST #1
THE ROBERT M. BALL PLAN

OVERVIEW

Robert M. Ball, a former commissioner of Social Security, advocates a plan that retains Social Security's current structure while making a series of adjustments to assure the system's long-term financial integrity and giving wage earners a way to save additional money for retirement. His plan is similar to a proposal endorsed in January 1997 by six out of thirteen members of the 1994–96 Advisory Council on Social Security. The Ball plan requires only limited benefit cuts and tax increases. It would invest a portion of the Social Security trust funds, now exclusively comprising U.S. Treasury securities, in private equities. All disability and life insurance benefits would be maintained at present levels. Benefits to retirees would continue to be guaranteed for life and indexed for inflation. Those who paid more in payroll taxes would continue to receive larger benefit checks, while the program also would continue to replace a greater portion of wages for low earners than for higher earners. In addition, beginning in 2000, wage earners would have the option of contributing up to 2 percent of their wages to voluntary private savings accounts.

SUMMARY OF KEY FEATURES

Benefit Changes. The Ball plan would avoid major benefit cuts. Like most other reform proposals, however, it does include minor changes in the cost-of-living adjustments to reflect corrections to the consumer price index recommended by the Bureau of Labor Statistics. Those changes, most of which are already scheduled to take effect, should reduce annual cost-of-living adjustments by about 0.25 percentage points a year. The Ball plan would also increase the number of working years counted to determine benefit levels from today's thirty-five to thirty-eight. Adding more years would reduce average benefits by about 3 percent because the average past salaries that benefits are based on would include more years when workers were young and earning less—or nothing at all. Those with long absences from the workforce—women more commonly that men—would end up with the largest reductions.

Tax Changes. The plan does not include major tax changes; but it would raise the ceiling on earnings subject to Social Security taxes (currently $68,400 per worker) at a rate faster than current law allows. The plan would seek to raise the portion of taxable wages from 85 percent of the national payroll to 90 percent—the traditional level of the program.

Structural Changes. The Ball plan would invest part of the Social Security trust funds, which now hold exclusively U.S. government securities, in stocks beginning in 2000. By 2015, 50 percent of the trust funds' assets would be invested in a broad index of equities. A Federal Reserve–type board would oversee these investments.

The plan would also move toward making Social Security universal by including all newly hired state and local government employees, some of whom are now covered under separate retirement systems. (Federal employees hired since 1974 are already covered under Social Security.) In addition, the Ball plan would allow workers to invest up to an additional 2 percent of their pay in voluntary supplementary retirement accounts administered through Social Security.

EVALUATING THE PLAN

Here's how Robert Ball's plan stacks up against those principles for prudent reform:

☑ PRINCIPLE 1

Social Security should continue to provide a guaranteed lifetime benefit that is related to past earnings and kept up-to-date as the general standard of living increases.

> **Analysis:** The Ball plan leaves intact nearly all basic features of the current system, including lifetime benefits based on past earnings (with adjustment to account for past changes in the cost of living).

☑ PRINCIPLE 2

American workers who have the same earnings history and marital status, and who retire at the same time, should receive the same retirement benefit from Social Security.

Analysis: None of Ball's changes would alter this basic feature of the current system. However, workers who chose to make use of voluntary supplementary retirement accounts usually could expect to receive higher overall benefits than those who did not.

✔ PRINCIPLE 3

Social Security benefits should continue to be fully protected against inflation, and beneficiaries should continue to rest assured that they will not outlive their monthly Social Security checks.

Analysis: By endorsing modifications to the cost-of-living adjustment recommended by the Bureau of Labor Statistics to correct for current overstatements of inflation, the Ball plan would slightly reduce the amount by which Social Security checks are increased each year. Still, this proposal would retain the current system's protections against inflation.

✔ PRINCIPLE 4

Retirees who earned higher wages during their careers should continue to receive a larger check from Social Security than those with lower incomes, but the system should also continue to replace a larger share of the past earnings of low-income workers.

Analysis: Again, the Ball plan maintains the current benefit structure of Social Security. Higher earners would continue to receive larger benefit checks than lower earners, but low-income retirees would receive checks that replaced a larger share of their average earnings.

✔ PRINCIPLE 5

Social Security's insurance protections for American families, including disability insurance, should be fully sustained.

Analysis: The Ball plan maintains all of Social Security's insurance protections and current benefit levels for the disabled and for family members of workers who die.

☑ PRINCIPLE 6

Social Security's long-term financing problem should not be aggravated by diverting the program's revenues to private accounts, and benefits should not be reduced to make room for private accounts; any such accounts should be supplementary to Social Security, treated entirely as an add-on.

Analysis: The Ball plan would not divert any of Social Security's payroll tax revenue into private accounts. However, it does feature voluntary, add-on accounts that would be administered by Social Security and that workers could use to build greater retirement savings. The Ball plan would also invest a portion of the Social Security trust funds in private equities, which historically have increased in value more rapidly than the Treasury securities the system now holds. This change would potentially help alleviate the long-term financing challenge facing the system. But because stocks can lose value during particular periods of time, the assets in the trust funds might decline during a bear market.

☑ PRINCIPLE 7

In addition to securing Social Security as the foundation of income support for retirees, their dependents, the disabled, and survivors, more needs to be done to encourage private savings and pensions.

Analysis: By creating add-on accounts supplementary to Social Security, the Ball plan would institute a new mechanism for workers to accumulate savings for retirement. This provision would be especially beneficial to Americans who have no private pensions or other retirement savings options. On the other hand, a variety of tax incentives currently in place to promote savings, such as tax breaks for individual retirement accounts and 401(k) plans, have not been sufficient to induce low- and moderate-income households to increase their anemic savings rates. It is unclear whether a voluntary program like Ball's would create significant new savings.

Checklist #2
Two Percent Personal Retirement Accounts

Overview

Harvard economist Martin Feldstein, a former chairman of the Council of Economic Advisers, has proposed reforming Social Security by creating "two percent personal retirement accounts." Feldstein's proposal, unlike most other plans, seems painless. It imposes no reductions in Social Security benefits or increases in taxes. In fact, its most distinctive feature is the creation of a new benefit: a fully refundable income tax credit, equal to 2 percent of each worker's earnings subject to the Social Security payroll tax, that would finance new personal retirement accounts. (This tax credit is fully refundable because workers with no income tax liability and those who owe less than 2 percent of their earnings would still receive the full 2 percent contribution to their account.)

Under the plan, workers would have flexibility to choose from a group of regulated stock and bond mutual funds that would be administered by private managers. After retirement, however, every $1 a retiree withdraws from his or her personal account would reduce that retiree's guaranteed Social Security benefit by $0.75. In cases where workers invested so badly or the market performed so poorly that little money was left in the accounts, they would continue to receive the benefits promised under today's system. Social Security's projected shortfall in the year 2032 would be deferred because the system would presumably owe less money to beneficiaries thanks to the accumulations in the investment accounts.

The Price Tag

According to the Congressional Budget Office, which recently released a critique of the Feldstein plan, the proposed tax credits would cost the government about $800 billion over the next ten years. Rather than raise taxes or reduce government spending over that period, Feldstein proposes allocating anticipated federal budget surpluses to pay for the tax credit. Whenever federal surpluses become insufficient, then Congress would determine how to raise the money. But for the near future, Feldstein argues, his proposal could be implemented without imposing either benefit reductions or revenue increases that other plans for strengthening Social Security include.

Since Social Security faces a projected shortfall in 2032, can the system really be strengthened painlessly? The Feldstein plan appears to do so by financing the new accounts with the surplus in general revenues, as opposed to the payroll tax that is dedicated to Social Security benefits, thereby tapping a new well of resources for mandatory retirement savings. But because current federal budget surpluses reduce the federal debt, creating a new tax credit and diverting the surpluses to private accounts would increase the government's long-term obligations and interest costs. Therefore, as the Congressional Budget Office report stated, "The policy would implicitly increase the tax burden on future workers if no further adjustments were made on the spending side of the budget."

EVALUATING THE PLAN

Here's how the Feldstein proposal for 2 percent personal retirement accounts stacks up against the principles for prudent reform:

☑ PRINCIPLE 1

Social Security should continue to provide a guaranteed lifetime benefit that is related to past earnings and kept up-to-date as the general standard of living increases.

> **Analysis:** Under the Feldstein plan, guaranteed Social Security benefits under the current formula, which is based on past earnings and takes into account cost-of-living changes, would become the minimum that workers receive. The actual payments that workers would collect, however, would depend to a significant extent on how the investments in their personal retirement accounts fared. Because the personal retirement accounts would be financed through a flat-rate income tax credit of 2 percent, the dollar amount of the contributions to the accounts would be higher for workers with larger incomes and would rise over time as a worker's earnings grew. Therefore, a retiree's total benefits would continue to be related to past earnings, although less so than under current law because of variations in the investment performance of his or her account.

⊘ PRINCIPLE 2

American workers who have the same earnings history and marital status, and who retire at the same time, should receive the same retirement benefit from Social Security.

> **Analysis:** The Feldstein 2 percent plan would produce new disparities in benefits earned by retirees with the same earnings history and marital status because some workers could be expected to make better investments than others. Variations in investment performance would be somewhat limited, however, because every extra $1 that workers accumulate in their personal retirement accounts would increase the benefits they receive by just $0.25 under the plan's formula. Distributions would be further reduced by the cost of administering the accounts, paying investment management fees, and integrating them with the rest of the Social Security system. Economist Peter Diamond has shown that the administrative costs in countries that have set up individual accounts (Britain, Chile, Argentina, Mexico) reduce benefits by 20 to 30 percent compared to what the U.S. Social Security system would pay given the same resources.

⊘ PRINCIPLE 3

Social Security benefits should continue to be fully protected against inflation, and beneficiaries should continue to rest assured that they will not outlive their monthly Social Security checks.

> **Analysis:** Because the baseline benefit would remain intact, beneficiaries would continue to receive some lifetime benefit. To date, however, the Feldstein 2 percent personal account plan does not specify whether and how the amounts accumulated in personal accounts would be converted into monthly payouts. Even if beneficiaries were required to annuitize their accounts (that is, convert the lump sums into smaller periodic payments based on life expectancy levels), the value of those payments would be eroded by inflation unless they were indexed to increases in the cost of living, as are today's Social Security benefits. The Feldstein plan does not indicate that the payments would be adjusted for inflation, however. If retirees were allowed to withdraw the money in a

lump sum, as they can with individual retirement accounts, for example, they might spend all that money before they die.

⊘ PRINCIPLE 4

Retirees who earned higher wages during their careers should continue to receive a larger check from Social Security than those with lower incomes, but the system should also continue to replace a larger share of the past earnings of low-income workers.

> **Analysis:** When the payouts from personal retirement accounts are included, the overall effect of the plan would be that higher earners would receive disproportionately greater increases in their total benefit package than lower earners. Brookings Institution economists Henry J. Aaron and Robert D. Reischauer show that a worker with a high income would see his or her combined Social Security and private account payment increase by more than twice that of a low-income worker.[1] That would happen mainly because 1) contributions to the accounts would be made at the same 2 percent rate regardless of income, but 2) guaranteed benefits, which would be reduced at the same rate for all retirees, replace a larger share of the past earnings of low-income workers. These calculations don't factor in the probability that high-income workers would invest more aggressively and successfully. The bottom line is that lower-income workers would benefit less from the proposed formula than upper-income workers. (Feldstein has said that this problem could be addressed by imposing a modest redistributive tax on the investments of higher earners.)

[?] PRINCIPLE 5

Social Security's insurance protections for American families, including disability insurance, should be fully sustained.

> **Analysis:** The Feldstein 2 percent account plan is not explicit about what changes, if any, would be made to the survivor's and disability features of Social Security. By skirting this issue, the plan leaves important questions unanswered. For example, if a worker died prematurely and left dependents, what formula would be used for paying out the proceeds of his or her personal retirement account and integrating these funds with Social Security survivor's benefits? If workers became

disabled, would they be entitled to gain access to the investments accrued in their accounts?

[?] PRINCIPLE 6

Social Security's long-term financing problem should not be aggravated by diverting the program's revenues to private accounts, and benefits should not be reduced to make room for private accounts; any such accounts should be supplementary to Social Security, treated entirely as an add-on.

Analysis: By creating a new, refundable income tax credit to finance personal accounts, the Feldstein plan avoids, for now, diverting payroll tax revenues earmarked for current benefits and the Social Security trust funds. But because the tax credit would create a new long-term government obligation, future Congresses would need to find a way to pay for the personal accounts when and if surpluses run out. One inviting target at that point would be the Social Security trust funds themselves, which are projected to have accumulated more than $2 trillion by early in the next century to finance guaranteed payments to the baby boomers. Any shifting of assets from the trust funds to private accounts would reduce the money available to pay for guaranteed benefits in the future. Another "fix" would be for Congress to allow the national debt to grow to keep the program whole.

[?] PRINCIPLE 7

In addition to securing Social Security as the foundation of income support for retirees, their dependents, the disabled, and survivors, more needs to be done to encourage private savings and pensions.

Analysis: Initially, the Feldstein plan would neither increase nor decrease America's low levels of national savings, which many economists believe should be raised to promote investment and long-term economic growth. Every federal surplus dollar shifted to investment in a personal account would remain a dollar saved. To gauge the effect of the plan on national savings when and if surpluses run out, one would need to predict what actions Congress would take in the absence of the plan—which obviously are unknown. Professor Feldstein assumes that, without his plan, Congress would spend any anticipated surpluses. Under that assumption, his plan would increase savings and, consequently, economic growth. But the Congressional Budget Office argues, at least as plausibly, that the new accounts would lead to higher government budget deficits and lower national savings because they constitute a new, costly, and unlimited commitment of federal resources.

Moreover, if the government guarantees prevailing Social Security benefits as a baseline regardless of how well each worker's personal account performs, it risks encouraging workers to take greater, perhaps imprudent, risks with their investments than they otherwise might. Under that scenario, akin to the savings and loan debacle of the 1980s, the government's future obligations would be even greater.

CHECKLIST #3
THE NATIONAL COMMISSION ON
RETIREMENT POLICY PLAN

OVERVIEW

The National Commission on Retirement Policy (NCRP), a bipartisan group convened by the Center for Strategic and International Studies, has endorsed a proposal that would fundamentally restructure Social Security. The plan channels two percentage points of the current payroll tax (12.4 percent of wages, divided equally between workers and their employers, with a cap at $68,400 in yearly income) into mandatory individual savings accounts. To compensate for the reduction in tax revenue and eliminate the projected shortfall in Social Security beginning in the year 2032, the NCRP plan cuts benefits substantially—in part by increasing the retirement age to seventy.

SUMMARY OF KEY FEATURES

Benefit Changes. According to the Congressional Research Service, the NCRP plan would reduce guaranteed benefit levels set under current law by 33 percent for an average-wage worker retiring at the age of sixty-five in the year 2025. By 2070, after the plan is fully phased in, benefits for the average worker (who retires at sixty-seven) would be 48 percent lower than under present law. The specific changes leading to those reductions include:

◆ Raising the normal retirement age from sixty-seven in 2029 (an increase that is already scheduled to be phased in under current law) to seventy. The plan would also increase the age of eligibility for reduced benefits from sixty-two to sixty-five by 2017. Raising the retirement age amounts to cutting benefits, since workers will receive lower lifetime benefits.

◆ Reducing benefits for middle-income and high-income retirees. The portion of preretirement earnings that Social Security pays middle-income beneficiaries would decrease from 32 percent to 21.36 percent by 2020. For higher-income beneficiaries, the reduction would be from 15 percent to 10.01 percent by 2020.

◆   Increasing the number of working years counted to determine benefit
    levels from today's thirty-five to forty by 2010. Adding more years would
    reduce benefit levels because the average past salaries that benefits would
    be based on would include more years when workers were young and
    earning less—or nothing at all. Those with long absences from the work-
    force—women more commonly than men—would end up with the largest
    reductions.

◆   Reducing benefits to dependent spouses from 50 percent of their spouses'
    benefits to 33 percent.

Tax Changes. The plan would not increase payroll taxes, raise the cap on
taxable earnings, or increase the taxation of benefits to help close the existing
financing gap. But it would divert two percentage points of the current payroll
tax into individual savings accounts.

Structural Changes. The NCRP proposal's structural changes to the Social
Security program include:

◆   Introducing individual savings accounts modeled on the Federal Thrift
    Savings Plan, which allows workers to invest in several broad-based
    funds. At retirement, workers would be required to annuitize the
    majority of funds in their accounts—that is, convert them from lump
    sums into monthly payments that are made for the duration of their
    lives.

◆   Expanding Social Security coverage to include all newly hired state and
    local government employees.

◆   Creating a new minimum benefit equal to 100 percent of the poverty
    line for those who have spent forty years or more working and 60 per-
    cent of the poverty line for those with twenty to thirty-nine years in the
    workforce.

EVALUATING THE PLAN

Here's how the National Commission on Retirement Policy plan stacks up
against the principles for prudent reform:

⊘ PRINCIPLE 1

Social Security should continue to provide a guaranteed lifetime benefit that is related to past earnings and kept up-to-date as the general standard of living increases.

> **Analysis:** Although the plan retains a guaranteed benefit based on a worker's past earnings, the size of that benefit would be cut by 33 percent for the average worker retiring at sixty-five in 2025. Those reductions would be offset somewhat by provisions for new individual savings accounts and minimum benefits of 100 percent of the poverty line for those who spent forty years or more working and 60 percent of the poverty line for those with twenty to thirty-nine years in the workforce. But, in the process, benefit levels would become less closely tied to past earnings and more dependent on the performance of the investments in each worker's individual savings account.

⊘ PRINCIPLE 2

American workers who have the same earnings history and marital status, and who retire at the same time, should receive the same retirement benefit from Social Security.

> **Analysis:** While workers with similar earnings histories and marital status would receive the same, reduced baseline benefit from Social Security, the introduction of individual savings accounts would produce significant variations in overall benefits. Those who enjoyed better luck with their individual accounts, who invested more aggressively, and who retired when their investments were at a peak would receive higher payments than workers who invested less wisely, opted for more conservative investments, or retired when their investments were down.

⊘ PRINCIPLE 3

Social Security benefits should continue to be fully protected against inflation, and beneficiaries should continue to rest assured that they will not outlive their monthly Social Security checks.

> **Analysis:** Although guaranteed benefits are cut substantially under the NCRP plan, they would still be indexed for inflation and continue until

death. However, payments from individual accounts would not be protected against inflation. The NCRP plan would require retirees to convert most of their individual savings accounts investments into annuities upon retirement, but it does not mandate that these annuities make payments that are indexed for inflation. Unless workers chose to convert the accumulations in their accounts into annuities that are indexed for inflation, the value of each payment would decline over time as inflation reduced the value of the dollar. Today, inflation-adjusted annuities are very expensive and not widely available in the private market.

✔ PRINCIPLE 4

Retirees who earned higher wages during their careers should continue to receive a larger check from Social Security than those with lower incomes, but the system should also continue to replace a larger share of the past earnings of low-income workers.

Analysis: The NCRP changes in the benefit formula would result in middle-income and higher-income retirees receiving a lower percentage of their past earnings than is currently the case. This would represent a substantial cut in their benefits. Still, workers who earned more would continue to receive somewhat higher benefits than individuals who had lower incomes. And the new guarantee of benefits equal to 100 percent of the poverty level for workers who spent at least forty years in the workforce and 60 percent for those who worked twenty to thirty-nine years would offer protection for some low-income retirees—though less than the current system does in most cases.

⊘ PRINCIPLE 5

Social Security's insurance protections for American families, including disability insurance, should be fully sustained.

Analysis: Although the NCRP plan would retain insurance coverage for the disabled and for surviving spouses, the reductions in guaranteed retirement benefits would dramatically reduce protections for workers whose earned income plummets for an extended period because of disability. The combination of delaying the retirement age, extending the number of working years counted in determining baseline benefits, and changing the formula for calculating those benefits would especially imperil those, such as the disabled, who leave the workforce for years at a time.

⊘ PRINCIPLE 6

Social Security's long-term financing problem should not be aggravated by diverting the program's revenues to private accounts, and benefits should not be reduced to make room for private accounts; any such accounts should be supplementary to Social Security, treated entirely as an add-on.

Analysis: The NCRP plan imposes significant benefit cuts to allow two percentage points of payroll tax revenue to be diverted to individual savings accounts. The reduction in guaranteed benefits is far greater than the cuts that would be needed to assure that the system will be adequately financed throughout the next century.

⊘ PRINCIPLE 7

In addition to securing Social Security as the foundation of income support for retirees, their dependents, the disabled, and survivors, more needs to be done to encourage private savings and pensions.

Analysis: The NCRP plan shifts assets accumulating in the Social Security trust funds to individual savings accounts, a process that would neither increase nor decrease national savings (the combined savings of the government, companies, and households) or personal savings levels. Many economists argue that increasing the nation's low savings level would help to promote long-term economic growth by supplying more capital for long-term investment.

CHECKLIST #4
THE MOYNIHAN–KERREY PLAN

OVERVIEW

Senators Daniel Patrick Moynihan (D-N.Y.) and Robert Kerrey (D-Neb.) have introduced legislation that would make significant changes in Social Security. Their plan would establish voluntary private retirement accounts while instituting major reductions in guaranteed benefits, a large, temporary payroll tax cut, and some tax increases. Most notably, the plan would reduce the payroll tax that finances Social Security from 12.4 percent (divided equally between workers and their employers) to 10.4 percent, giving individuals the option of either contributing the two-point difference to a savings account or keeping one percentage point to use as they see fit.

The guaranteed benefits received by today's retirees, currently adjusted for inflation as the consumer price index rises, would increase at a slower rate because in calculating benefits a percentage point would be subtracted from the rate of increase in the consumer price index each year. By the end of the average retirement period of twenty years, that change alone would leave beneficiaries with monthly checks about 25 percent below what they would be under current law. Economist Alicia H. Munnell of Boston College calculates that by the year 2070, when all the plan's changes would be fully phased in, the cut in guaranteed benefits for a worker with an average earnings history who retires at age sixty-five would amount to 31 percent. That's substantially more than the 25 percent across-the-board cut in guaranteed benefits that the government estimates will be required in the year 2032 if no changes whatsoever are made to Social Security in the interim.

SUMMARY OF KEY FEATURES

Benefit Changes. In addition to subtracting a full percentage point from the rate of increase in the consumer price index each year when adjusting retirement benefits for inflation, the Moynihan-Kerrey plan reduces benefits in the following ways.

◆   It would increase the age at which full retirement benefits could be collected by two months per year from 2000 to 2017, and by one month for every two years between 2018 and 2065. This means that workers who reach sixty-two in 2017 will not be eligible for full retirement benefits until age sixty-eight, and workers reaching sixty-two in 2065 will only become eligible at seventy. Under current law, workers reaching sixty-two in 2022 will be eligible for full retirement benefits at age sixty-seven.

♦ Benefit levels would be based on how much a worker earned over the course of thirty-eight years rather than over thirty-five years, which is the period currently used. On average, the change would reduce a worker's retirement benefits by about 3 percent because it includes in the average the earlier years in the worker's career when he or she likely earned less—or nothing at all. Because women are more likely than men to withdraw from the workforce for years at a time to raise children, this change would affect them disproportionately.

Tax Changes. The Moynihan-Kerrey plan's payroll tax cut would begin in 1999 and last through 2024. After that, the payroll tax would increase according to the following schedule:

♦ from 2025 to 2029, it would rise from 10.4 percent to 11.4 percent;

♦ from 2030 to 2044, it would return to the current level of 12.4 percent;

♦ from 2045 to 2054, it would be 12.7 percent;

♦ from 2055 to 2059, it would rise to 13.0 percent; and

♦ in 2060 and thereafter, it would be 13.4 percent.

Other tax increases would be imposed sooner, however:

♦ The cap on yearly earnings subject to the Social Security payroll tax would increase from $68,400 in 1998 to $97,500 in 2003, and thereafter would be indexed to wage inflation.

♦ Social Security benefits would become taxable to the extent that a retiree's benefits exceed his or her tax contributions to the system. This change would result in greater taxation of benefits than under current law, which taxes only half of benefits received by retirees with total yearly incomes in excess of $25,000 ($32,000 for married couples).

Structural Changes. The largest structural change is the incorporation of voluntary private retirement accounts. This new component of Social Security would give an individual earning $30,000 a year—who now pays $1,860 in Social Security payroll taxes—the option of investing $600 in a savings account or keeping an extra $300 in take-home pay. The individual could put the $600 either in investment funds that the government now offers to federal employees or in privately run accounts. Other structural changes include:

- Newly hired state and local government workers would be required to participate in Social Security. They are the last group of workers now excluded from Social Security.

- The earnings test, which may reduce current benefits for individuals who continue to work after electing to receive their Social Security benefits, would be eliminated beginning in the year 2003 for all beneficiaries aged sixty-two and over.

EVALUATING THE PLAN

Here's how the Moynihan-Kerrey plan stacks up against the principles for prudent reform:

✔ PRINCIPLE 1

Social Security should continue to provide a guaranteed lifetime benefit that is related to past earnings and kept up-to-date as the general standard of living increases.

> **Analysis:** Under the Moynihan-Kerrey plan, guaranteed retirement benefits would continue to be based on past earnings, adjusted for changes in the cost of living. But those benefits would be significantly lower than under reform proposals such as those put forward by former Social Security commissioner Robert M. Ball or Brookings

Institution economists Henry J. Aaron and Robert D. Reischauer. That's mainly because of the annual one-percentage-point reduction in the cost-of-living adjustment and the increase in the retirement age.

⊘ Principle 2

American workers who have the same earnings history and marital status, and who retire at the same time, should receive the same retirement benefit from Social Security.

> **Analysis:** While workers with the same earnings history and marital status would receive the same guaranteed benefits from Social Security, the introduction of personal retirement accounts would produce significant variations in overall benefits among workers with the same earnings history. Because these accounts are voluntary, some workers would choose not to participate. (Only 3 percent of Americans earning $30,000 or less, for example, have elected to open Individual Retirement Accounts despite considerable tax advantages in doing so.) Moreover, investment returns on the accounts are certain to vary widely. Investors with greater financial acumen and better luck, and those who retire when investment markets are strong, would receive higher payments than workers who invested less skillfully or retired during a bear market. As a result, under the Moynihan-Kerrey plan, Social Security would more closely resemble an investment program than retirement insurance.

⊘ Principle 3

Social Security benefits should continue to be fully protected against inflation, and beneficiaries should continue to rest assured that they will not outlive their monthly Social Security checks.

> **Analysis:** Under the Moynihan-Kerrey plan, Social Security would continue to pay guaranteed lifetime benefits indexed for inflation. However, by reducing the benefit adjustment tied to the consumer price index by one percentage point each year, the plan would hurt many low-income elderly who are already struggling with rising

medical costs (which rise more rapidly than the consumer price index). These costs have come to consume an ever-growing share of elderly Americans' personal expenses—20 percent of such expenses on average and an even higher share for poor seniors. Over the past fifteen years, adjustments in Social Security benefits have failed to take account of this rising burden. As for the assets accumulated in private retirement accounts, their value could be significantly reduced by a period of high inflation.

☑ PRINCIPLE 4

Retirees who earned higher wages during their careers should continue to receive a larger check from Social Security than those with lower incomes, but the system should also continue to replace a larger share of the past earnings of low-income workers.

Analysis: The Moynihan-Kerrey plan would retain this feature of the current program for determining guaranteed benefits.

☑ PRINCIPLE 5

Social Security's insurance protections for American families, including disability insurance, should be fully sustained.

Analysis: The Moynihan-Kerrey plan retains all of the disability and survivor's insurance features of the current Social Security program.

⊘ PRINCIPLE 6

Social Security's long-term financing problem should not be aggravated by diverting the program's revenues to private accounts, and benefits should not be reduced to make room for private accounts; any such accounts should be supplementary to Social Security, treated entirely as an add-on.

Analysis: By reducing the payroll tax in order to introduce personal retirement accounts, the Moynihan-Kerrey plan would deplete the asset buildup in the Social Security trust funds. This would shift a much greater share of the burden of financing Social

Security to future workers after the retirement of the baby boomers. The benefit cuts will reduce those obligations to some extent, but cutting revenues to the system now will add to, rather than lessen, the challenge of keeping Social Security sound in the next century.

Ø PRINCIPLE 7

In addition to securing Social Security as the foundation of income support for retirees, their dependents, the disabled, and survivors, more needs to be done to encourage private savings and pensions.

Analysis: The Moynihan-Kerrey plan includes no measures that would encourage private savings and pensions. Indeed, reducing payroll taxes (which by definition reduces the federal surplus or increases the deficit) without requiring households to save the money threatens to reduce further the nation's already low level of national savings.

CHECKLIST #5
THE GRAMM PLAN

OVERVIEW

Senator Phil Gramm (R-Tex.) is sponsoring a plan to transform Social Security by diverting nearly one-fourth of the payroll taxes that finance today's retirement insurance system into individual investment accounts. Under his proposal, workers would have the option of either retaining their current Social Security coverage and benefits or electing to shift three percentage points of their 12.4 percent Social Security payroll tax (split equally between workers and their employers) into their own investment account. Workers would not be allowed to opt out of the system altogether or transfer a different share of their payroll tax into the accounts. Those who opted for the investment accounts would be allowed to invest that money in a selection of privately managed mutual funds that would be certified and regulated by a new government oversight board. Initially, the accounts would be restricted so that no more than 60 percent of an investment portfolio could be in stocks, which can decline precipitously in value.

Upon retirement, workers with investment accounts would be required to convert the accumulated assets into an annuity that, like today's Social Security, would provide a lifetime monthly payment that increases as inflation rises. After the system was fully phased in, retirees who opted for the personal accounts would be guaranteed a total monthly benefit equal to the guaranteed payment promised under today's system plus 20 percent. If the assets accumulated in a retiree's personal account proved to be insufficient to pay the full 20 percent bonus, the government would make up the difference. Retirees who invested more successfully would be entitled to cash out any accumulations in excess of the 20 percent bonus as a lump sum, if they wanted to.

Senator Gramm claims that his plan would end prospects that Social Security will face a shortfall in the year 2032, when payroll taxes combined with system's trust fund assets are expected to become insufficient to pay guaranteed benefits in full. The main reason is that the assets accumulated in the private accounts would significantly reduce the benefits that the system would have to pay out from the remaining 9.4 percent payroll tax and the assets in the Social Security trust funds.

THE PRICE TAG

Diverting three percentage points of the Social Security payroll tax into private accounts for every worker who makes that choice would significantly reduce the anticipated growth in the Social Security trust funds, which currently are expected to tide the system over from 2013 to 2032—a period when promised benefits are expected to exceed payroll tax revenues. Because current retirees will have no private accounts to draw on and older workers will have little time to accumulate much in their private accounts, maintaining today's guaranteed benefits for them while payroll tax revenues decline by up to 24 percent (depending on how many workers opt for the new system) poses an expensive transition challenge.

Stephen C. Goss, deputy chief actuary of the Social Security Administration, calculates that if all workers opted for the private accounts, the cost to the federal budget and the Social Security trust funds would be an average of $140 billion a year from 2000 to 2009. Senator Gramm has said that those transition costs could be paid out of projected federal budget surpluses. Drawing on surpluses poses problems, however. First, surpluses are projected to be adequate to pay for only $81 billion of the $140 billion that would be needed. Second, if the projected surpluses were to be used to finance the transition to the new retirement system, actual surpluses would be substantially lower each successive year because the surplus from the previous year would not have been used to reduce the federal debt and thereby reduce interest obligations. Third, the projected federal budget surpluses through 2007 are almost entirely attributable to the surpluses in the Social Security trust funds. So paying for the transition with budget surpluses essentially means depleting 72 percent of the Social Security trust funds, which would raise the level of government debt.

Senator Gramm projects that it would take thrity-two years before his plan would become financially self-sustaining and fifty years before the assets accumulated in individual investment accounts would be sufficient to generate a benefit equal to 20 percent above the level promised by the existing system. If the investments in the private accounts don't increase in value as rapidly as Senator Gramm predicts—5.5 percent annually over and above the inflation rate—the system's long-term financial burdens could increase rather than decrease. Senator Gramm also claims that the government would gain additional revenues from higher corporate tax collections attributable to increased corporate profits that would arise from more money flowing into capital markets through the private accounts. There is little historical evidence, however, that higher levels of market capitalization generate increased corporate profits.

EVALUATING THE PLAN

Here's how Senator Gramm's proposal stacks up against the principles for prudent reform:

✔ PRINCIPLE 1

Social Security should continue to provide a guaranteed lifetime benefit that is related to past earnings and kept up-to-date as the general standard of living increases.

> **Analysis:** Guaranteed Social Security benefits under the current formula, which are based on past earnings after taking into account cost-of-living changes, would remain the minimum that workers would receive if they decided against opening their own accounts. If they opted for the accounts, they would be guaranteed a 20 percent bonus on top of a benefit that would still be based on past earnings. And because the personal retirement accounts would be financed through a 3 percent flat-rate contribution, the dollar amounts flowing into the accounts would be higher for workers with larger incomes and would rise over time as a worker's earnings grew. Workers who invested so successfully that they could collect even more than the 20 percent bonus would receive benefits less proportionate to past earnings, however.

⊘ PRINCIPLE 2

American workers who have the same earnings history and marital status, and who retire at the same time, should receive the same retirement benefit from Social Security.

> **Analysis:** Workers who elect to open private accounts gain a guaranteed 20 percent benefit bonus above the amount that those who decline the option receive. So the same past earnings history and marital status would not lead to identical benefits for workers who 1) made different decisions about whether to open an account and 2)

had different degrees of investment success. Those who earned more than the 20 percent bonus in their accounts would be able to collect the difference as a lump sum.

☑ Principle 3

Social Security benefits should continue to be fully protected against inflation, and beneficiaries should continue to rest assured that they will not outlive their monthly Social Security checks.

Analysis: The Gramm plan stipulates that the accumulations in the personal investment accounts would be required to be converted to lifetime, inflation-adjusted annuities akin to current benefits, and that those payments would be a minimum of 20 percent higher than the benefits currently promised. Although many questions could be raised about whether the plan adequately accounts for the cost of financing those benefits, the proposal adheres to this particular principle. An important ambiguity about the plan remains, however: it is unclear what benefits surviving spouses would receive. Under current law, survivors receive 100 percent of the benefit that their late spouse collected (presuming that benefit was higher than the payment the survivor was previously entitled to). The Gramm plan, as summarized to date, does not specify what happens upon the death of a beneficiary.

⊘ Principle 4

Retirees who earned higher wages during their careers should continue to receive a larger check from Social Security than those with lower incomes, but the system should also continue to replace a larger share of the past earnings of low-income workers.

Analysis: Workers whose private accounts grow enough to provide more than the 20 percent guaranteed bonus would receive larger payments relative to their past earnings than those who invested less successfully. In all probability, the most prosperous investors will be clustered at high income levels because 1) they have much greater experience and familiarity with investing, 2) they would have more money in their accounts to build on (since the contributions are a flat 3 percent rate), and 3) low-income workers with no investment experience may be more reluctant to open accounts in the first place.

⊘ PRINCIPLE 5

Social Security's insurance protections for American families, including disability insurance, should be fully sustained.

> **Analysis:** The Gramm plan stipulates that the survivor's and disability insurance features of the current system would be preserved in full. But Social Security actuary Stephen Goss points out that the proposal allocates only 1.5 percentage points of the 12.4 percent payroll tax toward maintaining those protections, even though that insurance now costs the system about twice as much—3 percentage points. Because the plan does not provide an explanation of how current disability and survivor's insurance could be maintained on half the funding it now receives, that aspect of the proposal deserves further scrutiny.

⊘ PRINCIPLE 6

Social Security's long-term financing problem should not be aggravated by diverting the program's revenues to private accounts, and benefits should not be reduced to make room for private accounts; any such accounts should be supplementary to Social Security, treated entirely as an add-on.

> **Analysis:** By diverting 3 percentage points of the payroll tax financing the current system into private accounts, for those who choose them, the Gramm plan compounds the challenge of alleviating the long-term financial pressures on Social Security. Because current retirees and those now near retirement age must continue to receive promised benefits from payroll taxes in the years ahead, the cost of creating the new accounts will, in essence, deplete the Social Security trust funds and the federal budget surplus while increasing the national debt and government interest costs. Although the accumulations in the investment accounts after several decades might indeed be sufficient to finance the more generous benefits proposed, that eventuality depends on a variety of uncertainties about the number of workers who opt for the accounts, the performance of the economy, and investment growth. In any case, no one disputes that the cost of making a transition to Senator Gramm's system would add to federal budgetary pressures.

⊘ Principle 7

In addition to securing Social Security as the foundation of income support for retirees, their dependents, the disabled, and survivors, more needs to be done to encourage private savings and pensions.

> **Analysis:** At first blush, the Gramm plan would seem neither to increase nor decrease national savings because payroll taxes would be moved from one category of savings—the Social Security trust funds—to private savings in the form of the personal accounts. But because of the need to finance the transition to the new system, the government will either have to borrow more, reduce promised Social Security benefits, or increase taxes. Increased federal borrowing by definition is the same as reduced government savings. And either reducing Social Security benefits or increasing taxes would cut the amount of money available to households to save.
>
> The government guarantee of a 20 percent bonus above today's benefits for those with investment accounts—even those that perform poorly—risks encouraging workers to take greater, perhaps imprudent, risks with their investments than they otherwise might. Under that scenario, akin to the savings and loan debacle of the 1980s, the government's future obligations could skyrocket since the bonus would be guaranteed whether the money was there or not.

NOTES

2

1. Social Security Administration, "Fast Facts and Figures about Social Security, 1997" (Washington, D.C.: Social Security Administration, 1997), p. 15. Hereafter cited as "Fast Facts." For later figures, there is a monthly benefits database maintained by the Social Security Administration, Office of the Actuary, Highlights of Social Security Data on http://www.ssa.gov/statistics/highlite.html.

2. *1998 Annual Report of the Board of Trustees of the Federal Old-Age and Survivors Insurance and Disability Insurance Trust Funds* (Washington, D.C.: Government Printing Office, 1998), pp. 2, 6. Hereafter cited as *1998 Annual Report of the Social Security Trustees*.

3. Ibid., p. 6.

4. "Fast Facts," pp. 14, 33.

5. Social Security Administration, *Annual Statistical Supplement to the Social Security Bulletin, 1996* (Washington, D.C.: Social Security Administration, 1996), p. 30; this includes work in Samoa, Guam, the Northern Mariana Islands, Puerto Rico, and the U.S. Virgin Islands; J. Patrick Skirvin, economist, Office of the Chief Actuary, Social Security Administration. The largest group of employees not covered under the Social Security program consists of state and local government employees who are covered under a retirement system. Robert M. Ball with Thomas N. Bethell, "Bridging the Centuries," in *Social Security in the 21st Century*, ed., Eric R. Kingson and James H. Schulz (New York: Oxford University Press, 1997), p. 289n. 2. Other workers excluded from Social Security include the following: federal civilian workers hired before January 1, 1984; railroad workers, who are covered under the railroad retirement system (which is coordinated with the Social Security system); household workers and farm workers whose earnings do not meet certain minimum requirements; and people with very low net earnings from self-employment (less than $400 per year).

6. Internal Revenue Service, "Circular E, Employer's Tax Guide" (Washington, D.C.: Department of the Treasury, 1997), p. 2. The ceiling for taxable wages is indexed and changed annually to reflect average wage changes in the economy.

7. For a general description of tax incidence, see Harvey S. Rosen, *Public Finance*, 4th ed. (Chicago: Irwin Press, 1995), chapter 13, especially pp. 285–86.

8. "Fast Facts," p. 1.

9. Social Security Administration, "Social Security: Understanding the Benefits," SSA Publication no. 05-10024, September 1997, p. 32.

10. Ibid., pp. 12, 9.

11. Deborah A. Stone, "Disability Insurance and the New Understanding of Disability," in *Social Insurance Issues for the Nineties*, ed., Paul N. Van De Water (Dubuque, Iowa: Kendall/Hunt Publishing Company, 1992), p. 204. Special rules apply to the blind. For instance, in 1996, blind individuals are considered disabled if their condition prevents them from earning at least $960 per month. *Annual Statistical Supplement to the Social Security Bulletin, 1996*, p. 76.

12. "Social Security: Understanding the Benefits," p. 21.

13. Social Security Administration, "How Work Affects Your Benefits," SSA Publication no. 05-10069, January 1997, p. 2.

14. *Annual Statistical Supplement to the Social Security Bulletin, 1996*, p. 53. The 1983 Social Security legislation guarantees that benefits will be indexed to the CPI unless the assets of the OASDI Trust Funds fall below 20 percent of annual expenditures. In that case, benefits will indexed to either the CPI or the national wage index, depending on which yields the smaller increase in benefits.

15. *Report of the 1994–1996 Advisory Council on Social Security*, vol. I (Washington, D.C.: 1994–1996 Advisory Council on Social Security, 1997), p. 88. Hereafter cited as the *Advisory Council Report, I*.

16. *1998 Annual Report of the Social Security Trustees*, p. 2.

17. Social Security Administration, *Social Security: Accountability Report for Fiscal Year 1997* (Baltimore, MD: Social Security Administration, 1997), p. 3.

18. Ibid., p. 2.

19. *1998 Annual Report of the Social Security Trustees*, p. 2.

20. U.S. Congress, House, Committee on Ways and Means, *Overview of Entitlement Programs: 1996 Green Book* (Washington, D.C.: Government Printing Office, 1996), p. 1226. Hereafter cited as *1996 Green Book*.

21. Census Bureau website: http://www.census.gov/hhes/poverty/poverty96/pv 96est1.html. (Visited March 9, 1998.)

22. U.S. Department of Commerce, *Statistical Abstract of the United States, 1996* (Washington, D.C.: U.S. Government Printing Office, 1996), p. 377.

23. "Fast Facts," p. 7.

24. Ibid., p. 8.

25. Ibid., p. 7.

26. For a recent treatment, see Steven H. Sandell and Howard M. Iams, "Women's Future Social Security Benefits: Why Widows Will Still Be Poor," paper prepared for presentation at the meeting of the Population Association of America, New Orleans, May 1996.

27. Older Women's League, "The Path to Poverty: An Analysis of Women's Retirement Income" (Washington, D.C.: Older Women's League, 1997), p. 5; this paper provides a good survey of the financial vulnerability of older women.

28. "Fast Facts," p. 20.

29. Susan Grad, "Income of the Population 55 or Older, 1994" (Washington, D.C.: Social Security Administration, 1996), p. 81.

30. Frank B. Hobbs with Bonnie H. Damon, *65+ in the United States* (Washington, D.C.: Current Population Reports, Special Studies, 1996), p. vi.

31. Ibid., p. 2.11.

32. Ibid., p. vi.

33. Testimony of Shirley Chater, U.S. commissioner of Social Security, U.S. Congress, Senate Finance Committee, *Hearing on Social Security and the Future of Retirees*, 104th Cong., 2d sess., March 11, 1996.

34. Elderly people without a work history whose incomes fall below the poverty line are eligible for federal Supplemental Security Insurance (SSI). (Some states also have an additional SSI payment for the most impoverished.) For general information about SSI, see "Social Security: Understanding the Benefits," pp. 23–26.

35. David Koitz, "Social Security: Brief Facts and Statistics," Congressional Research Service Report no. 94–27 EPW, Washington, D.C., 1997, p. 10.

36. Richard A. Posner, *Aging and Old Age* (Chicago: University of Chicago Press, 1995), p. 42; C. Eugene Steuerle and Jon H. Bakija, *Retooling Social Security for the 21st Century* (Washington, D.C.: The Urban Institute Press, 1994), p. 115.

37. Under the current system, states must pay some share of benefit and administration costs in the AFDC and Medicaid programs. (In addition, a number of states require local governments, usually counties, to share in the costs of the programs.)

38. Two examples highlight the interstate variation in other benefit programs. In 1996, the maximum AFDC benefit for a family of three ranged from $120 in Mississippi to $923 in Alaska, while the median state payment was $389; *1996 Green Book*, pp. 439–440. Similarly, Medicaid payments per beneficiary in 1991 ranged from $1,607 in Mississippi to $5,994 in Connecticut; Congressional Research Service, *Medicaid Source Book: Background Data and Analysis* (Washington, D.C.: Government Printing Office, 1993), p. 119.

39. James H. Schulz, *The Economics of Aging*, 6th ed. (Westport, Conn.: Greenwood Press, 1995), p. 109.

40. Benjamin I. Page and Robert Y. Shapiro, *The Rational Public: Fifty Years of Trends in Americans' Policy Preferences* (Chicago: University of Chicago Press, 1992), pp. 118–19.

41. Robert B. Friedland, "When Support and Confidence Are at Odds: The Public's Understanding of the Social Security Program," National Academy of Social Insurance, Washington, D.C., May 1994, p. 5.

42. Theodore R. Marmor, Jerry L. Mashaw, and Philip L. Harvey, *America's Misunderstood Welfare State: Persistent Myths, Enduring Realities* (New York: Basic Books, 1990), p. 134.

43. Jennifer Baggette, Robert Y. Shapiro, and Lawrence R. Jacobs, "The Polls—Poll Trends: Social Security—An Update," *Public Opinion Quarterly* 59 (1995).

44. Friedland, "When Support and Confidence Are at Odds," p. 5. For instance, according to most survey respondents, workers such as those for state and local governments should be eligible for participation in the Social Security program.

45. *1998 Annual Report of the Social Security Trustees*, pp. 179, 113.

46. Ibid, p. 178.

47. Ibid.

48. Ibid., p 4.

49. Ibid., p. 148; C. Eugene Steuerle, "Fiscal Policy and the Aging of the U.S. Population," in *The New World Fiscal Order: Implications for Industrialized Nations*, ed., C. Eugene Steuerle and Masahino Kawai (Washington, D.C.: The Urban Institute Press, 1996), p. 20.

50. *1998 Annual Report of the Social Security Trustees*, p. 145.

51. *Advisory Council Report*, p. 16.

52. Henry J. Aaron and Robert D. Reischauer, *Social Security's Future* (New York: The Century Foundation Press, forthcoming).

53. Calculated from the *1998 Annual Report of the Social Security Trustees*, p. 145.

54. *The 1998 Annual Report of the Board of Trustees of the Federal Hospital Insurance Trust Fund*, p. 2.

55. Ibid, p. 15.

56. Koitz, "Social Security," p. 7.

57. Steuerle and Bakija, *Retooling Social Security for the 21st Century*, p. 289.

58. One popular proposal aimed at increasing the rate of return for the Social Security Trust Funds is to shift money from investments in government securities to the stock market. In recent years, the growth in the stock market has been impressive—but such a performance cannot be guaranteed in future years. Shifting funds into the equity market is, by its very nature, a risk.

59. *Advisory Council Report, I*, pp. 221, 219.

60. Congressional Budget Office, *Assessing the Decline in the National Saving Rate*, CBO Study, Washington, D.C., April 1993, pp. 2–3.

61. William G. Gale, "The Aging of America: Will the Baby Boom Be Ready for Retirement?" *Brookings Review*, Summer 1997, p. 8.

62. For more extensive treatment of this subject, see George E. Rejda, *Social Insurance and Economic Security*, 3rd ed. (Englewood Cliffs, NJ: Prentice Hall, 1988); Martin Feldstein, "Social Security, Induced Retirement, and Aggregate Capital Accumulation," *Journal of Political Economy*, vol. 82, no. 5, September–October 1974, pp. 905–926; and *Report of the 1994–1995 Advisory Council on Social Security*, vol. II (Washington, D.C.: Government Printing Office, 1995), pp. 12–106, hereafter cited as *Advisory Council Report, II*.

63. *Economic Report of the President, 1997* (Washington, D. C.: Government Printing Office, 1997), p. 96.

64. U.S. Department of Commerce, *Statistical Abstract of the United States, 1953* (Washington, D.C.: U.S. Government Printing Office, 1953), p. 185; *Statistical Abstract of the United States, 1996*, p. 393.

65. *1996 Green Book*, p. 20.

66. Michael D. Hurd, "The Effects of Labor Market Rigidities on the Labor Force Behavior of Older Workers," in David A. Wise, *Advances in the Economics of Aging* (Chicago: University of Chicago Press, 1996). This chapter also contains a review of the factors other than Social Security that affect retirement ages—health insurance, private pension benefit plans, age discrimination, and labor market rigidities.

67. "Social Security: Understanding the Benefits," p. 15.

68. Ibid.

69. Ibid., p. 31.

70. Ibid., p. 14.

71. Robin L. Lumsdaine and David A. Wise, "Aging and Labor Force Participation: A Review of Trends and Explanations" in *Aging in the United States and Japan: Economic Trends*, ed., Yukio Noguchi and David A. Wise (Chicago: University of Chicago Press, 1994), p. 22.

72. Ibid., p. 23.

73. *World Population Prospects: The 1994 Revision* (New York: United Nations, 1995), pp. 168, 226, 238, 280, 284, 492, 494. The Group of Seven (G–7) is a forum for the largest industrialized countries to meet and coordinate economic policies. It is comprised of the United States, Canada, Japan, Germany, France, Britain, and Italy.

74. Social Security Administration, *Social Security Programs Throughout the World—1995* (Washington, D.C.: Government Printing Office, 1995), Table 3, p. xliii.

75. Ibid. This volume provides detailed information on this subject.

76. Sheetal K. Chand and Albert Jaeger, "Aging Populations and Public Pension Schemes," IMF Occasional Paper no. 147 (Washington, D.C.: International Monetary Fund, 1996), p. 12.

77. *Social Security Programs Throughout the World—1995*, pp. 61, 177, 348.

78. Chand and Jaeger, "Aging Populations and Public Pension Schemes," p. 17.

79. Ibid.

80. Testimony of Teresa Ghilarducci, associate professor of Economics, University of Notre Dame, U.S. Congress, House, Committee on Ways and Means, Hearing on the Future of Social Security for this Generation and the Next, 105th Cong., 1st sess., September 18, 1997.

81. Organisation for Economic Co-operation and Development (OECD), *Employment Outlook, July 1992* (Paris: OECD, 1992), p. 201; Organisation for Economic Co-operation and Development, *Labor Force Statistics, 1976–1996* (Paris: OECD, 1997), pp. 532–86.

82. The social security system in the United Kingdom explicitly encourages participation in private pension plans. Workers are allowed to "contract out" of the State Earnings Related Pension Scheme (SERPS) if they participate in an approved private pension scheme. Workers who "contract" pay reduced Social Security taxes.

83. Paul J. Yakoboski, research associate, Employee Benefit Research Institute (EBRI); this number was calculated from the U.S. Federal Reserve Board's Flow of Funds acounts; *Economic Report of the President, 1997*, p. 300. For more information on retirement in the United Kingdom, see Richard Disney, *Can We Afford to Grow Older?* (Cambridge, Mass.: MIT Press, 1996.

84. Disney, *Can We Afford to Grow Older?*, pp. 227–65.

85. Posner, *Aging and Old Age*, p. 265.

86. Marilyn Moon and Janemarie Mulvey, *Entitlements and the Elderly: Protecting Promises, Recognizing Reality* (Washington, D.C.: Urban Institute Press, 1996), Table 2.11, p. 33.

87. Organisation for Economic Co-operation and Development, *Ageing in OECD Countries*, Social Policy Studies no. 20, OECD, Paris, 1996, p. 54.

88. Chand and Jaeger, "Aging Populations and Public Pension Schemes," p. 8.

89. The information on the United Kingdom draws heavily on Disney, *Can We Afford to Grow Older?*, see especially pp. 69–84.

90. The information on Chile draws heavily on Robert J. Myers, "Social Security Reform in Chile: Two Views," in *Social Security: What Role for the Future?*, ed., Peter Diamond, David C. Lindeman, and Howard Young (Washington, D.C.: National Academy of Social Insurance, 1996), pp. 209–224.

91. The chair of the commission was Edward Gramlich. Other members were Robert M. Ball, Joan T. Bok, Ann L. Combs, Edith U. Fierst, Gloria T. Johnson, Thomas W. Jones, George Kourpias, Sylvester J. Schieber, Gerald M. Shea, Mark M. Twinney, Fidel A. Vargas, and Carolyn L. Weaver.

92. A technical note: The *Advisory Council Report* projected a gap of 2.17 percent of taxable payroll over the next seventy-five years. The figures generated for the percentage of the gap closed by various reforms were calculated using this earlier 2.17 percent figure, not the 2.23 percent estimate.

93. Moon and Mulvey, *Entitlements and the Elderly*, pp. 79–80.

94. This was the plan supported by Joan T. Bok, Ann L. Combs, Sylvester J. Schieber, Fidel A. Vargas, and Carolyn L. Weaver.

95. See Dean Baker, "Saving Social Security with Stocks: The Promises Don't Add Up" (New York: Twentieth Century Fund Press, 1997). Olivia Mitchell presents a comparison of the administrative costs of public and private retirement systems in "Administrative Costs in Public and Private Retirement Systems," NBER Working Paper no. 5734, National Bureau of Economic Research, Cambridge, Mass., August 1996.

96. Ball, "Bridging the Centuries," p. 286; John Mueller, "Three New Papers on 'Privatizing' Social Security, One Conclusion: Bad Idea," press release distributed at a press conference at the National Press Club, Washington, D.C., October 14, 1997, p. 4.

3

1. For the most part, the two groups are distinct. Most retired, disabled, and survivor beneficiaries do not work, but some engage in part-time work, and a few work full time. Overall, only 3.3 percent of beneficiaries have their pensions reduced or eliminated altogether because of earnings.

2. Robert M. Ball, "A Commentary on the Current Social Security Debate," unpublished paper, January 1998.

3. David M. Cutler and Ellen Meara, "The Medical Costs of the Young and Old: A Forty-Year Perspective," NBER Working Paper 6114, National Bureau of Economic Research, Cambridge, Mass., July 1997.

4. Over the 1990s, real per capita GDP grew at an average rate of 1.4 percent per year. Because the growth of the labor force is expected to slow more than population growth, the Congressional Budget Office, the Social Security Actuaries, and the Office of Management and Budget expect per capita growth to average 1.1 to 1.2 percent between 1998 and 2040.

5. Jonathan Gruber and David Wise, "Social Security Programs and Retirement Around the World," NBER Working Paper 6134, National Bureau of Economic Research, Cambridge, Mass., August 1997.

6. The age at which unreduced benefits will be paid rises two months a year starting for workers who turn age 62 in 2000 until it reaches 66 for those turning 62 in 2005. For the succeeding twelve years, the age of normal retirement will remain at 66. Then, it will be increased two months a year between 2017 and 2022. The increase in the "normal" age for claiming widows' and widowers' benefits begins and ends two years later.

7. There is no earnings test for those age 70 and older. Beneficiaries may receive unlimited amounts from private pensions, rents, royalties, and income from capital.

8. The cost of repealing the retirement test for those over age 64 would be modest because only a bit over half of those working and not receiving Social Security at this age will have earnings that exceed $30,000, the level the earnings test will reach in 2002. Furthermore, after 2005 when the delayed retirement credit fully compensates workers for benefits lost because of earnings above the threshold, the earnings test will have been effectively repealed. Repealing the earnings test means that workers receive the same expected lifetime benefits no matter when they retire. An actuarially fair delayed retirement credit has the same effect. However, the psychological effects of repealing the earnings test might well differ from those of an actuarially fair delayed retirement credit.

9. We explain why income testing is inadvisable in *Countdown to Reform*, Box 7-1.

5

1. Eric R. Kingson, B. A. Hirshorn, and John M. Cornman, *Ties that Bind: The Interdependence of Generations* (Cabin John, Md.: Seven Locks Press, 1986); Fay Lomax Cook and Edith J. Barrett, *Support for the American Welfare State: The Views of Congress and the Public* (New York: Columbia University Press, 1992); Fay Lomax Cook et al., "The Salience of Intergenerational Equity in Canada and the United States," in Theodore R. Marmor, Timothy M. Smeeding, and Vernon L. Greene, eds., *Economic Security and Intergenerational Justice* (Washington, D.C.: Urban Institute Press, 1994), pp. 91–129; Fay Lomax Cook, "Public Support for Programs for Older Americans: Continuities amidst Threats of Discontinuities," in Vern Bengtson, ed., *Continuities and Discontinuities in Adulthood and Aging* (New York: Springer, 1996), pp.327–46; Alan Walker, ed. *The New Generational Contract* (London: VCL Press, 1996); Virginia P. Reno and Robert B. Friedland, "Strong Support but Low Confidence: What Explains the Contradiction?" in Eric R. Kingson and James H. Schulz, eds. *Social Security in the 21st Century* (New York: Oxford University Press, 1996), pp.178–94.

2. An example of this type of reasoning can be found in Vern L. Bengtson, "Is the 'Contract Across Generations' Changing? Effect of Population Aging on Obligations and Expectations Across Age Groups," in Vern L. Bengtson and W. Andrew Achenbaum, eds., *The Changing Contract across Generations* (New York: Aldine de Gruyter, 1993), pp. 3–23.

3. Robert H. Binstock, "Transcending Intergenerational Equity," in Marmor, Smeeding, and Greene, *Economic Security and Intergenerational Justice*, pp. 155–68.

4. Subrata N. Chakravaty and Katherine Weisman, "Consuming Our Children?" *Forbes*, November 14, 1988, pp. 222–32.

5. Samuel H. Preston, "Children and the Elderly in the U.S.," *Scientific American*, December 1984, pp. 44–49. Preston argued that since the socioeconomic situation was improving for the elderly at the same time that it was becoming worse for children, it followed that the former was the cause of the latter.

6. Robert J. Samuelson, "The Withering Freedom to Govern: Soaring Costs for Elderly Curb President's Choices," *Washington Post*, March 5, 1978, pp. C1, C5.

7. Lester C. Thurow, "The Birth of a Revolutionary Class," *New York Times Magazine*, May 19, 1996, pp. 46–47.

8. The ratios vary, depending on the projection assumptions chosen and the start/end years used. The numbers in the text are from a Social Security Trustees' annual report and published in Joseph F. Quinn, *Entitlements and the Federal Budget: Securing Our Future* (Washington, D.C.: National Academy on Aging, 1996).

9. For a good explanation of this basic fact, see Donald O. Cowgill, *Aging around the World* (Belmont, Calif.: Wadsworth Publishing, 1986).

10. See, for example, Ben J. Wattenberg, *The Birth Dearth* (New York: Pharos Books, 1987).

11. Estimates of economist Robert Eisner, reported in Richard C. Leone, "Why Boomers Don't Spell Bust," *American Prospect*, January-February 1997, pp. 68–71.

12. James H. Schulz, Allan Borowski, and William H. Crown, *Economics of Population Aging: The "Graying" of Australia, Japan, and the United States* (New York: Auburn House, 1991). See also Donald J. Adamchak, "Demographic Aging in the Industrialized World: A Rising Burden?" *Generations* Winter 1993, pp. 6–9.

13. The basic projections were carried out using a real growth rate of 3.0 percent. Sensitivity testing was then carried out using lower and higher rates, demonstrating that burdens are very sensitive to economic growth rates but not to assumptions regarding population growth rates or labor force participation rates.

14. Most of Easterlin's many research studies on this topic are summarized in Richard A. Easterlin, "Implications of Demographic Patterns," in Robert H. Binstock and Linda K. George, eds., *Handbook of Aging and the Social Sciences*, 4th ed. (San Diego: Academic Press, 1995), pp. 73–93.

15. Population growth was a part of the first neoclassical growth models (e.g., Harrod-Domar) and the discussions of "optimal growth rates." But the main focus of these discussion was about saving/capital formation. A good survey of the literature can be found in Jack Habib, "Population Aging and the Economy," in Robert H. Binstock and Linda K. George, *Handbook of Aging and the Social Sciences*, 3d ed. (San Diego: Academic Press, 1990), pp. 328–45.

16. Lawrence H. Thompson, "Private and Public Aspects of Pension Management," *Asia and Pacific News Sheet* 36, no. 3 (September 1996): 18–25.

17. Martin S. Feldstein, "Social Security, Induced Retirement, and Aggregate Capital Accumulation," *Journal of Political Economy* 82, no. 5 (September-October 1974): 905–26. The errors were reported by Dean R. Leimer and Selig D. Lesnoy in "Social Security and Private Saving: New Time Series Evidence," *Journal of Political Economy* 90, no. 3 (June 1982): 606–29. An excellent summary of the literature on this controversy is in Congressional Budget Office, *Assessing the*

Decline in the National Saving Rate (Washington, D.C.: U.S. Government Printing Office, 1993).

18. See, for example, pp. 93–97 in *Ageing in OECD Countries*, Social Policy Studies no. 20 (Paris: Organization for Economic Cooperation and Development, 1996).

19. See the discussion of the literature in Richard Disney, *Can We Afford to Grow Older?* (Cambridge, Mass.: MIT Press, 1996).

20. Speech given at conference titled, "Coming of Age: The Economic and Political Impact of an Aging Society," sponsored by the World Affairs Council of Philadelphia, April 3, 1997. In his speech Volcker did make a passing reference to other factors affecting growth, but his main concern was increasing saving.

21. Bipartisan Commission on Entitlement and Tax Reform, *Interim Report to the President*, Washington, D.C., August 1994. Kerry and Danforth focus their remarks in both the interim and final report on saving and investment. No other growth factors are seriously considered.

22. *Economic Report of the President, 1997* (Washington, D.C.: U.S. Government Printing Office, 1997).

23. James M. Buchanan, "We Should Save More In Our Own Economic Interest," in Lee M. Cohen, ed., *Justice across Generations: What Does It Mean?* (Washington, D.C.: American Association of Retired Persons, 1993), pp. 269–82.

24. Robert A. Blecker, review of *Macroeconomic Policy after the Conservative Era: Studies in Investment, Saving and Finance* by Gerald A. Epstein and Herbert M. Gintis (Cambridge: Cambridge University Press, 1996), *Journal of Economic Literature* 35 (March 1997): 131–32.

25. Edward M. Gramlich, "How Does Social Security Affect the Economy?" in Kingson and Schulz, *Social Security in the 21st Century*, pp. 147–55. The neoclassical model Gramlich refers to is stated in Robert M. Solow, "A Contribution to the Theory of Economic Growth," *Quarterly Journal of Economics* (February 1956): 65–94.

26. Martin Feldstein, "Transition to a Fully Funded Pension System: Five Economic Issues," NBER Working Paper no. 6149, National Bureau of Economic Research, Cambridge, Mass., 1997.

27. Solow's modeling was much more "general" than is sometimes thought. For example, some attempt is made to take account not just of physical capital and the amount of labor but also of changes in the quality of labor (due to better education, health, etc.). The literature on technological change is large. See, for example, the review article by Wesley Cohen and Richard Levin, "Empirical Studies of Innovation and Market Structure," in R. Schmalensee and Daniel Levinthal, eds., *Handbook of Industrial Organization* (New York: North Holland, 1989), pp. 1059–1107.

28. David M. Gordon, "Putting the Horse (Back) before the Cart: Disentangling the Macro Relationship between Investment and Saving," in Epstein and Gintis, *Macroeconomic Policy after the Conservative Era*, pp. 57–108.

Some prominent economists argue, in fact, that it is sometimes not so much a shortage of saving in the United States that has limited investment but a shortage of investment opportunities in the face of economic uncertainty, low profits, or reduced market expectations. Nobel laureate Franco Modigliani, for example, asserts that "when a country needs capital to drive rapid growth, capital will be forthcoming." Franco Modigliani, "The Key to Saving Is Growth, not Thrift," *Challenge* 30 (May-June, 1987): 24–29.

29. Bryn Davies, *Better Pensions for All* (London: Institute for Public Policy Research, 1993).

30. "Introduction," in Epstein and Gintis, eds., *Macroeconomic Policy after the Conservative Era*.

31. See, for example, the findings of V. Bhaskar and Andrew Glyn, "Investment and Profitability: The Evidence from the Advanced Capitalist Countries." In Epstein and Gintis, *Macroeconomic Policy after the Conservative Era*, pp. 175–96.

32. Richard Nelson, "How New Is New Growth Theory?" 40, no. 5, *Challenge* (September/October 1997): 29–58.

33. Jane Katz, "The Joy of Consumption," *Federal Bank of Boston Regional Review* 7, no. 1 (Winter 1997): 12–17.

34. W. C. Dunkelberg, "Analyzing Consumer Spending and Debt," *Business Economics* 24, no. 3 (July 1989): 17–22.

35. "Give Card Companies Some Credit for Delinquency," *USA Today*, September 24, 1997.

36. Dagobert L. Brito and Peter R. Hartley, "Consumer Rationality and Credit Cards," *Journal of Political Economy* 103, no. 2 (April 1995): 400–433.

37. Credit is not necessarily used for consumption expenditures. Household appliances, cars, and housing are often viewed as investment (depending on how they are used).

38. A book on saving by a prominent economist working in the area has only this to say about credit: "Economic [tax] incentives combined with appealing market strategies to create a booming demand for credit. In the absence of tax breaks [that were repealed by Congress], marketing will become more problematic, and the credit industry will probably decline." B. Douglas Bernheim, *The Vanishing Nest Egg: Reflections on Saving in America* (New York: Priority Press Publications, 1991), p. 116. Given contemporary events, it is difficult to agree with Bernheim's prediction. More important, there is absolutely no discussion in the Bernheim book about how the accessibility of credit cards may have negatively influenced household saving in the United States. In his chapter "Why Do Americans Save So Little?" there is only one sentence that mentions credit: "For example, the development of a consumer credit industry may tempt individuals to invade certain mentally 'reserved' accounts in order to spend." (p. 71).

39. "Credit Card Debt May Present Growing Problem," *USA Today*, December 17, 1997, p. B-1. In 1996, the average amount of credit card debt for *all* households (i.e., those with revolving debt and those without) was $2,500. David R. Francis, "Easy Credit Fuels Rise in Bankruptcy," *Christian Science Monitor*, April 11, 1997, pp. 1, 8.

40. Ibid.

41. James Medoff and Andrew Harless, "Missing the Turn," *Challenge* 40, no. 2 (March-April 1997): 6–12.

42. The implications of the rising rate of bankruptcies are not entirely clear. As pointed out by Edgar Fiedler, "the rising rate of bankruptcies, which has been going on not just in recent years but for decades, is, I strongly believe, due almost entirely to changes in bankruptcy law (making it an easier process), rather than to rising incidence of consumers taking on an excessive debt burden." Edgar Fiedler, personal correspondence with author, January, 1998.

43. See, for example, the discussion of this point by Lester Thurow, "Tax Wealth, Not Income," *New York Times Magazine*, April 11, 1976, p. 32.

44. World Bank, *Averting the Old Age Crisis* (Oxford: Oxford University Press, 1994).

45. Arthur Okun, *Equality and Efficiency: The Big Trade-off* (Washington, D.C.: Brookings Institution, 1975).

46. Alfred Marshall, *Principles of Economics: An Introductory Volume* (New York: Macmillian, 1948).

47. An increasing number of economists argue that investment should be defined explicitly to include expenditures on research and "human capital."

48. "Silicon Valley," survey, *Economist*, March 29, 1997.

49. Ibid.

50. Richard R. Nelson, *The Sources of Economic Growth* (Cambridge, Mass.: Harvard University Press, 1996). With regard to the development of new technology, Nelson points out that there are four aspects of the process that are supressed or ignored in most economic models: (1) the uncertainty involved; (2) the fact that there are many different firms in various industries exploring opportunities for research and development; (3) the fact that "when R & D is done competitively, the regime of property rights in technology significantly influences, and warps R & D incentives," (p. 32) and (4) the documented fact that in many technologies, learning by doing is an important complement to R & D.

51. Theodore W. Schultz, *Investing in People: The Economics of Population Quality* (Los Angeles: UCLA Press, 1981). See also Schultz's *Restoring Economic Equilibrium: Human Capital in the Modernizing Economy* (Oxford: Basil Blackwell, 1990).

52. "Education and the Wealth of Nations," *Economist*, March 29, 1997, pp. 15–16.

53. Robert Eisner, "U.S. National Saving and Budget Deficits," in Epstein and Gintis, *Macroeconomic Policy after the Conservative Era*, pp. 109–42.

54. Schultz, *Restoring Economic Equalibriums*.

55. Israel M. Kirzner, "Entrepreneurial Discovery and the Competitive Market Process: An Austrian Approach," *Journal of Economic Literature* 35 (March 1997): 60–85.

56. Thus, a recent study of growth determinants states: "We conclude that differences in levels of economic success across countries are driven primarily by the institutions and government policies (or infrastructure) that frame the economic environment in which people produce and transact." Robert E. Hall and Charles I. Jones, "Levels of Economic Activity across Countries," *American Economic Review*, Proceedings 87, no. 2 (May 1997): 173–80.

57. Disney, *Can We Afford to Grow Older?*

58. Michael Cichon, "The Ageing Debate in Social Security: Barking up the Wrong Tree?" in *Protecting Retirement Incomes: Options for Reform*, ISSA Studies and Research no. 37 (Geneva: International Social Security Association, 1996), pp. 83–99.

59. Peter G. Peterson, *On Borrowed Time: How the Growth of Entitlement Spending Threatens America's Future* (San Francisco: Institute for Contemporary Studies Press, 1988).

60. Bipartisan Commission on Entitlement and Tax Reform, *Interim Report to the President*.

61. For a more extensive discussion of this point, see Robert J. Myers, "Social Security and the Federal Budget: Some Mirages, Myths, and Solutions," *Journal of the American Society of CLU & ChFC* (March 1989): 58–63.

62. Prior to the Tax Reform Act of 1983, federal income tax brackets were not indexed. As inflation in the economy occurred, it tended to increase money incomes of individuals. Thus, a portion of rising taxable income did not represent *real* income. Workers, however, were pushed by rising wages (granted in part to compensate for inflation) gradually into higher tax brackets, with more of their income being taxed at higher marginal rates. This was a relatively invisible way of augmenting tax revenues over time—minimizing the political issues that inevitably arise around increasing taxes. The indexing of the brackets was enacted to stop this practice, making it more difficult to generate the revenues necessary to pay for federal expenditure increases in future years arising, in part, out of the same inflationary pressures.

63. See the extensive discussion of this point in Kingson and Schulz, *Social Security in the 21st Century*.

64. Another argument made for privatization of pensions is to promote greater equity and to deal with an alleged problem of giving future retirees their "money's worth." Discussion of this topic is beyond the scope of the chapter. For an extensive overview of the topic, see "Are Returns on Payroll Taxes Fair?" in ibid.

65. Andrew Glyn, "Stability, Inequalitarianism, and Stagnation: An Overview of the Advanced Capitalist Countries in the 1980s," in Epstein and Gintis, *Macroeconomic Policy after the Conservative Era*, pp. 18–56.

66. The discussion that follows is treated more extensively in James H. Schulz, "To Old Folks with Love: Aged Income Maintenance in America," *Gerontologist* 25, no. 5 (October 1985): 464–71; James H. Schulz and John Myles, "Old Age Pensions: A Comparative Perspective," in Binstock and George, *Handbook of Aging and the Social Sciences*, 3d ed., pp. 398–414.

67. The traditional reasons given for government pensions are information inefficiencies, adverse selection, and the "free rider" problem. See, for example, Zvi Bodie and Olivia S. Mitchell, "Pension Security in an Aging World," in Zvi Bodie, Olivia S. Mitchell, and J. A. Turner, eds., *Securing Employer-based Pensions: An International Perspective* (Philadelphia: University of Pennsylvania Press, 1996), pp. 1–30. Our emphasis here is on the influence of chronic unemployment on policies to encourage retirement through pensions.

68. James H. Schulz, "Epilogue: The 'Buffer Years': Market Incentives and Evolving Retirement Policies," in John Myles and Jill Quadagno, eds., *States, Labor Markets, and the Future of Old-Age Policy* (Philadelphia: Temple University Press, 1991), pp. 295–308.

69. Dan Jacobson, "Optional Early Retirement: Is It a Painless Alternative to Involuntary Layoffs?" in S. Bergman, G. Naegele, and W. Tokarski, eds., *Early Retirement: Approaches and Variations* (Israel: Brookdale Institute of Gerontology and Human Development, 1988), pp. 11–24.

6

1. "Social Security: The Credibility Gap," survey by Frank Luntz and Mark Siegel, Third Millennium, September 1994.

2. Michael X. Delli Carpini and Scott Keeter, *What Americans Know about Politics and Why It Matters* (New Haven: Yale University Press, 1996).

3. These results were confirmed by several additional surveys conducted in 1997, which reported that nearly 60 percent of Americans felt confident in their understanding and knowledge about the program. A March 1997 *Washington Post* poll asked: "Would you say you know a lot, a fair amount, very little, or nothing about Social Security?" Five percent selected "a lot," 51 percent "a fair amount," 40 percent "very little," and 4 percent "nothing." The Employee Benefit Research Institute (EBRI) asked: "Would you say that you are very confident, somewhat confident, not too confident or not at all confident . . . that you have a good understanding of how the Social Security system works?" Twenty-one percent selected "very confident," 41 percent "somewhat confident," 23 percent "not too confident," 13 percent "not at all confident," and 2 percent reported "not knowing."

4. An alternative hypothesis is that lower-income groups are more likely to deceive themselves about a program that they have heard of but which they do not understand to the same depth as the more affluent.

5. The proportion who indicated that they followed Social Security "very" or "fairly" closely in the news fell from 64 percent in January 1997 to 49 percent in February.

6. Similar results were reported in a 1997 survey by the Public Agenda Foundation, which showed that 84 percent believed that "the government is mismanaging Social Security so badly that the money is going to waste," and 67 percent were convinced that "too many people are cheating the program." See "Miles to Go: A Status Report on American Plans for Retirement," Public Agenda Foundation, 1997.

7. "Miles to Go: A Status Report on Americans' Plans for Retirement," Public Agenda Foundation. DYG, found a similar pattern in its two surveys in 1995 and 1996. "Social Security and Medicare: An Ongoing Study of Public Values and Attitudes," conducted by DYG, Inc. for the American Association for Retired Persons (AARP), fall 1996.

8. "Social Security and Medicare: An Ongoing Study of Public Values and Attitudes," DYG, Inc. DYG, in its surveys for the AARP found that 70 percent to 80 percent of Americans agreed that "everyone who pays into Social Security should receive it, no matter what other income they have."

9. Princeton Survey Research Associates asked: As a taxpayer, please tell me whether you generally approve or disapprove of having your tax dollars used to help pay for each of the following. What about . . . Social Security for better-off retired people?"

10. "Social Security and Medicare: An Ongoing Study of Public Values and Attitudes," DYG, Inc.

11. Table 10 also offers evidence that the most advantaged can be strong defenders of Social Security, despite what would seem to be their self-interest. See Fay Lomax

Cook and Edith Barrett, *Support for the American Welfare State* (New York: Columbia University Press, 1992).

12. The survey asked: "Under the existing Social Security plan workers and their employers each contribute equally to total payroll taxes of 12.4 percent, which is paid on $65,400 of workers' annual salary. Do you favor or oppose the existing Social Security plan?" Sixty-four percent favored the existing arrangement and 29 percent opposed it.

13. Virginia Reno and Robert Friedland, "Strong Support but Low Confidence: What Explains the Contradiction," in *Social Security in the 21st Century*, ed. Eric Kingson and James Schulz (New York: Oxford University Press, 1997).

14. "Miles to Go: A Status Report on Americans' Plans for Retirement," Public Agenda Foundation.

15. "The National Piggybank: Does Our Retirement System Need Fixing?" National Issues Forums Report on the Issues, conducted by John Doble Research Associates, 1997.

16. "Miles to Go: A Status Report on Americans' Plans for Retirement," Public Agenda Foundation, p. 24.

17. Lawrence Jacobs and Robert Shapiro, *The News Media's Coverage of Social Security*, report prepared for the National Academy of Social Insurance, March 1995; Lawrence Jacobs, Mark Watts, and Robert Shapiro, "Media Coverage and Public Views of Social Security," *Public Perspective* (April/May 1995).

7

1. Robert Myers, "Dispelling Myths about Social Security"; Myers's paper will appear (as will this one) in a volume edited by Robert N. Butler, *Aging in America*, a Century Foundation book (New York: The Century Foundation Press, forthcoming); Eric M. Engen and William G. Gale, "Social Security Reform and Saving," in Robert Triest, ed., *Social Security Reform: Links to Saving, Investment, and Growth* (Boston: Federal Reserve Bank of Boston, 1998, 103–42).

2. The shift in the composition of pensions toward defined contribution plans has tended to blur the distinction between the second and third legs of the retirement income stool.

3. James M. Poterba, Steven F. Venti, and David A. Wise, "Targeted Retirement Saving and the Net Worth of Elderly Americans," *American Economic Review* 84, no. 2 (May 1994): 180–85.

4. B. Douglas Bernheim and John Karl Scholz, "Private Saving and Public Policy," in James M. Poterba, ed., *Tax Policy and the Economy*, vol. 7 (Cambridge, Mass.: MIT Press, 1993).

5. However, the appropriate figure will vary depending on a household's specific situation.

6. Poterba, Venti, and Wise, "Targeted Retirement Saving."

7. B. Douglas Bernheim, "Is the Baby Boom Preparing Adequately for

Retirement?" Technical Report, Merrill Lynch & Co., Inc., New York, September 1992; B. Douglas Bernheim, "The Merrill Lynch Baby Boom Retirement Index: Update '95," Merrill Lynch & Co., Inc., New York, February 1995.

8. These are not unreasonable estimates of Social Security and pension benefits. According to TIAA-CREF, a worker with thirty-five years of covered service in Social Security, a spouse, and a final salary of $40,000 would have initial Social Security benefits equal to 47 percent of final earnings ("Making Sense of Social Security," Teachers Insurance and Annuity Association/College Retirement Equities Fund, New York, 1994). If retirement income needs are, by rule of thumb, 75 percent of final earnings, Social Security benefits constitute 63 percent (47/75) of retirement income needs. The replacement rate would be even higher for workers with lower earnings. Andrew A. Samwick, "Retirement Incentives in the 1983 Pensions Provider Survey" (mimeo, Massachusetts Institute of Technology, April 1993), estimates that expected private pension benefits in the 1983 Survey of Consumer Finances average 20–30 percent of final earnings. Using the rule of thumb above, private pension benefits would constitute 27–40 percent of retirement income needs for workers who have such benefits.

9. "Pension and Health Benefits of American Workers: New Findings from the April 1993 Current Population Survey," U.S. Department of Labor, 1994.

10. Samwick, "Retirement Incentives in the 1983 Pensions Provider Survey."

11. B. Douglas Bernheim, "The Adequacy of Personal Retirement Saving: Issues and Options," in David A. Wise, ed., *Facing the Age Wave* (Stanford, Calif.: Hoover Institution Press, 1997).

12. David M. Cutler, "Re-examining the Three-Legged Stool," in Peter A. Diamond, David C. Lindeman, and Howard Young, eds., *Social Security: What Role for the Future?* (Washington, D.C.: National Academy of Social Insurance, 1996).

13. Bernheim and Scholz, "Private Saving and Public Policy."

14. Christopher Ruhm, "Bridge Jobs and Partial Retirement," *Journal of Labor Economics* 8, no. 4 (October 1990): 482–501.

15. N. Gregory Mankiw and David N. Weil, "The Baby Boom, the Baby Bust, and the Housing Market," *Regional Science and Urban Economics* 19, no. 2 (May 1989): 143–203; James Poterba, "House Price Dynamics: The Role of Tax Policy and Demography," *Brookings Papers on Economic Activity* 2 (1991): 143–203.

16. This issue is distinct from the point that models that do not include the reduction in mortgage payments as households pay off their homes will overstate retirement needs.

17. Sylvester J. Schieber and John B. Shoven, "The Consequences of Population Aging on Pension Fund Saving and Asset Markets," NBER Working Paper no. 4665, National Bureau of Economic Research, Cambridge, Mass., March 1994.

18. Employee Benefit Research Institute, "Employment-Based Retirement Income Benefits: Analysis of the April 1993 Current Population Survey," *EBRI Special Report SR-25*, Washington, D.C., September 1994, Table 2. This participation rate includes salary reduction plans as well as more traditional defined benefit and defined contribution plans.

19. Poterba, Venti, and Wise, "Targeted Retirement Saving," Table 1. At the aggregate level, reserves in private pension funds have accounted for more than 20 per-

cent of net worth in the household sector in recent years ("Balance Sheets for the U.S. Economy," Board of Governors of the Federal Reserve System, 1995). Private pensions and other tax-deferred accounts, such as IRAs, Keoghs, and 401(k) plans, have accounted for more than 90 percent of net personal saving since 1987. Refer to John Sabelhaus, "Public Policy and Saving Behavior in the U.S. and Canada," mimeo, Congressional Budget Office, February 1996; John B. Shoven, *Return on Investment: Pensions Are How America Saves* (Washington, D.C.: Association of Private Pension and Welfare Plans, September 1991).

20. Alfred M. Skolnik, "Private Pension(s) no Plans, 1950–74," *Social Security Bulletin*, Social Security Administration, June 1976, pp. 3–7.

21. Daniel J. Beller and Helen H. Lawrence, "Trends in Private Pension Plan Coverage," in John A. Turner and David J. Beller, eds., *Trends in Pensions 1992* (Washington, D.C.: U.S. Department of Labor, 1992), pp. 59–96.

22. For further discussion, see Robert L. Clark and Ann A. McDermed, *The Choice of Pension Plans in a Changing Regulatory Environment* (Washington, D.C.: American Enterprise Institute Press, 1990); William G. Gale, "Public Policies and Private Pension Contributions," *Journal of Money, Credit, and Banking* 26, no. 3, part 2 (August 1994): 710–32; Richard A. Ippolito, "Selecting and Retraining High-Quality Workers: A Theory of 401(k) Pensions," unpublished paper, Pension Benefit Guaranty Corporation, Washington, D.C., April 1993; Douglas S. Kruse, "Pension Substitution in the 1980s: Why the Shift toward Defined Contribution Pension Plans?" NBER Working Paper no. 2882, National Bureau of Economic Research, Cambridge, Mass., October 1991.

23. Ippolito, "Selecting and Retraining High-Quality Workers."

24. Richard Thaler, "Anomalies: Saving, Fungibility, and Mental Accounts," *Journal of Economic Perspectives* 4, no. 1 (Winter 1990): 193–205; B. Douglas Bernheim, "Rethinking Savings Incentives," in Alan Auerbach, ed., *Fiscal Policy: Lessons from Economic Research* (Cambridge, Mass.: MIT Press, 1996), p. 25.

25. B. Douglas Bernheim, "Personal Saving, Information, and Economic Literacy: New Directions for Public Policy," in *Tax Policy and Economic Growth in the 1990s* (Washington, D.C.: American Council for Capital Formation, 1994): 53–78.

26. William G. Gale, "The Effect of Pensions on Wealth: A Re-Evaluation of Theory and Evidence," mimeo, Brookings Institution, Washington, D.C., June 1995. In some cases, the biases can generate an estimated positive effect of pensions on nonpension wealth, even when the true relation is that a dollar increase in the pension wealth causes a one-dollar reduction in other wealth.

27. Bernheim and Scholz, "Private Saving and Public Policy"; Gale, "Effect of Pensions on Wealth."

28. The literature is reviewed in Bernheim, "Rethinking Savings Incentives"; Eric M. Engen, William G. Gale, and John Karl Scholz, "The Illusory Effects of Saving Incentives on Saving," *Journal of Economic Perspectives* 10, no. 4 (Fall 1996): 113–38; James M. Poterba, Steven F. Venti, and David A. Wise, "How Retirement Savings Programs Increase Saving," *Journal of Economic Perspectives* 10, no. 4 (Fall 1996): 91–112.

29. For further discussion, see Zvi Bodie, Alan J. Marcus, and Robert C. Merton, "Defined Benefit versus Defined Contribution Pension Plans: What Are

the Real Tradeoffs?" in Zvi Bodie, John B. Shoven, and David A. Wise, eds., *Pension in the U.S. Economy* (Chicago: University of Chicago Press, 1988), pp. 139–60; Andrew A. Samwick and Jonathan Skinner, "How Will Defined Contribution Pension Plans Affect Retirement Income?" mimeo, Dartmouth College, June 1995.

30. James M. Poterba, Steven F. Venti, and David A. Wise, "Lump-sum Distributions from Retirement Saving Plans: Receipt and Utilization," NBER Working Paper no. 5298, National Bureau of Economic Research, Cambridge, Mass., October 1995.

31. Samwick and Skinner, "How Will Defined Contribution Pension Plans Affect Retirement Income?"

32. These tabulations were carried out by Joel Dickson at the Federal Reserve Board. A number of studies reach similar conclusions. See Emily S. Andrews, "The Growth and Distribution of 401(k) Plans," in Turner and Beller, *Trends in Pensions 1992*; Leslie E. Papke, Mitchell Petersen, and James M. Poterba, "Did 401(k) Plans Replace Other Pensions?" NBER Working Paper no. 4501, National Bureau of Economic Research, Cambridge, Mass., October 1993; "Current 401(k) Plan Practices: A Survey Report," Buck Consultants, Secaucus, N.J., 1989.

33. Leslie E. Papke, "Are 401(k) Plans Replacing Other Employer-Provided Pensions? Evidence from Panel Data," mimeo, Michigan State University, August 1996.

34. Similar effects of 401(k)s on outright plan termination appear to have been a relatively rare response in the early 1980s (see Kruse, "Pension Substitution in the 1980s"), perhaps because converting already existing thrift plans would be a much less disruptive way to add a 401(k).

35. The following congressional testimony, by an executive of a major corporation, is not atypical: "A recent major change occurred in 1995. We generally reduced the value of our defined benefit plan. . . . Correspondingly, we increased the match in our 401(k) plan." Donald H. Sauvigne, "Statement of the American Savings Education Council before the House Education and Workforce Subcommittee on Employee-Employer Relations," U.S. Congress, House, 105th Cong., 1st sess., February 12, 1997.

36. Daniel I. Halperin, "Tax Policy and Retirement Income: A Rational Model For the 21st Century," in Jack L. Vanderhei, ed., *Search for a National Retirement Income Policy* (Homewood, Ill.: Richard D. Irwin, Inc., 1987), pp. 159–95.

9

1. See, for example, C. E. Steuerle and J. M. Bakija, *Retooling Social Security for the 21st Century: Right and Wrong Approaches* (Washington, D.C.: The Urban Institute, 1994).

2. O. S. Mitchell, J. M. Poterba, and M. J. Warshawsky, "New Evidence on the Money's Worth of Individual Annuities," National Bureau of Economic Research

Working Paper #6002 (Cambridge, Mass.: National Bureau of Economic Research, 1997.)

3. Alternatively, one could subtract the cost of purchasing an annuity from the retirement wealth accumulated in private savings instruments.

4. One reason it is likely that real valued annuities will become increasingly common is that the federal government just began offering real valued government bonds. These bonds pay an interest rate that moves along with the inflation rate. The availability of these bonds enables financial institutions to offer real valued annuities without accepting the inflation risk themselves. They can use the income from real valued bonds to support the payouts, thereby transferring the inflation risk back to the government.

5. Adverse selection results from a situation in which only individuals with long life expectancies buy insurance. Under such circumstances, an insurance company has to set its price for every individual as though he were a person with a long life expectancy. This causes people with normal life expectancies to pay a substantial premium.

6. In 1996, administrative costs of the insurance industry averaged 18.1 percent of the money that went to either current benefits or reserves. These costs were 25.6 percent of the money that was actually paid out in benefits for the year (American Council of Life Insurance, *1997 Life Insurance Fact Book Update*, [Washington, D.C.: American Council of Life Insurance, 1997], p. 41).

7. This sort of insurance would, in effect, imply that workers paid a certain portion of their wages in annual premiums but would receive a large percentage back in retirement benefits if they had a low lifetime earnings history, and a low percentage back if they ended up with a high lifetime earnings history.

8. *Annual Report of the Board of Trustees of the Federal Old-Age and Survivors Insurance and Disability Insurance Trust Funds* (Washington, D.C.: Government Printing Office, 1998), p. 103.

9. See Dean Baker, *Saving Social Security with Stocks: The Promises Don't Add Up* (New York: Twentieth Century Fund, 1997).

10. Steuerle and Bakija, *Retooling Social Security for the 21st Century: Right and Wrong Approaches;* C. E. Steuerle and J. M. Bakija, *Social Security Disability Insurance: Fiscal Imbalance and Lifetime Value* (Washington, D.C.: The Public Policy Institute of the American Association of Retired Persons, 1995).

11. For example, see *Annual Report of the Board of Trustees of the Federal Old-Age and Survivors Insurance and Disability Insurance Trust Funds*, p. 183.

12. Steuerle and Bakija, *Retooling Social Security for the 21st Century: Right and Wrong Approaches* and *Social Security Disability Insurance: Fiscal Imbalance and Lifetime Value.*

13. Social Security Advisory Council, *Report of the 1994–1996 Advisory Council on Social Security* (Washington, D.C.: U.S. Department of Health and Human Services, Social Security Administration, 1997).

14. Steuerle and Bakija, *Retooling Social Security for the 21st Century.*

15. Since the mortality and disability rates differ for men and women, it makes a difference which spouse is assumed to be the higher wage earner. The assumption that the man is the higher wage earner in each case reflects the current pattern of earnings.

16. *Annual Report of the Trustees of the Federal Old-Age and Surviviors Insurance and Disability Insurance Trust Funds*, p. 183.

17. These numbers are derived from the benefit levels that are received by new retirees as shown in Social Security Administration, *Annual Statistical Supplement to the Social Security Bulletin* (Washington, D.C.: U.S. Department of Health and Human Services, Social Security Administration, 1995), Table 6.B.

18. This is the discount rate that was used in both of the Steuerle and Bakija studies, and has often been used in assessing Social Security benefits and tax payments.

19. *Annual Report of the Board of Trustees of the Federal Old-Age and Survivors Insurance and Disability Insurance Trust Funds*, p. 113.

20. The tax increase used in these calculations was 1.8 percentage points. This incorporates the impact of recent changes in the consumer price index that should reduce the long-term shortfall by approximately 0.35 percentage points in the next Trustees Report.

21. Earnings for years after the worker turns age sixty are also included in the calculation, but they are added in with a slightly different formula.

22. Actually, the value of disability benefits should fall somewhat in this scenario, since these will be affected by the timing of earnings. This calculation does not include any adjustment for this fact and therefore somewhat overstates the value of disability benefits in this scenario.

23. For example, see *How Do Individual Accounts Stack Up? An Evaluation Using the EBRI-SSASIM2 Policy Simulation Model* (Washington, D.C.: Employee Benefit Research Institute, 1998), and E. Wolff and H. Chernick, *The Distributional Effects of Raising the Retirement Age and Partially Indexing Social Security Benefits* (Washington, D.C.: Economic Policy Institute, 1996).

24. See, for example, M. Feldstein and A. Samwick, "The Economics of Prefunding Social Security and Medicare Benefits," National Bureau of Economic Research Working Paper #6055 (Cambridge, Mass.: National Bureau of Economic Research, 1997); W. Shipman, "Retiring with Dignity: Social Security vs. Private Markets" (Washington, D.C.: The Cato Institute, 1995).

25. Baker, *Saving Social Security with Stocks.*

26. Employee Benefit Research Institute, *How Do Individual Accounts Stack Up?*

27. The EBRI study made its comparisons based on payback ratios, the discounted value of benefits relative to the discounted value of the taxes paid into the system, rather than rates of return (Employee Benefit Research Institute, *How Do Individual Accounts Stack Up?*).

28. Mitchell, Poterba, and Warshawsky, "New Evidence on the Money's Worth of Individual Annuities."

29. Steuerle and Bakija, *Retooling Social Security for the 21st Century: Right and Wrong Approaches;* Steuerle and Bakija, *Social Security Disability Insurance: Fiscal Imbalance and Lifetime Value.*

30. Social Security Administration, *Annual Statistical Supplement to the Social Security Bulletin* (Washington, D.C.: U.S. Department of Health and Human Services, Social Security Administration, 1997), p. 182.

31. Steuerle and Bakija, *Social Security Disability Insurance*, Tables A1 and A2.

10

1. Social Security reserves were approximately $757 billion at the end of 1998—enough to support benefits for only about two years. Reserve accumulation is projected to continue until 2020, at which point reserves will be sufficient to pay for benefits for two and one-half years. Relative to benefits, reserves will peak in 2011, when they will be equal to about three and one-quarter years of benefits.

2. For example, some proposals would permit individuals to "opt out" of Social Security, that is, to shift their funds to personal retirement accounts. For reasons set forth in Box 3–6, such an approach is inherently unstable. The problem is that high earners would find it financially more attractive to leave Social Security than low earners would. While payroll taxes are proportional to earnings, benefits rise less than proportionately with earnings. In addition, high earners are more likely to be familiar with the operation of financial markets and would face proportionately lower administrative charges because their private account balances would be larger. As a result, voluntary withdrawal would leave Social Security largely with low earners. Since low earners receive larger benefits in relation to their payroll tax payments than do high earners, voluntary withdrawal would create deficits, necessitating one of two responses. The payroll tax rate necessary to support benefits for workers who remain inside the system would have to rise, causing still more workers to withdraw. Or subsidies from general tax revenues would have to be provided to support the social assistance provided by the Social Security system. What this all means is that the proposal to permit workers to "opt" out of Social Security is not a complete plan. It buries the transition costs that most privatization plans honestly face by failing to analyze the inevitable consequences of permitting workers voluntarily to leave the system.

3. This represents the returns to the average wage worker, not the real return earned on the balances of the trust funds, which is estimated to be 2.8 percent over the long run.

4. If IRAs, Keogh plans, and the cash value of life insurance are excluded, fewer than one in eight families have liquid assets that exceed their annual income. Federal Reserve Board, *Survey of Consumer Finances*, Washington, D.C., 1995.

5. Caroline Daniel, "A Look at . . . The Future of Social Security: Taxing Reforms for British Retirees," *Washington Post*, Outlook, August 9, 1998, p. C3.

6. We assume that, subject to private (or public) offsets, described in the text below, the accumulation of funds in pension funds leads to smaller increases in consumption than do additions to income in other forms.

7. Almost all of the reserves are invested in special Treasury securities not sold to the public that have an important advantage. The Social Security trustees can sell their special issues to the Treasury at par regardless of the current market price of Treasury bonds of the same yield and maturity. This feature spares Social Security a risk that private investors face, of suffering a capital loss if compelled to sell bonds when interest rates were higher and bond prices lower than at issue.

8. B. Douglas Bernheim and Daniel M. Garrett, "The Determinants and Consequences of Financial Education in the Workplace: Evidence from a Survey of Households," NBER Working Paper 5667, Cambridge, Mass., July 1996; Patrick J.

Bayer, B. Douglas Bernheim, and John Karl Scholz, "The Effects of Financial Education in the Workplace: Evidence from a Survey of Employers," NBER Working Paper 5655, Cambridge, Mass., July 1996.

9. Eric M. Engen and William G. Gale, "The Effects of Fundamental Tax Reform on Saving," in *Economic Effects of Fundamental Tax Reform*, edited by Henry J. Aaron and William G. Gale (Washington, D.C.: The Brookings Institution, 1996), Table 3–2, p. 86.

10. Peter D. Hart Research Associates, "Americans View the Social Security Debate," Washington, D.C., July 1998.

11. These estimates are drawn from Lawrence Thompson, "Risks of Mid-career Economic and Demographic Changes" (draft), September 23, 1997, for the International Social Security Association. Thompson's calculations show that the variability in contribution rates based on the experiences in Germany, Japan, and the United Kingdom would have been somewhat less extreme than those in the United States. Whether contribution rates would have to rise or fall depends on whether growth of wages is accelerating or decelerating and whether interest rates are rising or falling.

12. The costs of disability insurance, which are larger than those of retirement and survivor insurance, are not included in this figure because privatization plans typically do not encompass disability insurance.

13. Before 1995, the Social Security Administration provided reports only to those participants who requested information. As a result of legislation enacted in 1989 and 1990, SSA began sending information on past earnings and estimated benefits to all participants age 60 and older. By 2000, SSA will be required to provide information periodically to all workers age 25 and over who are not receiving benefits.

14. Olivia S. Mitchell, James M. Poterba, and Mark J. Warshawsky, "New Evidence on the Money's Worth of Individual Annuities," NBER Working Paper 6002, National Bureau of Economic Research, Cambridge, Mass., April 1997.

15. Such information would be needed if private account balances were divided upon divorce. If private accounts are treated as the sole property of the worker, divorced women could experience a substantial reduction in retirement incomes compared to the current situation.

16. One way to counteract this effect would be to impose a tax on funds not used to buy annuities, the proceeds from which would be used to subsidize annuities. The tax would offset the unfavorable selection into the annuity pool.

12

1. In public discussions this option has often been referred to as "privatization." This is inaccurate. Privatizing Social Security would mean assigning the management of the existing Social Security system to a private corporation.

2. See M. Feldstein, "Social Security and Saving: New Time Series Evidence," National Bureau of Economic Research Working Paper # 5054, 1995.

3. Barry Bosworth and Gary Burtless, "Effects of Tax Reform on Labor Supply, Investment, and Saving," *Journal of Economic Perspectives* 6, no. 1 (1992), pp. 3–25.

4. Congressional Budget Office, *The Economic and Budget Outlook: An Update* (Washington, D.C.: Congressional Budget Office, 1995), p. 53.

5. By comparison, the Bureau of Labor Statistics (BLS) recently corrected an error in the methodology used to compute the consumer price index. This correction has led to an increase in the projected growth of real wages of 0.21 percent a year. Adjusting for this error raises the real wage projected for 2030 by 8.0 percent. This is more than *four times* the size of the gain resulting from the tax increase prescribed by the Schieber-Weaver plan. See Bureau of Labor Statistics, "Extending the Improvements in CPI Sample Rotation Procedures and Improving the Procedures for Substitute Items" (Washington, D.C.: Bureau of Labor Statistics, 1996).

6. American Council of Life Insurance, *1995 Life Insurance Fact Book Update* (Washington, D.C.: American Council of Life Insurance, 1995), p. 37.

7. Social Security Trustees, OASDI, *Annual Report of the Board of Trustees of the Old-Age and Survivors Insurance and Disability Trust Funds* (Washington, D.C.: U.S. Government Printing Office, 1995), p. 54.

8. See, for example, Robert J. Shiller, "Who's Minding the Store?" in *The Report of the Twentieth Century Task Force on Market Speculation and Corporate Governance* (New York: The Twentieth Century Fund Press, 1992); Robert J. Shiller, *Market Volatility* (Cambridge, Mass.: MIT Press, 1989); and W. DeBondt and R. Thaler, "Does the Stock Market Overreact?" *Journal of Finance* 39 (1985), pp. 793–805.

9. This assumption is made explicitly in *Report of the 1994–95 Advisory Council on Social Security, vol. 2: Reports of the Technical Panel on Trends and Issues in Retirement Savings and Presentations to the Council* (Washington, D.C.: U.S. Government Printing Office, 1996), p. 38. Although I use the term "profit share" here, it is only for simplicity. A more accurate term is "capital share of corporate GDP," which I discuss later in this section.

10. The economic growth rates and the returns projected for stockholders are all *real* returns. This means that they subtract increases in price that are simply due to the effect of inflation.

11. This number is calculated by dividing the market value of domestic corporations (Federal Reserve web site, www.bog.frb.fed.us, Flow of Funds Table L213, line 18) by total dividend payouts (Bureau of Economic Analysis web site, www.bea.doc.gov, National Income and Product Accounts table 1.14, line 25). The data used are for the second quarter of 1996.

12. These ratios were calculated by taking the Federal Reserve Board's data on the market value of domestic corporations (Federal Reserve web site, www.bog.frb.fed.us, Flow of Funds Table L213, line 18) and dividing by the after-tax profits including inventory valuation and capital consumption adjustments (Bureau of Economic Analysis web site, www.bea.doc.gov, National Income and Product Accounts table 1.14, line 20 minus line 23).

13. The numbers used in these calculations are based on stock prices at the end of the second quarter of 1996. Stock prices are more than 10 percent higher as of November 1996, with initial reports actually showing a small decline in earnings for the third quarter. This means that current price-to-earnings ratios would be more

than 10 percent higher than the price-to-earnings ratio used in this analysis.

14. These calculations assume that in each year, the difference between the expected rate of return (6, 7, or 8 percent) and the dividend payout is made up by an increase in the share price. These numbers become explosive, because the rise in the share price outpaces the growth in dividends, thereby requiring larger percentage increases in share prices year by year.

15. These calculations assume that the share of profits paid out as dividends remains constant. This means that percentage growth in profits each year is the difference between the targeted rate of return and the current dividend-to-price ratio (2.87 percent). The percentage decline in wages is calculated by taking the implied increase in the capital share of income as a percentage of the current labor share.

16. Other factors could affect this basic picture, but it is extremely unlikely they would alter it in any fundamental way. For example, the nonfinancial corporate sector—that is to say, businesses other than banks, insurance companies, and so on—increased its net holdings of financial assets at an annual rate of $36.6 billion in the second quarter of 1996 (Federal Reserve web site, www.bog.frb.fed.us, Flow of Funds Table F102 line 15). If this money had instead been paid out as dividends, it could have increased the dividend-to-price ratio by approximately 0.5 percent, raising returns by the same amount. However, net investment remains very low by historical standards, at less than 2 percent of GDP. If corporations were to raise the share of net investment in GDP back to just 3.0 percent, the level in the 1980s, dividend payouts would have to be cut and/or borrowing would have to rise. The former lowers dividends directly, the latter reduces the share of capital income that goes to profits, as more would be paid out in interest.

It is possible that profits could rise without higher growth or an increased capital share if interest payments fell. However, interest is already quite low as a share of capital income. Currently, just 17.4 percent of capital income goes to corporate interest payments, the lowest share since 1978. Since corporate debt continues to rise at approximately the rate of growth of corporate GDP, it is difficult to envision any significant reduction in this share.

Another possibility is that the profits of U.S. corporations could increase more rapidly than the overall rate of growth if American companies received a higher rate of return on foreign than on domestic investments. Although the return on foreign investments may be higher, the volume of foreign investment is still not very large relative to domestic investment. Also, an increasing portion of profits generated in the domestic economy is being taken by foreign corporations. These two trends tend to offset each other. The net international flow of profits (foreign profits of U.S. corporations minus U.S. profits of foreign corporations) has not increased relative to the size of domestic profits. In the second quarter of 1996, this net flow came to 11.8 percent of capital income in the corporate sector. By comparison, the net flow was 12.0 percent in 1978 and 14.2 percent in 1988, the peak profit years of the last two business cycles.

One last possibility is that the growth of profits in the corporate sector could exceed the growth of the economy as a whole. In principle this could occur for a short period of time, but since the corporate sector already accounts for 63.7 percent of GDP, even a small difference in growth rates would quickly eliminate the rest of the economy. If growth in the corporate sector exceeded the overall growth rate by 1 per-cent a year, in forty-six years the government sector, the nonprofit sector, and the unincorporated business sector would completely disappear. There has been no clear trend in the corporate share of GDP over the postwar period, but the 63.7 percent share hit in the second quarter of 1996 is the highest level attained to date. This might make it more likely that the corporate share will decline in the future, rather than rise.

In all these instances, there may be some opportunities for profit growth to exceed GDP growth, but all of them are very limited. Furthermore, in each case recent trends indicate that these factors are at least as likely to depress corporate profits in the future, so that their growth rate may actually be less than the growth rate of GDP.

17. The large premium that has historically accrued to stockholders is discussed in N. Kocherlakota, "The Equity Premium: It's Still a Puzzle," *Journal of Economic Literature* 34 (1996), pp. 42–71.

18. These calculations assume that each of the four variables—capital share, tax share, dividend-to-price ratio, and price-to-earnings ratio—moves back to its average since 1959 at a constant pace. The averages are 14.4 percent, 41.2 percent, 3.65 to 1, and 15.1 to 1, respectively. This assumption does not exactly equalize rates of return over the period. Also, average returns would be affected by the timing of these move-ments. For example, average returns would much lower if the fall from the current price-to-earnings ratio of 20.3 to 1 to the longer-term average of 15.1 to 1 were to occur in the last year before retirement.

19. The following calculation was used to generate figure 3:

1) To measure additional value—The projected real growth rate used for all years was 4.14 percent (7 percent minus 2.86 percent). This was assumed to take the form of higher productivity and wage growth (wage growth equals productivity growth), not higher labor force growth. The ratio of Social Security tax revenue to pay-roll was assumed to be the same as in the Trustees Report.

2) I approximate the impact of more rapid growth on social security costs in year t, c_t^1, by adding an additional term a_t, to the estimates of the growth rate of costs in the Trustees intermediate projections for time t, c_t^0; g_t^1 represents the higher growth rate of output at time t needed to maintain a 7 percent real return, and g_t^0 the growth rate of output given by the Social Security Trustees intermediate cost projections.

$$a_t = \sum_{i=0}^{17} \left(g_{t-i}^1 - g_{t-i}^0 \right) / 18 = \text{increment to } \overset{0}{c}_t \text{ at time } t$$

$$c_t^1 = a_t + c_t^0 = \text{new growth rate of costs at time}$$

The assumption is that approximately one-eighteenth of the beneficiaries of Social Security are new retirees each year (the current life expectancy at age 65 is about 17.0 years, but this will rise to about 20.3 years by the end of the planning horizon). The higher growth rate (if fully reflected in higher wages) will raise the benefits paid to new retirees by approximately the same amount, but leave the benefits for earlier retirees unaffected. Once eighteen years have passed, costs will be rising in step with the new, higher rate of growth. This formula ignores differences in the size of age cohorts and the actual differences in the way in which increased productivity growth might be translated into higher wages for each wage cohort. It probably understates the impact of the added growth on costs in the early years (when average life expectancies are slightly shorter than 18 years) and overstates it somewhat in later years.

3) The annual surplus is calculated by multiplying the cumulative surplus in the fund at the end of the previous year by the interest rates projections in the Trustees report and adding in the annual difference between revenues and costs, plus 0.5 x the projected interest rate x the sum of the annual interest earnings and the current year difference between revenue and cost.

20. Andrea L. Prochnia, "The Best Mutual Funds For Reaching Your Goals," *Fortune*, August 19, 1996, pp. 142–54.

21. Pat A. White, Paul Kupiec, and Gregory Duffee, "A Securities Transaction Tax: Beyond the Rhetoric, What Can We Really Say?" *Finance and Economics Discussion Series* (Washington, D.C.: Division of Research and Statistics Division of Monetary Affairs, Federal Reserve Board, August 1990), p. 17.

22. *Plan Sponsor*, February 1996, p. 75, reprinted in Olivia Mitchell, "Administrative Costs in Public and Private Pension Systems," National Bureau of Economic Research, Working Paper no. 5734, 1996.

23. The appropriate analogy here is probably to the current practices of banks regarding checking accounts. There is usually a monthly service charge plus a charge per check for accounts that do not maintain a minimum balance over, say, $3,000.

24. Z. Bodie and R. Merton, "Pension Benefit Guarantees in the United States: A Functional Analysis" in *The Future of Pensions in the United States*, Ray Schmitt, ed. (Philadelphia: University of Pennsylvania Press, 1992), p. 218.

25. The fee structure used in this analysis assumes that low- and moderate-income workers pay considerably less per account than high-income workers in absolute terms, even though the percentage charge is higher for the former. Assuming the accumulations are proportionate to their wages, a low-income worker will be paying roughly 40 percent as much as a high-income worker for each account, and a middle-income worker will be paying approximately 67 percent as much.

26. A recent study by the Employee Benefit Research Institute (EBRI) found that a significant percentage of participants in the retirement plans of three major corporations had accounts with little or no equity holdings.

27. A. Kling estimated that the bid-ask spread on long-term Treasury bonds averaged 0.063 percent, and 0.02 percent on Treasury bills. If a fund were evenly divided between the two assets and turned over 200 percent a year, total commissions would be 0.083 percent of the assets. See A. Kling, "Futures Markets and Transactions Costs" in *Financial Futures and Options in the U.S. Economy*, Federal Reserve System Staff Study (Washington, D.C.: Board of Governors of the Federal Reserve System, 1986).

28. *Plan Sponsor*, February 1996, p. 75, reprinted in Olivia Mitchell, "Administrative Costs in Public and Private Pension Systems," National Bureau of Economic Research, Working Paper no. 5734, 1996.

29. The assumption of a 2 percent real return is probably somewhat high, given the earlier analysis, but applying a lower rate of return would not significantly alter the calculations.

30. These numbers assume that the worker is single.

31. A recent study found that insurers charge a yearly premium of between 4.21 and 6.13 percent on annuities. See B. Friedman and M. Warshawsky, "The Cost of Annuities: Implications for Saving Behavior and Bequests," *Quarterly Journal of Economics* 105 (1990), pp. 135–54. Insurance companies charge a substantial premium for issuing annuities because of the problem of adverse selection. If an average person at age sixty-five can be expected to live twenty years but the only people who buy annuities are ones who can expect to live twenty-five years based on their family histories, the insurance company has to charge fees consistent with a life expectancy of twenty-five years. This problem of adverse selection is likely to grow considerably worse in the future as developments in genetics allow individuals much greater knowledge of their life expectancy.

13

1. *1997 Annual Report.* In Social Security, costs are usually calculated as a percent of payroll, since workers' earnings (payrolls) are the main source of financing. This way of discussing the capacity of the financing of the system to pay expected benefits avoids the complications that would attend using dollar figures to measure one set of benefits in one time period versus another set of benefits in a different time period.

2. Whether these changes are politically feasible at the present time is unclear. Four years ago, when the administration and the Congress agreed on a modest increase in taxation of benefits by making up to 85 percent of Social Security benefits subject to the income tax—a change affecting only higher-income beneficiaries—this action became the basis for attacks on incumbent Democrats in the 1994 elections. Although taxing benefits to the extent they exceed what the worker paid in is a change that warrants consideration on the merits, I suspect that it could be passed only with strong bipartisan support. And repeal of the special exemption might be attacked by opponents as singling out low-income people for a benefit cut, even though this change is equitable and restores the principle of equal treatment for taxpayers of the same income level. Again, bipartisan support would be necessary to get the vote.

3. *Report of the 1994–1996 Advisory Council on Social Security*, Volume I: Findings

and Recommendations (Washington, D.C.: Government Printing Office, 1997), pp. 97–99.

4. There is no strong theoretical argument against this proposal, which when combined with other quite minimal changes would bring the system into exact balance over the entire 75-year estimating period. Whether it could attract sufficient support for enactment is another question. At one point the Carter administration proposed such a change, but because of employer opposition it developed little support in Congress, and this could well be the fate of any such proposal today.

5. *Report of the 1994–1996 Advisory Council*, pp. 83–86 and 100–101 (discussion of Maintain Benefits plan).

6. Some critics argue that Congress might interfere with the principle of neutrality in investments. My view, however, is that a system of very broadly indexed investments would protect Congress against pressure to favor one corporate constituent over another, and that most members of Congress would welcome this protection.

7. The fund would build faster as a result of investing in stocks, but the additional national savings accruing from Social Security investment in stocks would be very considerably offset by other savers having to increase their holdings of government bonds as compared to investment in stocks. This offset would be less than 100 percent, however. In comparing Social Security investment in stocks to stock investments by individual accounts, it bears noting that, unlike the build-up in the Social Security fund, returns from stock fund investments by private investors would not be entirely saved but would be partly taken out of savings and spent.

8. This part of the proposal may strike a particularly responsive chord. A reduction in the level of Social Security taxes is welcomed by some policymakers as a progressive move, but whether it is or not depends on what is proposed as a substitute or whether, as in this instance, there is no substitute at all, thus forcing a benefit cut.

A proportional tax on wages would not be a fair way to raise money for general purposes. The Social Security tax is the same rate on wages that count toward benefits whether one has a high or low income. Although this, of course, means that the amount of taxes rises with wages up to the maximum wage counted for benefits, such a proportional tax is more burdensome on those with the lowest incomes. As a payment toward Social Security benefits that are heavily weighted in favor of the low-paid, however, it is fair. The total system of Social Security—contributions and benefits—is highly progressive, and the deduction from workers' earnings earmarked for Social Security strengthens the earned right to benefits in a way that no other method of financing can duplicate.

This is not to say that some general revenue subsidy for Social Security is out of the question, but it is to say that the major source of support should continue to come from deductions from workers' earnings and employer contributions that at least match those of their employees.

9. The Moynihan plan would affect more than Social Security. By making a 1 percent reduction in the Consumer Price Index—which governs both the Social Security cost-of-living adjustment and automatic changes in income tax brackets—it would, for example, very significantly increase income tax revenues.

14

1. In the table below, Social Security benefits correspond approximately to the average replacement rates of low and maximum earners—56 percent and 25 percent, respectively. Each worker contributed proportionately to individual accounts and, therefore, receives a pension proportionate to earnings. When Social Security benefits are reduced by three-quarters of the pension based on the individual account, the low earner's pension goes up 12 percent, and the high earner's by 21 percent.

	AVERAGE EARNINGS	SOCIAL SECURITY	INDIVIDUAL ACCOUNT	TOTAL PENSION	CHANGE IN PENSION
Low Earner	1,000	560	240	620	+ 11%
High Earner	5,600	1,375	1,340	1,720	+ 25%

About the Contributors

HENRY J. AARON is a senior fellow at the Brookings Institution, chair of the board of the National Academy of Social Insurance, and president of the Association of Public Policy and Management. He has been a student of Social Security for thirty-five years and chaired the 1979 Advisory Council on Social Security.

GREG ANRIG, JR., is vice president, program, at The Century Foundation and previously was Washington bureau chief for *Money* magazine.

DEAN BAKER is a senior research fellow of The Century Foundation and the Preamble Center. He is the author of *Defusing the Demographic Time Bomb: Income Projections for the 21st Century* and *Getting Prices Right: The Battle over the Consumer Price Index* and is the coauthor (with Mark Weisbrot) of *Social Security: The Phony Crisis*, which will be published in 1999.

ROBERT M. BALL was commissioner of Social Security from 1962 to 1973, serving under Presidents Kennedy, Johnson, and Nixon. He was a member of the 1982-83 National Commission on Social Security Reform and a member of the 1989-91 and 1994-96 Advisory Councils on Social Security.

THOMAS N. BETHELL is a Washington, D.C., writer and editor who has worked with Robert M. Ball previously on the final report of the 1994–96 Advisory Council on Social Security.

WILLIAM G. GALE is the Joseph A. Pechman Fellow in the economic studies program at the Brookings Institution and a former senior staff economist for the Council of Economic Advisers.

LAWRENCE R. JACOBS is associate professor of political science at the University of Minnesota and author of *The Health of Nations: Public Opinion and the Making of American and British Health Policy.*

RICHARD C. LEONE, president of The Century Foundation, has served as chairman of the Port Authority of New York and New Jersey and state treasurer of New Jersey. His analytical and opinion pieces have appeared in the *New York Times,* the *Washington Post,* the *Los Angeles Times, Foreign Affairs,* and the *Nation.* Dr. Leone also was the president of the New York Mercantile Exchange and a managing director at Dillon Read, an investment banking firm.

JOHN MUELLER is senior vice president and chief economist at Lehrman Bell Mueller Cannon, Inc., and worked as economic counsel to the House Republican caucus under Jack Kemp.

ROBERT D. REISCHAUER is a senior fellow at the Brookings Institution and was director of the Congressional Budget Office from 1989 to 1995. Currently the chair of the Restructuring Medicare for the Long-term project of the National Academy of Social Insurance and chair of the board of the Manpower Demonstration Research Corporation, he has testified and written extensively on social insurance policy issues.

JAMES H. SCHULZ is professor of economics in the Florence Heller School at Brandeis University and holds the Meyer and Ida Kirstein Chair in Aging Policy. Past president of the Gerontological Society of America and a founding fellow of the National Academy on Social Insurance, he has testified before various congressional committees, the President's Commission on Pension Policy, and the National Commission on Social Security.

ROBERT Y. SHAPIRO is professor of political science at Columbia University, a member of the board of directors for the Roper Center, and the author of *The Rational Public: Fifty Years of Trends in Americans' Policy Preferences.*